The Changing Bedouin

The Shiloah Center for Middle Eastern and African Studies
Tel Aviv University

The Shiloah Center is, with the Department of Middle Eastern and African History, a part of the School of History at Tel Aviv University. Its main purpose is to contribute, by research and documentation, to the dissemination of knowledge and understanding of the modern history and current affairs of the Middle East and Africa. Emphasis is laid on fields where Israeli scholarship is in a position to make a special contribution and on subjects relevant to the needs of society and the teaching requirements of the University.

Collected Papers Series

The books published in this series consist of collections of selected papers, presented mostly in seminars and conferences of the Shiloah Center. The views expressed in these papers are entirely those of the authors.

M. Confino and S. Shamir (eds.) / *The U.S.S.R. and the Middle East*
I. Rabinovich and H. Shaked (eds.) / *From June to October: The Middle East between 1967 and 1973*
S. Shamir (ed.) / *The Decline of Nasserism, 1965-1970: The Waning of a Messianic Movement* (Hebrew)
H. Shaked and I. Rabinovich (eds.) / *The Middle East and the United States: Perceptions and Policies*

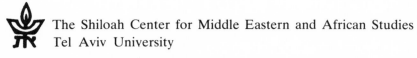

The Changing Bedouin

Edited by

Emanuel Marx
Avshalom Shmueli

Transaction Books
New Brunswick (USA) and London (UK)

Published in collaboration with the Shiloah Center

Library of Congress Catalog Number: 83-17936
ISBN: 0-87855-492-0 (cloth)
Printed in the United States of America

Library of Congress Cataloging in Publication Data
Main entry under title:
The Changing Bedouin.

(Collected papers series / Shiloah Center for Middle Eastern and African Studies)
Bibliography: p.
Contents: Economic change among pastoral nomads in the Middle East / Emanuel Marx — The desert frontier in Judea / Avshalom Shmueli — The Islamization of the Bedouin family in the Judean desert . . . / Aharon Layish — [etc.]
1. Bedouins—Isreal—Addresses, essays, lectures. 2. Israel—Social life and customs—Addresses, essays, lectures. I. Marx, Emanuel. II. Shemu'eli, Avshalom. III. Series: Collected papers series (Mekhon Shiloah le-heker ha-Mizrah ha-tikhon ve-Afrikah)
DS113.7.C52 1983 305 83-17936
ISBN 0-87855-492-0

Avshalom Shmueli died suddenly, just as the manuscript was going to press. We all miss him, for Avshalom was more than a colleague and collaborator; we could conceive of this lively, warm and generous person only as a friend. And as such he was seen by literally hundreds of people, in every walk of life. His network of friends included army generals, nomadic Bedouin, government ministers, kibbutz members, geographers in numerous countries, retired farmers and many more. He acquired these friends in his several consecutive careers, as member of a kibbutz, as army officer, and as university lecturer. At the age of forty-four, he retired from the army and made a fresh start. He read geography at the Hebrew University, and devoted both his M.A. and Ph.D. theses to the settlement of Bedouin. During the last few years he taught geography at Tel Aviv University. Into the short span of ten years he crammed numerous research projects, and edited an impressive number of books. It was as if he knew that his time was measured.

The study of Bedouin always remained his chief interest. Only a few months before his death his book *The End of Nomadism* appeared in Hebrew. And now this book concludes the cycle of his work. We fondly dedicate it to Avshalom's memory.

Emanuel Marx

It will not be found that there is consistency in name spelling. I agree with Lawrence, who in *Seven Pillars of Wisdom* says: "Arabic names won't go into English, exactly, for the consonants are not the same as ours, and their vowels, like ours, vary from district to district. There are some scientific systems of transliteration, helpful to people who know enough Arabic not to need helping, but a wash-out for the world. I spell my names anyhow, to show what rot the systems are".

I could not agree more. When compiling my map I had great trouble in securing agreement among experts. One expert — a great expert — revised my place names and six months later, when again seeing his version of spelling, altered many of them. So I gave it up and spelled names anyhow so long as they sounded the same. As further proof of absurdity, there are over thirty ways of spelling Jedda.

Birds of Arabia

Colonel R. Meinertzhagen, D.S.O.

And so it has been with the compilation of this volume.

Contents

Acknowledgements

We thank the Faculties of the Humanities and the Social Sciences of Tel Aviv University, The Shiloah Center for Middle Eastern and African Studies of Tel Aviv University, and the Desert Research Institute of Ben-Gurion University at Sede Boqer, for their generous contributions toward the publication of this book. We are also grateful to the Bronfman Program at the Shiloah Center for its help in the publication of this book.

We would also like to thank Anthony Grahame for his copy-editing work on the articles, and Ms Edna Liftman, of the Shiloah Center, who has assisted at all stages of the book's publication.

Preface

This book is concerned wih recent developments among the Bedouin of Israel and the surrounding areas. It deals with a variety of groups in the Galilee, in the Tel Aviv metropolitan area, in the Judean hills, in the Negev and in South Sinai. Rapid economic change has affected their whole life style. Everywhere they are absorbed in industrial urban society; they settle in towns or villages, and wage labor becomes their main source of income. And yet they maintain traditions and tribal frameworks. This apparent contradiction is examined in several chapters. All the contributions were written especially for this volume, and are concerned with contemporary change.

Israel, the West Bank, the Gaza Strip and Sinai have a population of over five million. Three million Jews and two and a half million Arabs share this area between them. The Bedouin are a small minority of the Arab population: there are about 200,000 of them (i.e., they make up 8 percent of the Arab population). The customary threefold division of Arabs into Bedouin, peasants and town-dwellers has always been too categorical; now it has become almost meaningless, for the whole population is gradually becoming urbanized, even where they continue to reside in camps and villages. Wage labor is the main source of income. Roads and motorcars as well as modern settlements established in the desert have brought jobs and services closer to the Bedouin and the villagers. The whole population is rapidly acquiring literacy and technical skills. Health services have improved, and life expectancy has grown accordingly. These factors have contributed to an annual population increase of about 4 percent, that is almost without parallel anywhere.

Researchers from various disciplines have for some years been interested in these processes. A number of Israeli social anthropologists, geographers and historians have worked in this field, and have collaborated fruitfully across disciplinary boundaries. Much of their research has centered on the integration of Bedouin into large and diversified societies. In particular the research has been concerned with economic change. The subject obtruded itself on the authors, although most of them were first attracted by other aspects, such as the richness of Bedouin culture, the roving way of life that reduces material belongings to a minimum, and the fierce loyalty to kinsmen and tribesmen. These themes are treated in various chapters, side by side with the major concern of economic change.

The articles show that the Bedouin still practise the traditional occupations of herding and farming. But now they also work in building, road construction, industry, transport and security, while the traditional economy supplies only a fraction of their income. Even the nature of herding has changed: it has become a large-scale, almost industrial operation, run by well-connected capitalists. Most Bedouin seem to become migrant or commuting wage laborers, who return as frequently as they can to their home base. There they feel secure among tribesmen and kinsmen, and their small flocks, fields and gardens serve as an economic reserve. This, claims Marx's introductory essay, is the picture throughout the Middle East. There are, however, regional variations and even within Israel distinctions can be discerned. Thus while the Ḥjerāt discussed by Eloul are mostly employed in industry and in the security forces, among the Jawarish described by Kressel there are many farm workers and self-employed tractor and truck drivers. The Bedouin of the Judean desert-border in Shmueli's article are mostly commuting wage laborers, while the Bedouin of South Sinai in Marx's concluding article are largely migrant laborers. Obviously these differences can be attributed to the kind of work available and to the ease of access to urban centers of employment.

These conditions have several consequences. First, the Bedouin settle in more or less nucleated villages where they are close to water, shops, health services and transportation. In most places the settlement is nowadays spontaneous; only the Negev Bedouin described by Lewando-Hundt's article live in a government-sponsored suburb. Second, they are increasingly controlled by the government. One aspect of this is the gradual encroachment of the *shari'a* court on tribal justice, as set out in Layish's article. Another aspect is police intervention in tribal blood disputes. This does not stop feuding, argues Ginat: the wish to keep the group united in spite of divergent economic interests may cause the leaders to provoke and exacerbate disputes. Third, where the members of the tribe are so widely dispersed, stable tribal leadership becomes a necessity. The leaders are not usually powerful, and the strong Ḥjerāt chief in Eloul's article is rather an exception than the rule; but their homes provide a meeting place, a center of communication, for the tribesmen. Fourth, the position of married women changes radically. They participate less in economic production and are more tied to the house, but their legal status improves and they are open to new ideas. They are no longer content with their household duties, and stand up for their rights of privacy and property. All this comes out clearly in Lewando-Hundt's article.

Finally, it must be borne in mind that these changes are stages in a process and that further developments are in store. There are indications that in future Bedouin will find more diversified, secure and better-paid employment, and that many of them will become fully urbanized. Bedouin youth is today preparing for the future: boys and girls attend school, and more and more of them become qualified professionals. A handful of Bedouin doctors, lawyers, social scientists and army officers are in the vanguard of these trends.

Emanuel Marx
Avshalom Shmueli

Economic Change Among Pastoral Nomads in the Middle East

Emanuel Marx

This paper discusses two seemingly contradictory trends among pastoral nomads in the Middle East.[1] New urban and rural development resulting from economic growth has cut into the critically important summer pastures of the nomads, while at the same time traditional economic pursuits within the old frameworks have persisted despite the vast economic changes.

The trend resulting from economic development has created numerous employment opportunities for unskilled and semi-skilled laborers. In consequence many of the smaller herdsmen are seeking employment in urban centers. Wage labor has become the major source of income for these nomads. Another result of economic development has been a great increase in the price of meat. In response to the demand, individual entrepreneurs among the nomads have begun to raise animals on a large, almost industrial scale. In this manner they can cover their considerable overheads and obtain the necessary summer pastures. The tribesman's economy has thus become diversified and transformed.

From the trend described above one might assume that because of these conditions, pastoral nomadism as one knew it was doomed. It is true that some nomads leave their tribes for good, that the herds and fields of most tribesmen are neglected, and that the range and frequency of nomadic movement have become very limited. Nevertheless, pastoral nomadism continues and the tribal framework is maintained intact, though both have changed in the process. The general trend among pastoral nomads is that:

1. Nomads who have taken up employment in towns congregate in tribal residential enclaves and tend to concentrate in a limited number of work places.

2. They maintain strong ties with kinsmen who remain in tribal territory, and many even keep their homes and families there.

3. Even where few of the nomads still rely on pastoralism for a living, corporate descent groups remain intact and tribal territory is protected.

4. They raise small flocks and till land in the tribal territory, even though they may lose money on these ventures.

I shall argue that these two trends are not as contradictory as they might at first seem. While wage labor outside the tribal area is the major source of cash income, traditional affiliations and economic pursuits are maintained for reasons of security. Economic and political conditions are insecure, and people are aware that they are likely to lose their urban jobs at any time. The dependence on external sources of employment over which no control can be exerted, entails serious risks. These are perhaps magnified by the nomad's conception of an inconstant ever-changing world. The uncertainty of the desert environment makes them aware of the precariousness of life in general. They safeguard the tribe, their territory and the indigenous economy, so that they can resume a pastoral way of life at short notice.

Some nomads achieve a large measure of economic security in town and break away from the tribe: they neglect the kinsmen they left behind, their herds and gardens, and even their tribal friends in town. Sometimes even close kinship relations are allowed to lapse. But others, usually the majority, belong to two worlds, Unable to achieve a permanent foothold in the world of wage labor, they make every effort to insure against an expected loss of employment. They maintain a "basic economy" in their tribal area which can be built up into a subsistence base, and maintain a set of multiplex relationships for mutual assistance in their home grounds.

In order to understand the processes it is necessary to do away with certain widely accepted notions such as that: under strong government nomadic pastoralists settle; sedentary nomads become peasants; under the impact of a modern economy tribal organization breaks down. The literature is replete with statements of this type. Here is one example: "Traditional relationships and groups lose ground and are replaced (usually forcibly) by new superordinated systems, and the old personal allegiances of members to the 'small group' are replaced by a new anonymous link of the individual to the big society" (Scholz 1974, p. 53). Such sweeping statements cannot easily be verified as long as the conditions in which they apply are not specified. But among the pastoral nomads of the Middle East today they do not seem to apply.

INTEGRATION IN THE WIDER ECONOMY

The nomadic pastoralists in the Middle East have always maintained exchange relations with differentiated external economies. They raised animals for sale in rural and urban markets, and in return bought farm produce and manufactured goods. Because there were no limits to the number of animals that the market could absorb the nomads constantly sought to maximize production, and considerable differences in wealth ensued. Yet they had to maintain egalitarian corporate groups, both for their personal defense and to maintain control over tribal territory. So, whenever inequalities became so glaring as to jeopardize the functioning of the corporate groups, some of the wealth was redistributed.

During the present century, and especially since the Second World War, the Middle East has changed rapidly. The economy has grown and become diversified, and the population of the region has multiplied. This has had serious repercussions on the nomadic pastoralists. They have been absorbed in the external economy, working outside the tribal area in many different types of work. Their indigenous economy has also become differentiated, one aspect of which is that they acquire modern means of transportation which allow many of them to establish permanent homes. The main reason for all these changes have been the economic opportunities which have provided attractive alternatives to pastoralism for many of the smaller herdowners. These economic changes have also encouraged the larger herdowners to build up their herds.

The intensity of interaction between any aggregate of pastoral nomads and the external economy can be plotted on a scale. At one end societies, such as some East African cattle breeders, produce for their own subsistence and have no access to markets. Then there are pastoralists who exchange their animals and animal products on the market. They are linked with an external economy, and can still select points of contacts with it (Baxter 1975). This is the traditional market exchange, so often described in the literature as relations between desert and town (Patai 1969, chapter 3; Barth 1973; Musil 1928, p. 90; and in greater detail Swidler 1973). Then a time arrives when the external economy can no longer be kept at bay. This is the other end of the scale where nomadic societies have become fully integrated in the wider economy. This may assume a variety of forms, yet in the Middle East today these appear to include neither the transformation of pastoralists into peasants, nor the breakdown of corporate organizations and tribal affiliations. Everywhere pastoralists are reported to be working in towns or industrial plants, yet reports also indicate that corporate and tribal allegiances are maintained. While the tribesman earns his living in town, his family often remains in the tribal area, migrates with the herds and may continue to live in tents. Variations on this theme include the family remaining in tents, but giving up animal husbandry, or the family moving into more permanent dwellings, such as mud huts or stone houses, and yet keeping animals. Some examples will be discussed below.

The shift from market exchange to encapsulation in the wider economy is far-reaching in its effects, but they are less destructive of "traditional" organization than one might expect. This is due to the insecurity of much of the work available to the pastoralists in urban conditions. Not that the pastoral economy is all that secure. Droughts, epidemics, floods and raids can destroy a man's wealth almost overnight. But tribal life provides two separate and partly overlapping systems of mutual assurance — agnation and kinship — as well as common access to specified natural resources found in tribal territory. These are valuable assets which the pastoralist wishes to safeguard even when he earns his living in urban pursuits. Henceforth the main purpose of tribal life is, for him, to maintain these connections.

The absorption of the pastoral nomads in the external economy cannot be explained as a transition from a "primitive" to a "modern" economy, from security due to strict frugality to the insecurity due to unlimited wants (Sahlins 1974, p. 37). The pastoral nomads of the Middle East have always been competitive producers and also developed some types of conspicuous consumption, such as keeping horses and the exercise of lavish hospitality. In this sense their outlook has always been "modern." The shift of the pastoral nomads to urban diversified employment has not received enough attention in anthropological literature. As far as I am aware there exists only one monograph that examines this recent trend in detail (Kressel 1976), although frequent reference to it is made in other works (e.g., Abou-Zeid 1963; Bujra 1973; Cole 1975; Lancaster 1975 and Lewando-Hundt 1978). The limited academic coverage may be influenced by the continuing concern of the nomads with pastoralism. They often view economic diversification as the end of tribal life, wage labor outside the tribe as a temporary occupation suitable for young men, and pastoralism as the major occupation and the main source of income of the tribe. The field worker too is tempted to concentrate his attention on the well-integrated culture of the pastoralists, the "real" tribesmen. He finds it hard to follow the migrations of numerous men of one tribal unit dispersed in various workplaces in different locations. Furthermore, he is reluctant to view the dilapidated shanty towns as social units that deserve to be studied in their own rights. Yet it is to be hoped that once the permanence of the economic change and the significance of wage labor and shanty towns are fully appreciated, more attention will be paid to their study. Only then will the realities of life in the tribal area be seen in a new light.

Typically, the poorer and younger unmarried men seek work outside the tribal area. Even the menial temporary employment they obtain is better than being dependent on their kinsmen at home. When more lucrative work becomes available those with property and families also go out until sometimes most of the male working population is affected. That is the case in South Sinai today. These nomads possess few skills that townspeople can use, and so inevitably they enter the lowest ranks of unskilled work. They become domestics, farmhands, construction workers or watchmen, often in small establishments, and are paid less than the going rates. In most cases the workers take care of their own food and lodgings. Judging from their own accounts, the nomads may spend several years in the service of one employer, but however long they stay they are always liable to be dismissed at short notice. They are well aware of their insecure tenure and are always ready to change jobs when required. Yet they also know that they are earning more than they would in the tribal area.

After working some years in town they acquire a limited range of skills and other experience. They learn how to deal with employers and find alternative jobs. Their income usually rises and some men obtain reasonably secure employment. These men may reach a point where they ask themselves whether they should remain permanently in town and bring their families there, or whether they should terminate their urban employment after a while and return to their families who stay in the tribal territory. Whatever the decision, it is usually reversible. And whatever it is, it does not contradict the tendency for the town migrants to maintain links with the tribe. Most of them opt for keeping their families in tribal territory, but even those who move their families to town do not usually relinquish tribal links. Thus about half the members of the ‘Aleqat tribe of South Sinai have settled in Egypt proper with their families, yet ties of kinship are constantly renewed by marriages with tribesmen from Sinai and by mutual visits. Only a few men sever their ties with the tribe, and the best indicator of such intentions is when they cease sending remittances to their families back home. All others try to live in two complementary worlds: they become townsmen whose roots are still in the countryside.

The move to town is facilitated by kinsmen who have preceded the new migrant. They provide hospitality during the first months, and often the kinsmen remain together for years. At the very least, they try to obtain lodgings in the same neighborhood. The old established emigrant also finds the newcomer a first place of work. This is likely to be with his own firm, in the same area of work, or in the same type of work. Thus the newcomer remains close to kin and tribesmen who exercise considerable social control over him. Only the dynamics of the urban economy gradually lead to a wider distribution of the tribesmen. Employment fluctuates seasonally or cyclically, workplaces expand or close down, and workers may accumulate skills and some capital. As each man in the course of his duties makes numerous acquaintances in town, he may move from one place of employment to another, and gradually drift away from his fellow tribesmen. Yet the insecurity is so great that most of these mobile people stay in the old residential neighborhood, and in their turn try to bring kinsmen from back home to their new places of work.

When these townspeople acquire wealth they invest it in either polygynous marriages, in jewelry for their wives, or in automotive machinery, such as trucks, pick-ups and tractors. All these items appear to have a common denominator: they protect their owners against expected political or economic change. Wives bear children, and the more sons a man has the wider he spreads the risks of future unemployment. Both jewelry and automotive equipment are portable and should conditions in the place become unsuitable, such items can assist in the move to a new location. In one important respect the nomads do not behave like other insecure populations: they do not invest in formal education and professional training. While they are aware that most professional qualifications are mobile commodities, they lack the necessary headstart. Their limited educational background, many of them are illiterate, effectively prevents this. Even their children cannot usually make sufficient progress. There are of course exceptions, such as the Bedouin boy who became university lecturer (Diqs 1967). It often turns out that highly educated Bedouin are the sons of the wealthier members of the tribe, who themselves were literate.

Kressel (1976) examined an urban community of Bedouin from the Negev, which settled in the Tel Aviv metropolitan region.[2] The hamlet of Jawarish was set up by the state in 1952 for a group of Bedouin. Until the early 1960s the population remained stable. A military administration had tried till then to confine the Negev Bedouin in a reservation, where they pursued traditional herding and cultivation. Those were days of severe unemployment, and in this manner the Bedouin were kept out of the labor market. By the early 1960s the situation had changed. There was full employment and the restrictions on movement were lifted (Marx 1967, pp. 46-47). But when the Bedouin flocked to the centers of employment, only the lowliest manual jobs were left to them. They became seasonal farm hands and worked in other unskilled temporary jobs. These were often obtained without the mediation of the Labor Exchange and were thus illegal. In 1968 work-hungry Arabs from the recently occupied Gaza area and the West Bank of Jordan moved in and undercut the local Bedouin whose income had by then risen considerably. As a result the employment structure of the people of Jawarish was transformed. A number of them became mediators of work for Arabs from the occupied areas, others bought trucks and tractors and took over the cultivation and harvesting of Jewish farms. Some began to farm on their own account, making use of the cheap labor. Again much of this work was wrought with risks, either because it infringed the prerogatives of the Labor Exchange, or because the land for cultivation could only be obtained by devious means. Insecurity there was, but at the same time capital and skills accumulated which made it easier for the Bedouin to adapt to further changes. The trend toward economic diversification was unmistakable.

The increased prosperity in the late 1960s resulted, among other things, in a sharp rise of polygyny (Kressel 1976, pp. 134-36). Kressel argues that this is a peculiarly Arab type of conspicuous consumption. But another interpretation fits his data: namely that Jawarish men marry a second wife and assume the attendant increased household responsibilities because they wish to raise more progeny. In this way they invest in their future economic security, and do not indulge in conspicuous spending. Cole's (1975, pp. 143-44, 153-54) short discussion of new economic developments among the Al Murra Bedouin of Saudi Arabia points in the same direction. "Many tribespeople have settled in shanty town complexes ... At least three such shanty towns belong to and are predominantly inhabited by members of the Al Murra ... all of them have settled because of their activities in industrial occupations". The settlers also operate trucks and taxis. Only few of them engage in farming. The oil industry appears to have provided so many opportunities of lucrative employment that the Bedouin are drawn toward its centers. Yet here too they do not simply disperse in towns, but stay close to their fellow tribesmen and indicate in other ways that they do not wish to forgo the security of the tribal framework.

Economic diversification takes place in tribal territory as well. Herding and farming are no longer the main sources of income of all the tribesmen. In many areas wage labor becomes the most important occupation, and the number of full-time pastoralists declines. But some people now become pastoralists on an industrial scale. They maintain herds of sheep and goats — camels become less important — amounting to hundreds and even thousands, and employ other tribesmen as herders. Only such a large-scale operation can successfully overcome the obstacles set by the expanding urban and rural settlements. The critical late summer pastures are nearly always located in well-watered, and therefore settled, areas, and pasture rights now are negotiated with the owners, either government or big landowners. But once such arrangements are made, the animals can graze most of the year in areas where there is plenty of water and pasture, and no longer need return to the distant desert. Thus many of the large Bedouin flocks of the Negev now stay all year round in the area around Tel Aviv. The Bedouin cannot lease waste land from the government, and overcome this difficulty by joining up with Jewish partners. Sometimes the Jew leases government land, while the Bedouin provides the flock and the shepherd. The two then share the profits according to an agreed formula. In other cases the Bedouin signs an agreement with a Jewish village. Such an agreement may also include additional clauses; for instance, the Bedouin may guard the settlement's orchards.

Once again Cole's material seems to validate this argument. He argues that fewer people now engage in herding but that the overall number of animals has not declined (Cole 1975, p. 158). Sheep and goats have replaced the camel, because of the insatiable demand for mutton among the urban population. Many herdsmen now spend the summer camped at a permanent well, and migrate during the rest of the year from one pasture to the next. Water is brought to the animals by truck, so that they can range in the desert at some distance from the deep permanent wells (p. 159). The herds may even stay all year round outside the tribal territory. One may assume that the same trucks which supply water to the flocks also eventually haul the animals to the urban markets. The organization of herding has thus altered radically.

To sum up the main argument: in recent years, a fast-growing external economy has offered the poorer tribesmen attractive work of various types outside the tribal area. The tribesmen's major source of income now is wage labor. The labor migrants reduce their investment in pastoralism and cultivation but, as I shall show, do not altogether neglect them. They also maintain their tribal affiliations. Some of the wealthier tribesmen have developed an industrialized type of pastoralism around permanent wells. The income of the tribesmen from all these sources has increased, but they consider this income to be less secure than their traditional mode of pastoralism and cultivation. They trust in their tribal affiliations. Their efforts to maintain a secure base in the tribe will be described in the following section.

MAINTAINING TRADITIONAL FRAMEWORKS

Many pastoral nomads obtain most of their income by activities in the external economy. But they do not rely on it in the long term. They are keenly aware of the political and economic factors affecting it, and know that upheavals of any kind adversely affect people in the bottom rung, like themselves. A Bedouin construction worker in Sharm al-Sheikh, South Sinai, spoke quite explicitly about two kinds of insecurity to which every Bedouin was exposed: "Any Jewish workman can throw you out of work, even if you have been three years on the job and he arrived only just now. We are not safe here; what will happen if there should be another war? When the October (1973) War broke out, we were left stranded here and walked three days in the mountains without food or water before reaching home. In the mountains we are safe, so we prefer our families to remain there" (Marx 1978). A similar attitude was expressed by a Bedouin of the Saudi Arabian Al Murra, many of whom work in the oil industry: "The oil wells can be blown up in thirty minutes and, with no money, all those people in Dhahran and Riyadh would die from lack of food. Why, they would not even have enough gasoline to leave and go back to their homelands" (Cole 1975, p. 155).

Both speakers implied that back home they had a secure economic base that would at least feed them and their families. I claim that much of the nomad's tribal economy and social organization, in the tribal area and in town, can only be understood in these terms. Tribesmen stick to their traditional economic pursuits even when they earn good wages outside the tribe, and even when their flocks and gardens do not yield profits. They do so in the knowledge that in times of need they can fall back on their traditional economy, and by devoting all their efforts to it could make it work again. Their subsistence would thus be assured. It is for related reasons that they foster their kin and agnatic relationships, and maintain the tribe. Even the tribal neighborhoods in towns and the tribal shanty towns serve this purpose. Taken together, these economic and organizational patterns indicate how deeply the nomad is concerned about providing a secure livelihood for his family.

I shall now examine the various elements of this "secure economic base" one by one. First, I discuss the tribal enclaves set up in towns. The Negev Bedouin settled in Jawarish again provide the best illustration. They preserve their tribal identity; they reside in residential clusters, cooperate as groups in local politics, and maintain visiting and marital links with their groups of origin. In a violent local dispute they call on their agnates from the Negev for help, and in the end the quarrel is patched up by their respective tribal chiefs from the Negev (Kressel

1976, p. 86). The local associations of migrants, here as elsewhere, serve numerous ends; they help the new arrival to find his bearings, and provide mutual assistance. It is significant, however, that among these former nomads the associations take the form of offshoots of agnatic descent groups in the area of origin. The links with the groups in the Negev can be useful in two ways; first, members of the group can be enlisted for help in disputes (that is of course a two-way traffic); and second, the line of retreat to the Negev is always kept open. Thus, whenever there is a threat of war between Israel and her Arab neighbors, residents of Jawarish return to the Negev. The view that the Negev is the warm womb to which one can return is held by these Bedouin in spite of the fact that they do not possess a territory. Their tribal area there is largely made up of small parcels of land leased by individuals from the state, with annually renewable contracts.

The link between the local groups of migrant laborers and their tribe is even more pronounced among nomads who actually possess a tribal territory. Here there is constant movement between the town and the tribal base, the stay in town viewed by many of the migrants as just a temporary episode. Among the Bedouin of South Sinai this is expressed mainly in two ways. First, many migrants do not set up house in town; they lodge either with other tribesmen, or a number of them jointly rent cheap lodgings, or they stay overnight in their place of work. Often they do not possess so much as a corner where they can leave their few belongings. Second, they do not usually bring their families to town. Their homes are then clearly in the tribal area. This pattern of behavior has been observed in such urban centers as Eilat and Sharm al-Sheikh.

The Al Murra seem to stand halfway between Jawarish and South Sinai Bedouin. The wage laborers of this tribe reside in shanty towns located on the fringe of cities, among members of their tribe. "There is no village or town organization and a man looks to his nomadic tribal leader and would plan to intermarry with his nomadic kinspeople rather than with other families in the settlement" (Cole 1975, p. 154). Yet the migrants do build houses. At first they are constructed of scrap materials, but each year some improvements, "such as concrete floors and plywood walls inside the rooms" are introduced (p. 153). Then gardens are planted, and the urban settlement seems to consolidate. In spite of all this, the ties with the tribal territory are faithfully maintained. "About half the households keep tents, and their families, especially the women and younger sons, move out to graze their sheep and goats in the desert during part of the winter and spring. During summer vacation, most of the young sons and many of the women enjoy a visit with their camel-owning relatives at their wells deep in the desert" (p. 154).

Up to now the discussion has centered on the settlements of wage laborers. Therefore the illusion that the tribal economy and organization was sound and healthy could be maintained. How else could one explain the labor migrants' view that their home and political center, as well as their means of economic survival, were located out there in tribal territory? But when the focus of attention shifts to the tribe another picture emerges. It turns out that the traditional economic pursuits of the tribesmen are neglected; one is told that the land is deteriorating and can no longer sustain the flocks, that the palm trees are not profitable and that the people depend on the income from wage labor. Not only the tribal economy seems to be on its last leg, but the tribe as well. Most of the men are away at work and return for short visits. Only the old men, women and children stay at home. All this is, of course, true, but must be seen in a different perspective. For what one sees is not a slow deterioration of the tribe, but rather a large scale maintenance operation. This involves three main interrelated aspects: the maintaining of kinship ties, of agnatic descent groups and tribal affiliation, and of a "traditional" economy. For most of the year these activities are carried out by the people back home, but their successful accomplishment requires the periodic cooperation of the wage laborers. They must return for defined periods and join in the activities. Thus the secure home base is kept ready for reactivation in time of need. As in so much of human endeavor, when times are good the maintenance operations are carried out only half-heartedly. Only when bad times are envisaged are they carried out in earnest and their full significance emerges.

This argument can be illustrated by observations made among Jebaliya Bedouin of South Sinai.[3] They live in the high mountains in the center of the peninsula, a harsh desert that permits horticulture only in a few oases and in the mountain valleys. Grains and most of the other basic foods are imported and not even dates are produced in sufficient quantity to satisfy local demand. Bedouin have acquired few specialized skills; there are some builders, well-diggers, truck-drivers, mechanics and some other artisans, and a handful of shopkeepers. But wherever one moves in the area one encounters women and girls herding flocks of black goats, with here and there some sheep interspersed. These flocks vary in size from a few heads to fifty or more. They are so ubiquitous that one may easily gain the impression that pastoralism is the chief source of income for these people, and that the women are the main providers. In fact, herding is practised on a limited scale, mainly because Bedouin consider that they either make no profit or actually sustain losses from it. The average Bedouin owns an estimated 5-6 goats and one camel. Yet it is an undisputable fact that many Bedouin households raise animals.

Horticulture is even more important for the Jebaliya as it can more easily be expanded and because, even in these days of wage labor, it provides some of the Bedouin's subsistence. I shall discuss this below in somewhat greater detail. Practically all the adult males of the tribe are engaged in wage labor. They tend to stay at work for two to three weeks at a time, without rest days, and then to return home for a short, often unspecified period of rest, which often becomes longer than initially planned. During their home leave they visit relatives and friends, who in their absence have taken care of their families and economic affairs. The Bedouin generally maintain joint households into which go the labor migrant's wages. Joint households are often maintained by the families of brothers, but households of brothers-in-law or cousins are also frequently found. The extent of cooperation varies but some of the joint households arrange and finance the marriages of members, nurse members through long illness, and provide for widows and orphans. These groups may cooperate for long periods, and where that is the case they provide members with basic security in case of death, illness and poverty. Joint households are, of course, found outside the desert as well, but they can thrive only where economic survival is assured.

As long as Bedouin labor migrants continue to fear wholesale dismissals from work, perhaps in the wake of a political upheaval, the joint households must remain in the mountains. There gardens and flocks guarantee at least some income, and the members can support each other for an extended period. Here physical proximity is most important. The children of migrants can be properly cared for when they live next door. Their flock will be taken to pasture in turns by the girls of the other members of the household only if it is kept with the other animals. Provisions for the migrant's family can be bought and stored when they live nearby. There is thus a tendency for members of joint households, and of other kin, to settle in a cluster, usually near a place where food and services are available. This arrangement reduces the mobility of the individual households. It also affects the small flock, which no longer determines the migrations of the households. The flock is taken to pasture in the vicinity of the hamlet where the food supply is soon exhausted. The animals' diet has to be supplemented for about six months every year by feeding them expensive imported corn. No wonder the Bedouin claim that they lose money on their flocks: they therefore try to keep them as small as they can, but they do not abandon them.

Tribal membership is still important for the pastoral nomad because it gives him the right to exploit certain resources within tribal territory, and other resources outside of it. The individual acquires membership of the tribe indirectly, by belonging to a patronymic group of agnates (patrilineal descent group) which is recognized as part of the tribe. The outward sign of a group's belonging is usually a place in the tribal genealogy. These groups, which were said to characterize the pastoral nomads in the Middle East, have little work to do in today's conditions. Cultivable land is generally owned by individuals and pasture by the tribe; blood disputes are not often prosecuted by these groups; self-help and vengeance are frowned upon by police forces. So the remaining purpose of the agnatic descent groups is to mediate the individual's membership of the tribe.

The tribe reserves for its members certain rights over the strategic resourdes found in its territory such as water for the irrigation of gardens, housebuilding sites, pasture, and employment opportunities, or any other combination of rights. Due to the extensive concern with wage labor some of these rights may not be fully exploited by tribesmen. Tribesmen devote considerable efforts to the preservation of the tribe to make sure that the rights do not lapse. In the absence of joint activities they can do so chiefly by organizing gatherings, at which tribal solidarity is reaffirmed. This annual meet is set to coincide with the date harvest or the ripening of other produce, so as to attract as many people as possible. Many of the labor migrants leave their employment at such times and return to the tribal area. In South Sinai hundreds of tribesmen congregate in the major oases of Dahab, Nuweba and Wadi Firan, and in some smaller ones. At the end of the date harvest the gatherings culminate in tribal pilgrimages, each tribe gathering at the tomb of a saint (Marx 1977). Among the Al Murra there are the beginings of such tribal gatherings. Cole (1975, p. 153) states that the four oases in the tribe's territory now "play an important role in the maintenance of tribal solidarity... Since the advent of wage labor ... many [tribesmen] have begun to invest some of their income in the construction of summer homes in the oases... Those who are engaged in full-time wage labor return during summer vacations to the oases where they have a chance to renew their relationship with the rest of their lineage and clan."

I have made some reference to the nomads' maintenance of traditional economic pursuits in order to have something to fall back on. An example that has been studied in some detail is the horticulture of the Jebaliya of Mount Sinai.[4] The Jebaliya are the second largest tribe in South Sinai with about 1,200 members. Practically every household owns one or more orchards in the mountain valleys, where they grow fruit trees of apricots, apples, pears, almonds, quinces and pomegranates, and some vegetables. Each orchard has its own well and is surrounded by a dry stone wall. These orchards can, if necessary, supply the Jebaliya's basic food requirements. Up to the 1950s many households lived on the produce of their orchards. Part they consumed and part, especially a robust variety of pear, they transported on camel-back to urban centers. The proceeds were used to purchase enough grain to last them through the year.

During periods of abundant wage labor the Jebaliya view their gardens as pleasant summer retreats. They spend part of the hot summer months in the shade of the trees. The gardens are watered fairly regularly, and from time to time men carry out some maintenance. But they consider neither the fruit nor the vegetables as valuable economic resources. They are viewed as delicious additions to the diet, but not as subsistence. For wage labor has brought them higher incomes and reduced the relative value of the garden produce. Yet they do tend the orchards, so that they bear fruit. If necessary, they would again rely on the proceeds of the orchards, just as they did in the old days.

Such a contingency actually arose after the October 1973 War between Egypt and Israel, when most Israeli economic activities in South Sinai were interrupted for about five months. During that period the Bedouin used up their money and food. Most families, it turned out, had stored basic foods such as wheat, sugar and oil, for such an eventuality. People who had large stocks of food shared them with kinsmen. As everyone was back home, social relationships were intensified. Soon the interest in orchards also increased. Some men planned to acquire orchards or to plant new ones, and to improve existing ones. Tribal pilgrimages in 1974 were very well attended. This flurry of activity was part of the Bedouin's attempt to reactivate their secure economic base. Not everyone was fully prepared for the sudden change, but all the Bedouin shared in the mutual assurance provided by a social and economic organization designed to serve this purpose.

The behavior of the pastoral nomads in wage labor and in the tribe may thus be described as all of one piece. If for purposes of exposition I have talked about two types of economy, wage labor and the traditional economic base, this distinction can now be dropped. What is clear, however, is that the nomads seek to strike a balance between their wish to maximize money income and their wish to provide full social security for their families.

NOTES

1. The paper is partly based on field work in South Sinai, carried out from 1971 onwards. This work was generously supported by the Ford Foundation, through the Israel Foundation Trustees. An earlier version was presented at a conference of the Commission on Nomadic Peoples of the International Union

of Anthropological and Ethnological Sciences, in London, in 1978. I gratefully acknowledge comments received from S. Hartman, G. Kressel and S. Weir.

2. Kressel's 1976 book, published in Hebrew, is titled *Individuality against Tribality: The Dynamics of a Bedouin Community in a Process of Urbanization.* The paper presented by Kressel in this volume, "Changes in Employment and Social Accomodations of Bedouin Setting in an Israeli Town" concentrates on just one aspect of the original Hebrew book and is a translation of a section of the 1976 book. The summary and references to Kressel's paper that follow refer the reader to the 1976 book.

3. See the other paper in this volume by Marx, "Changing Employment Patterns of Bedouin in South Sinai," which also discusses the Jebaliya Bedouin of South Sinai.

4. See the paper referred to in note 3.

The Desert Frontier in Judea

Avshalom Shmueli

A desert frontier is a transitional zone between the actual desert and pastoral areas, and the cultivated and settled areas. The combination of physical features and human activity encountered in these zones gives them a singular character. In the Fertile Crescent the width of the desert frontier differs from country to country, depending on the physical conditions in the area concerned.[1] However, throughout history, human activities have been a major factor of change in the contours of desert frontiers. There have always been dynamic political military boundaries between nomads and permanent settlers (Aharoni 1962, p. 6; Weulersse 1946, pp. 61-65).

The main physical feature affecting the border region is rainfall since certain areas receive no water from streams, rivers or wells. The average annual rainfall influences soil-types and their fertility as well as the abundance and variety of plant-life found there. Average annual rainfall at the frontier is representative of those areas able to sustain dry farming (i.e., 300 mm.-400 mm.). However, annual variations and distribution are critical, and influence "border movement" between cultivated and grazing lands (Nir 1973, pp. 21-26). The soil types found in the frontier, an area in which both Mediterranean-type flora and desert scrubs (mainly Irano-Turanian) grow, represent the typical changes to be seen between fertile land and barren, saline, desert soils. (Zohari 1955, pp. 51-52, 382; Dand and Raz, 1970, pp. 17, 22, 24).

In the human sector, the frontier is a contact-zone for shepherds and farmers practising either dry farming or irrigated agriculture. Two different cultural groups, permanent settlers and nomads, maintain a broad basis of contact in trade, economic matters, social life and warfare. From the aspect of settlement, this is the area where in the past settlements, fortresses, strongholds and colonies of discharged soldiers were set up, in addition to fortified lines protecting the settled land (Gichon 1975, pp. 149, 151, 162). The frontier was also the site of "exchange centers" — cities where shepherds and settlers bartered their goods. These centers also served as stations for international trade caravans.[2] The settlement layout and the frontier border depended on the general political situation in the Fertile Crescent and the balance of power between nomads and permanent settlements. Occasionally, the frontier area was employed as a zone for the assimilation of nomads and their eventual absorption in the permanent settlers' culture. However, fresh waves of nomads coming from the desert, always kept the strife alive (Ibn Khaldun 1966, pp. 77-78).

Judea constitutes the southern part of the Holy Land's central mountain range in its Mediterranean part. It is bordered by two arid regions — the Judean Desert and the Negev. The Dead Sea, 400 meters below sea level, the Judean Desert lying in the lee, and the Jordanian Rift Valley, are all topographical deserts, and constitute Judea's eastern border. The Negev borders the Judean mountains in the south and southwest. Southwards, the two southern ranges of the Hebron Hills, and those of Dahariya and Yatta meet in the Beersheva–Arad basin. To the southwest, the Judean mountains border the semi-arid regions of Arad, Tel Shoket, Lahav and Shoval, all of which have been a longtime domain of the desert nomads.

In the past traditional technology in the desert frontier clearly limited economic alternatives. Bedouin and fellahin survived from a combination of various agricultural activities and grazing. When the Bedouin tribes were in control they survived from dry farming, pasture lands and other sources of income including transporting work-animals, raids and plunder. When the region was at peace and the tribes under central control, the fellahin worked at developing plantations on the hillsides, practising dry farming on the hills and in the frontier, and grazing their flocks on the margins of the frontier and the desert itself. The main difference between these two cultural groups stemmed from political control of the frontier settlements. During times of strong central rule, settlements expanded and new settlements emerged in the frontier. When the nomdas had the upper hand, permanent settlements disappeared in the frontier area, and tents dominated the classical farm landscape.

In the latter half of the twentieth century, when industrial economy had spread to the margins of settled areas thus influencing social set-up and the Bedouin economy, it was apparent that a revolutionary change had occurred in the frontier. Bedouin settled permanently and worked as hired laborers in nearby cities. This reduced the economic influence of the desert and the desert frontier.

This article examines the events that have occurred and the processes that are developing in the Judean Desert's frontier area. We shall also attempt to examine whether the relationship between settlers and nomads is representative of the general situation which emerges at frontier areas throughout the Middle East, as contended by Natan Shalem.[3]

HISTORICAL ASPECTS OF FRONTIER AREA OF THE JUDEAN DESERT

Owing to the size, nature and location of the two deserts bordering Judea, the Negev and the Judean Desert, the frontier area has exerted different influences on them throughout the course of history.

Up until the Arab era (7th century A.D.), there were no nomad tribes in the Judean Desert or in the vicinity of the Dead Sea. With the settlement of Israelite tribes in the Holy Land around 1,200 B.C., man began to utilize various available natural resources, thus initiating a new era. Extensive utilization took place in the Dead Sea vicinity and the Judean Desert. The state, at that time, was able to integrate the region and its resources within the total administrative and economic system.

The resources were many, the principal being the pastures of the Judean Desert. Owing to the topographical structure of the Judean Hills and Desert, it was possible to maintain a seasonal migration between the lower areas in the east where grazing took place in winter and spring, and the higher areas in the west where the herds went in summer. The Dead Sea area yielded salt and asphalt for export, both products being extremely valuable in ancient times. Salt was required for purposes of cooking, preserving and manufacturing, and asphalt was used for embalming and medicine. Furthermore, there were healing springs along the shores of the Dead Sea, and these were used for medicinal cures (Harel 1971, pp. 17-18). The most profitable agriculture lay in the Dead Sea shores: dates, medicinal herbs and perfumes (Feldman 1977). Dry farming was also practised in the frontier zone during times of heavy rainfall. All economic activity concerning these products took place via a road network connecting the producing areas via the Dead Sea shores and the capital Jerusalem with the chief urban concentrations in the mountains. This road network also functioned as an international trade route between Judea, Moab and Edom.[4]

To protect this valuable region and the state against the Moabites and Edomites (1st Temple era) and the Nabateans (2nd Temple era), a system of fortifications and fortified lines was set up in the Judean Desert. These were developed more extensively in the days of the

Hasmoneans and Herod. The forts played an important port in internal policies and civil wars (Klein 1939, pp. 193-94). The Israelites were able to establish settlements in the desert and along the shores of the Dead Sea during early stages of their sedentarization, and these included the Biblical towns of Beit HaArava, Sekhakha, Madin, Nibshan, Salt City and Ein Gedi.

From archaeological surveys conducted after the Six Day War, three of these cities were identified in the Hyrkania Basin (Judean Desert) and Harel argues that the City of Salt corresponds to Khirbat Kumran (Harel 1971, pp. 173-74, 180, 188-89, 193-94). A settlement in Ein Fashha dating from the Second Temple era was uncovered, and sites and forts from the same period were found along the western shore of the Dead Sea. This information indicates that during the First and Second Temple eras, the mountains and desert of Judea and the desert oases constituted an integrated economic unit when the central authority was interested in keeping it that way. Consequently the frontier's inhabitants could take advantage of two kinds of lands, the desert and the sown, and sustain diversified farming. Generally speaking, there were no traditional nomad-settler wars.

Recourse to both the desert and the town land by the same ethnic group has been mentioned in the Bible. For example, the story about Nabal, and the prophecies of Amos and Jeremiah. Nabal, living in the frontier-settlement of Ma'on, raised flocks: "And there was a man in Maon, whose possessions were in Carmel.... and he had three thousand sheep, and a thousand goats...." (1 Sam. 25:2). Amos from Tekoa in the desert frontier, raised flocks and grew sycamores: "The words of Amos, who was among the herdsmen of Tekoa... (Amos 1:1). "But I am an herdsman; and a gatherer of sycamore fruit; And the Lord took me as I followed the flock...." (Amos 7:14-15). Jeremiah, from Anatot in the frontier, uses descriptions and images taken from both desert and Mediterranean landscapes (for example, Jeremiah, chapter two). However, it is necessary to point out that at certain times the frontier was a favorite hiding place, especially during King David's reign and also during the Hasmonean (Harel 1971, pp. 56, 65) and Roman eras.

The administrative division of the country in these times gives us an understanding of the degrees of importance the central authorities attached to different sub-areas and places in these regions (i.e., they functioned as district capitals and central places). Klein has submitted a detailed analysis of the administrative structure of Judea from the days of exile from Babylon (circa 538 B.C.) to the end of the first century A.D. (Klein 1939, chap. 9). According to Klein, Judea's administrative division comprised toparchies, apparently dating from Nehemiah's days.

This system continued into the Hasmonean and Roman eras, there having been eleven toparchies in Judea (24 in the whole country), although some changes were made in the size of the different units. From this it would appear that the frontier and the Judean Desert had considerable political weight. There were two "lines" of toparchies; one south of the Jordan Valley and the western shores of the Dead Sea, and the other line being on the desert frontier to the west.

TOPARCHIES OF THE DESERT OASES AND DESERT FRONTIER

Jericho (Klein 1939, pp. 202-7, 212-16, 256-57) had been the capital of the Kikar District since Nehemiah's days. This district had been known as the District of the Jericho Basin prior to the Hasmonean era, and according to this administrative division it was one of the seven districts in the country. The Mishna mentions Jericho as being capital of the "valley" — a region which included the Jericho–Ein Gedi vicinity and settled areas of the Judean Desert. Josephus and other sources from the end of the Second Temple era refer to Jericho as the capital of one of the eleven toparchies in the country. Josephus and various apocrypha refer to Ein Gedi as a capital of one of the country's eleven toparchies (Klein 1939, pp. 213-15).

The toparchies of the desert frontier include the districts of Tekoa, Efron and Herodion. The capitals of these toparchies were somewhat less stable than Jericho, even though the region was part of the country's administrative system throughout the entire period under investigation. Tekoa was the district capital during Nehemiah's time. Later the capital was transferred to Herodion during Herod's rule and, according to Josephus, remained so till the end of the Second Temple era. Plinius also refers to Herodion as a toparchial capital (Klein 1939, pp. 213-16). Efron is apparently Ofra or the contemporary Taiyiba. During the Hasmonean era Efron in the desert frontier acted as the capital of one of Judea's seven districts and, later on, was included in the "Mount" (the Jerusalem area). At the end of the Second Temple era, Akrabata or Akrabatine became the capital of a frontier district in the Samarian Desert and most probably replaced Efron (Klein 1939, pp. 204-6, 213-14, 218-19).

THE NOMAD TAKEOVER OF THE JUDEAN DESERT AND DESERT FRONTIER

At the close of the Byzantine era the desert frontier settlers were already having to defend themselves against the nomads' raids (Harel 1977, p. 40). With the Arab invasion in 700 A.D. the nomads penetrated the erea. But the nomad influx only became consistent in the latter half of the eighth century "and the country experienced a continuous and stable process of nomadization" (Sharon 1977, p. 548). Further waves of nomads entered the lands in the Middle Ages when it was a politically disputed area between Iraq and Egypt. More significant were the nomad invasions that occurred during Mameluke and Ottoman eras — especially between the sixteenth and nineteenth centuries — these having considerable influence on the country's population structure.

Most of the tribes in the Judean Desert and its frontier during the second half of the present century or those groups who formed tribes in the area, entered the country from about 5 A.D. onwards. Weak central rule and insecurity characterized the Ottoman period thus enabling nomads to over-run the area and gain control over considerable lands near the chief cities of Judea, namely Bethlehem and Hebron (Shmueli 1974, pp. 74-75). The tribes in this area are listed according to the geographic layout from north to south (see map 1). It must be emphasized that part of the following information is traditional and has been handed down by word of mouth, thus presenting difficulties as to its authenticity.

The Sawahra tribe originated in the area about 1,500 A.D., most likely growing from elements of the Beni Okba tribe in Arabia, and also some local elements (including rural ones). Today there are some 6,000 members of this tribe.

The founding fathers of one hamula of the 'Ubadiya tribe — the Raddayda — were Greek in origin. According to tradition they reached the Holy Land as slaves of the Mar-Saba Monastery during 86 A.D. The founding fathers of the remaining hamulas arrived at the close of the fourteenth century or the beginning of the fifteenth. They are now 6,000 strong (Shmueli 1970, pp. 32-33).

The nucleus of the Ta'amra tribes (now 13 tribes) reached the area during 600 A.D. They absorbed fellahin elements such as the inhabitants of the Beit Ta'amir village (which has since ceased to be a village). They now number some 20,000.

The Rashayda tribe is a small, low-status tribe, one of the oldest in the region. It includes 400 members and has lately settled southeast of Tekoa (Shmueli 1970, pp. 30-31; Segev 1977, pp. 567-71).

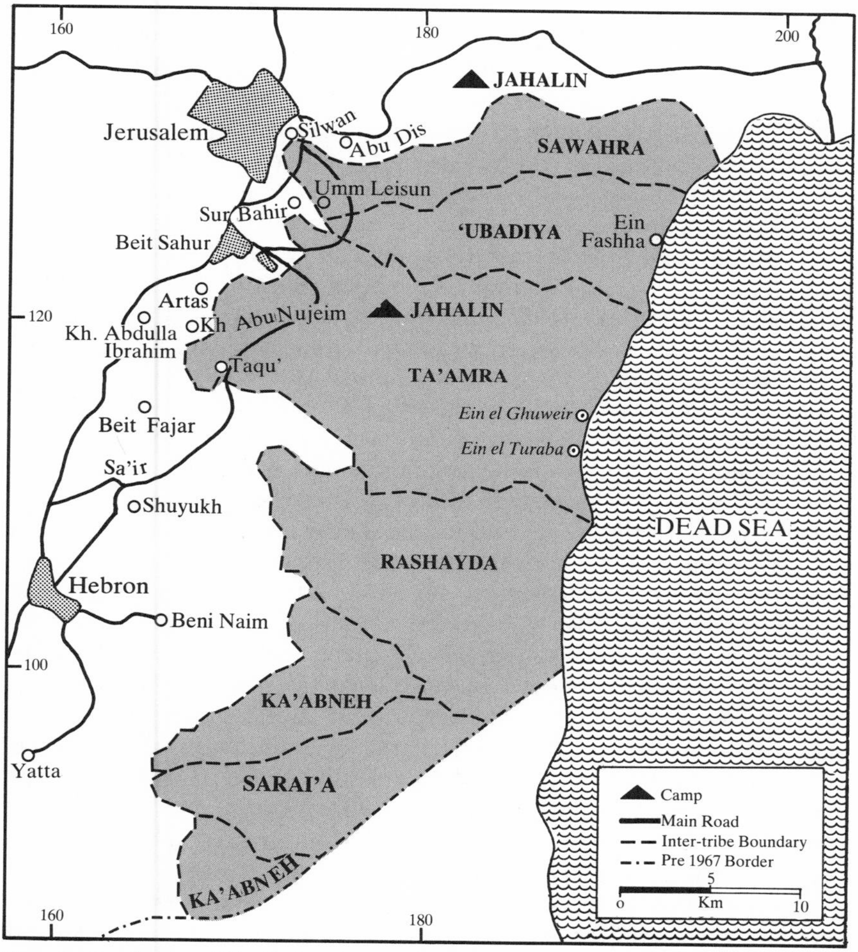

Map 1: Territories of the Judean Desert Tribes 1967

As early as the sixteenth century, a part of the Ka'abneh tribe had invaded the area. The remainder followed on slowly, well into the 19th century (Sharon 1977, pp. 548-549). The tribe has settled in the frontier area of the Judean Desert and includes some 800 members.

The Jahalin tribe is older than its neighbor, the Ka'abneh (Sharon 1977, pp. 548-49), and entered the area during the 16th century. Most of its members (total 1,100) are situated in Za'atra (near Herodion) and in 'Azaria near the Jerusalem–Jericho road. The Sarai'a, who originate from the Jahalin, are organized into two tribal frameworks.

Once the nomads had entered the Judean Desert, and taken over a considerable area, a situation developed during the sixteenth to nineteenth centuries which rendered passage through these zones unsafe. If the tribes permitted a journey, and it was paid for, and their own transportation services were employed, it was then considered "safe." The relative strength of the tribes enabled them to expand their spheres of influence. They demanded protection money from the local villages and pressurized the nearby inhabitants of Bethlehem (Shmueli 1970, pp. 32, 122). This state of affairs affected the ownership of land in the desert. A number of villages located in the hills and the frontier that had previously made use of the desert as pasture land, could do so no longer. Growing nomad strength on one hand and the transition to an urban economy by the villages on the other hand (e.g., tourism, manufacturing souvenirs, and employment and businesses in Jerusalem), lessened dependence on these areas (Shmueli 1970, pp. 43-44). Some villages, including Yatta, which were stronger than the tribes in their vicinities, held on to the desert grazing lands just by virtue of their strength. Sometimes these conflicts were quite violent. Occasionally the rights for land and water were purchased by the nomads for money.

The signs of "nomadization" of the Judean Desert were also to be seen at the frontier, especially in types of settlement and land use. Some permanent settlements stood fast in the face of nomad power and some retreated. This retreat is particularly evident in the fertile highland region of Tekoa (825 m.). Tekoa had been a *khirba*, destroyed since the Ottoman regime, and the nomads advanced through it towards the Mediterranean part of Judea (Shalem 1974, p. 149).

The fellahins' permanent settlements in the east of the Judean mount opposite the frontier, were not located with respect to criteria concerning physical features such as topographical height, rainfall and soils. An examination of the settlement line from north to south shows gaps between the settlements — this being unjustifiable in the light of the physical conditions. (See map 2.) These gaps were created by the

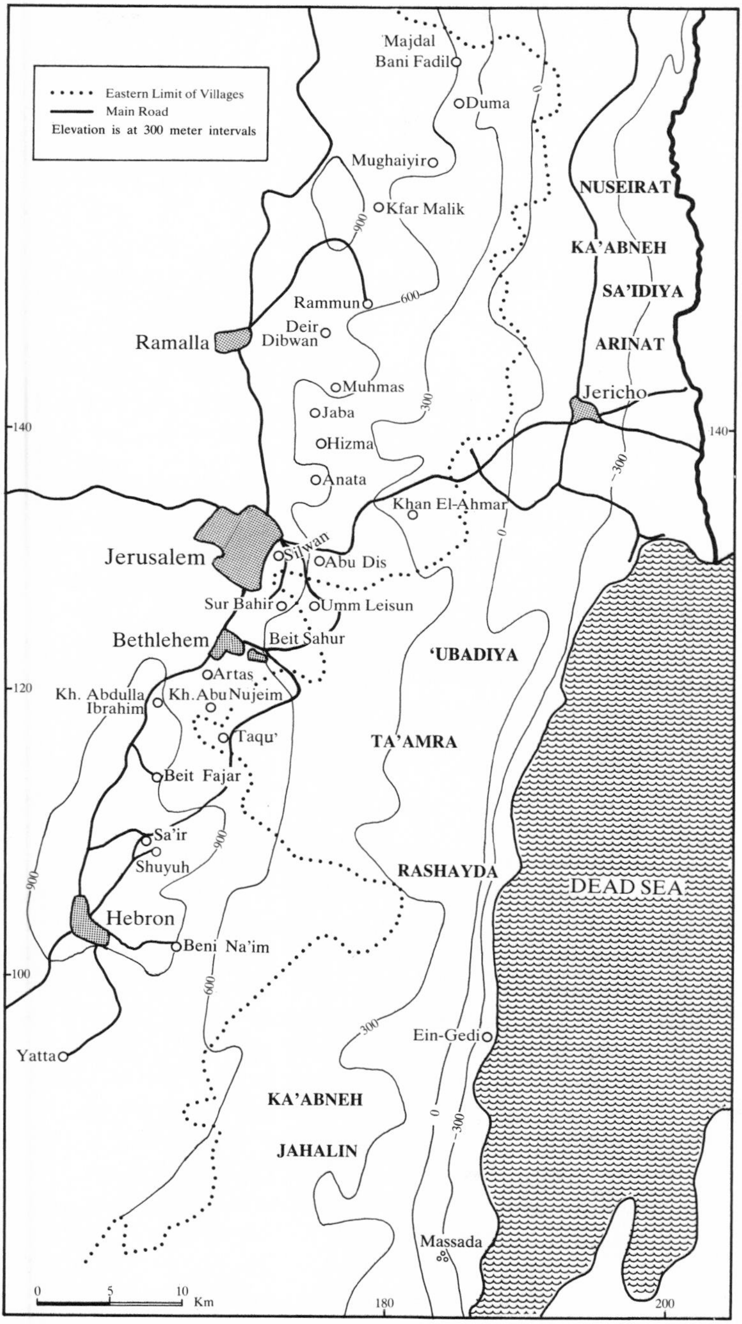

Map 2: Eastern Border of Permanent Settlement in the Desert Frontier

nomads in their advance toward the desert frontier and the Mediterranean part of Judea, causing permanent settlements to retreat (Shmueli 1970, pp. 43-44). The intrusion took two forms: force or purchasing lands. In some instances the settlers bought back the land from the nomads.

The nomads' advance had its effects on the land use itself. Part of the area was designated for pasture, and part for growing cereal crops, and included both the rural and Bedouin community. There was a two-fold danger in sowing seeds at the frontier: the possibility that rainfall would be insufficient, and even if there was enough the crops would be devoured by Bedouin flocks. Fights between farmers and shepherds were common, and some eventually developed into bloody confrontations.[5] The frontier's landscape was influenced by Bedouin presence and power. Hill-side terraces which had formerly been used for different crops were neglected, places suitable for dry farming plantations (e.g., figs, vineyards and olives) were deserted. The entire area was devoid of trees and scrub, and fell into ruin.[6]

The frontier was important for the seasonal migration of the flocks. Because of the differences in topography and rainfall in the lands between Judea and the Dead Sea, each piece of land was used for pasture according to the season (i.e., the lower areas in winter and spring and the higher regions during the summer). This system caused the nomads to be dependent on the higher regions to the west of the frontier (Shmueli 1970, pp. 26-27).

THE DESERT FRONTIER VILLAGES OF JUDEA AND THE NOMADS

"The South" witnessed extensive Jewish settlement after the fall of the Second Temple. According to Avi-Yonah it stretched from Ein Gedi to the Western Negev. He also notes that after the war of Bar Kochba there were many large villages in the south, including the village of Carmel (1952, p. 3). Contemporary frontier settlements in the southeast and east of the Hebron Hills are located within the borders of the historical "South". Shalem points out that steadfast frontier settlements formed a defensive ring around Hebron which was surrounded by deserts from three directions. In the region under study, Shalem makes special reference to Yatta, Beni Na'im and Sa'ir (Shalem 1968, p. 138). Due to the many wars and struggles with the nomads, there are many ruins of former settlements in the frontier. Shalem points out that in the frontier of the Hebron and Tubas Hills, the number of ruins is actually larger than the number of settlements that exist (Shalem 1968, pp. 130, 134;

Kochavi 1972). Agricultural prosperity in the Middle East, according to Reifenberg, is in keeping with the ability of the state to defend the settlers (Reifenberg 1960, p. 91).

Extensive and Densely Populated Villages

The frontier villages located near the nomads of the Judean Desert had to come to grips with this reality. On one hand there was the difficulty of raising crops on semi-arid land and on the other hand, the danger of pressure from the nomads in areas where the "state" failed to properly defend its farmers. The weaker villages lost the struggle and had to surrender their lands, breaking the territorial continuity of the settlements (north-south line) and leaving gaps into which the nomads advanced. The villages that managed to exist and to hold their lands in the desert (grazing) and frontier (grazing and dry farming) did so by physical power and by "signing" a treaty between various villages calling for a common defense against the nomads. Amiran has investigated the presence of several settlements and villages in the Hebron Hills. Only large areas and densely populated villages employed this system (Amiran 1948, pp. 30-38; Meshel 1969, p. 119). In the northern part of Samaria — the desert frontier — the large village of Tubas managed to stay its ground because of its size and strength. Shalem devotes special attention to the extent of the villages' pasture lands and their importance in the rural economy. Meshel also mentions the importance of large villages but, according to him, dry farming was the most important component. However, it is necessary to remember that these two pieces of work were written forty years apart, and it is clear that considerable changes took place in the interim period (Shalem 1968, p. 131).

The 1922 census throws light on the importance and size of desert frontier villages. Several villages can be considered as representative of the demographic and settlement developments that took place. At that time the district of Ramalla included 37,320 inhabitants who lived in 73 rural settlements and two urban settlements. The fifth largest rural settlement in the district was Taiyiba located in the desert frontier. In 14 of the settlements the number of inhabitants exceeded 700, and three of these were in the desert frontier. In 1922 the district of Jerusalem included 42,219 inhabitants who lived in 32 rural settlements and one urban settlement. The settlement of Abu Dis on the desert frontier was the third largest rural settlement in the district. With the exception of one settlement, all those supporting a population larger than 900 people were located east of the watershed in the desert frontier, and in its vicinity.

The district of Bethlehem included 25,464 inhabitants in 1922 and they occupied 15 rural settlements and 2 urban settlements. The desert frontier village of Beit Fajar was the second largest rural settlement in the district. The village of Beit Sahur, which later became a town, is also located in the desert frontier. The district of Hebron in 1922 was occupied by 53,571 inhabitants who lived in 35 rural settlements and one urban settlement (Hebron). Its desert frontier settlements, Yatta, Dahariya, Samoa and Sa'ir ranked second, fifth, eighth and ninth respectively as regards size. The chief rural settlement, Dura, was considered to be the largest settlement in the western part of the Bedouin desert frontier.

Facing the Desert

The villagers of frontier villages adopted a farming-system based on three types of land-use: plantations and dry farming in the Mediterranean part, grazing and dry farming in the frontier, and grazing in the desert. In the frontier villages part of the population would live by putting flocks out to graze — an essential occupation for large villages. A diversified economy and selective utilization of various lands befits a description of older times (i.e., prior to the nomadic infiltration) excluding, of course, defense systems in the forntier and desert, and trade and transportation throughout the Judean Desert.

By keeping flocks in the frontier or even in the desert itself, contact was established with the nomad culture. This factor exerted considerable influence on rural economic and social affairs. At the end of the winter and in spring herd-raising villagers and their families would set up tents in the desert and frontier, whereas during other seasons they lived in the temporary lodgings (*khirba*) (Shmueli 1969, pp. 125-29).

From Natan Shalem's survey in the late 1920s and early 1930s, it is possible to learn about the occupation of people living in frontier villages. Shalem notes that Yatta is virtually empty when the inhabitants put their flocks to pasture in spring, and they would sleep out in tents and caves. Yatta has eight *khirba*s where there were water holes and man-made caves. Major *khirba*s include Carmel, Ma'on and Jinbah, and the shepherds sometimes reached Nahal Tzeelim (Shalem 1968, pp. 142-43 and 1974, p. 411). The fellahin of Beni Na'im are called Arab-Na'im by the Bedouin because they spend more time in their tents than the rest of the frontier villagers (Shalem 1968, p. 146). In the frontier north of Jerusalem, other villages practise the same custom. The migration of fellahin from Dir Dibwan, Ramon, Mukhmas, Dir Jarir and Kafr Kalikh village took them as far as the Jordan Rift Valley (Shalem 1968, pp. 24-25).

These occupations are an integral part of economic life in the desert frontier. In this respect there is no real difference between fellahin and Bedouin — each one growing and cultivating his own land alloted according to the amount of rainfall at the beginning of each year. The frontier villagers north of Jerusalem (excluding the Tubas region) have long and narrow strips of land which stretch as far as the Jordan Rift Valley, as nomad presence here was relatively weak. South of Jerusalem the frontier presents a different picture since certain villages had virtually lost control over pasture lands in the desert and even in the frontier. For example, the village of Samoa owns no pasture lands in the desert though the rest of southeast Hebron's villages have been able to maintain wide areas of land in both the desert and frontier (Yatta, Beni Na'im and Sa'ir). In the Yatta region, the Ka'abneh and Jahalin tribes have maintained a narrow strip of land bordering dry farming fields (Shalem 1968, p. 138).

Two examples will serve to give an idea of the size of the lands held by the frontier villages: Sa'ir: 95,423 dunams and Yatta: 174,172 dunams. This is comparable to a regional council in Israel. For example, Menashe R.C. (1972) has 65,000 dunams, 21 settlements and 7,000 inhabitants.

The frontier settlers have adopted some elements of the nomad way of life, including that of clothing, household and working materials. In common with other Bedouin they migrated to other parts of the Holy Land in times of drought. For example, in the winter of 1973 in the village of Masha, southwest Samaria, I encountered shepherds from Samoa in southern Judea. This similarity, between nomad and settler, is especially evident in the inhabitants of the Samoa, Yatta, Beni Na'im and Sa'ir villages (Shalem 1968, p. 36; Shmueli 1969, pp. 127-29).

The Struggle with the Bedouin

Sharon describes the Bedouin sovereignity over southeast Hebron region beginning with the Jahalin tribe. Only in the latter half of the nineteenth century did the Ka'abneh tribe take control. Sharon argues that this demonsration of power is expressed by the fact that the Bedouin demanded protection money from the villages, the inhabitants of Hebron, caravans and tourists (Sharon 1977, pp. 548-49). However, it is hard to accept that this was the order of the day. According to records concerning the "qais" area of the Hebron Hills, it is highly unlikely that large frontier villages and the city of Hebron were permanently subject to Bedouin demands (Conroyer 1951, pp. 75-91; Karmon and Shmueli 1970).[7] The ability of the larger villages such as Yatta to protect their large populations is explained by their control and protection over cultivated patches and pasture lands.

The Ta'amra managed to repress frontier villagers along the Bethlehem–Beit Fajar front, and later had to base themselves on the Mediterranean lands of Judea, whereas there were villagers in southeast Hebron region who managed to maintain their lands in the frontier and even the desert. In examining the relative power between the villages and the Bedouin in the southeast Hebron region in comparison to that of the Ta'amra tribe and the villagers of Bethlehem, it is more than clear that the villagers of southeast Hebron region were the most powerful (Shalem 1968, pp. 5-6).

The struggle between Bedouin and villagers over pasture lands and preventing flocks from entering sown fields, were a permanent struggle in the desert frontier. Shalem points out that up to the First World War there were quarrels over pasture land between the inhabitants of Yatta and the Jahalin tribe and that the village of Samoa had serious contentions with the Bedouin. Shalem further mentions that in these wars between Yatta and the sub-confederation of Zullam from the Arad Basin, the inhabitants of Dura supported Zullam (Shalem 1968).

Yatta's strength and its ability to stand up to violent continuous confrontation in Tel Arad district with the Zullam Bedouin over lands during 1900-1912, reflects the character of frontier settlements. Up until 1900, the plains of Tel Arad were divided between Yatta and the Zullam Bedouins, but owing to warfare the Turkish authorities were compelled to intervene and in fact declared the lands to be under their territory — as "Jiftlik" lands (Brasslavsky 1946, pp. 52-63). The fact that up to 1900 the inhabitants of Yatta could go 20 kilometers further south in order to cultivate their lands, shows the powers of resistance of border villages. Bloody quarrels were commonplace during both the Ottoman regime and British Mandatory rule, even under Jordanian rule. Quarrelling between the Sawahra Bedouin and the inhabitants of Abu Dis justified the intervention on the part of the authorities.

During the British Mandatory period, and Jordanian rule, there were violent outbreaks between the villagers of Sa'ir and the Rashayda tribe, and the authorities were compelled to intervene. There were similar disputes between the Ta'amra Bedouin and the village of Sa'ir.

Twentieth Century Changes in the Desert Frontier

It has been previously mentioned that the importance of the desert frontier and the desert in rural economics was greater in the past than during the 1950s and 1960s. Nowadays the importance of plantations in the Mediterranean parts is increasing. This corresponds to the expansion of the Holy Land's market which took place during the British Mandatory period, and opportunities of exporting agricultural produce to the East Bank and Arab oil producing countries which increased during Jordanian rule (Karmon and Shmueli 1970, pp. 85-86, 98). Another major source of rural income is being hired out to work in modern industry that first developed during British Mandatory rule. Later on, the villagers found similar employment in the East Bank and the oil producing countries. Rural demographic growth and the need to seek more profitable employment brought about a wave of migration to ex-regional centers. These phenomena are not singular to frontier villages, it was common to the entire population of Judea and Samaria, Bedouin and townsmen alike (Karmon and Shmueli 1970, pp. 74-80; Shmueli 1970, pp. 56-58).

Table 1 shows the rate of population growth in some selected villages. This gives a clear indication of natural increase ratios as it does not include the number of emigrants. For example, the village Sa'ir had 1,477 inhabitants in 1922 and by 1963 it had increased to 4,172. Another 4,000 immigrants and their offspring can be added to this figure. The growth pattern in Sa'ir is representative of that in other villages. According to the 1931 census, the average number of people to a house in frontier settlements reached 4.6, and today this figure stands at 7. There was also more than a twofold increase in the number of houses.

The beginning of British Mandatory rule was marked by an increase in settlement activity in the frontier. Shalem's surveys in the areas of Beit Sahur (east of Bethlehem) and Ein Rogel (east of Jerusalem) indicate a "transgression" of settlement toward the desert and the transformation of pasture lands to plantations and cultivated areas (Shalem 1974, pp. 375-76, 400; Avi-Yona 1952, p. 3). In the south, according to Brasslavsky, nuclei of settlements in the *khirba*s of Yatta, Samoa and Dahariya were emerging during the 1940s but these did not appear on governmental maps of that period (1966, p. 356). The expansion of settlements and cultivated areas in the desert frontier common to both the fellahin and the Bedouin, originated from demographic growth and the relative public security imposed by the British throughout the country. Fellahin settlement development included transforming the *khirba*s into permanent settlements and not using them as seasonal lodgings. The Bedouin east of Jerusalem and Bethlehem underwent a process of sedentarization at the end of the 1920s.[8]

In the sub-district of Bethlehem there are 33 settlements which were not recognized as "established" settlements in the 1922 and 1931 census. In several of them, various development enterprises had been initiated by British Mandate authorities. Many of the settlements were accounted for in the Jordanian census of 1961, and several of those that were excluded, were sub-settlements of the tribe's "main settlement" and

Table 1

**Selected frontier villages:
Population growth patterns 1922-1967**

Settlement	*1922 census*	*1931 census*	*1967 census*	*Comments*
Dura	5,834	7,255	4,954	1931 Census: 1,537 houses West Hebron is presented for comparison. The 1967 Census excluded 70 *khirba*s that emerged as independent settlements
Samoa	1,600	1,882	3,784	1931 census: 370 houses
Yatta	3,200	4,000	7,281	1931 census: 767 houses 1967 census: excluding *khirba*s
Beni Na'im	179	1,646	4,271	1931 census: 320 houses
Sa'ir	1,477	1,976	4,172	1931 census: 388 houses 1967 census: 831 houses
Beit Fajar	766	1,043	2,474	1931: including Umm Tzalmona, Marah-Rabah and Marah-Malah 1931 census: 258 houses
Abu Dis	1,029	1,297	2,640	1931 census: 272 houses
Taiyiba	961	1,125	1,419	1931 census: 262 houses

were included in the latter's estimate. Estimates concerning the districts of Jerusalem and Bethlehem refer to tribes and not settlements. The new fellahin settlements in the Bethlehem district are not mentioned but estimates of their population are included in those of their main settlements. The census also includes information pertaining to the suburbs of Bethlehem.

The combined forces of demographic growth, migration, ex-rural employment and developing plantations on the Mediterranean-type lands of the village eventually brought about changes in the functioning of the desert frontier. Between the end of the 1940s and the end of the 1960s, utilization of the frontier for purposes of agriculture and pasture lessened, and a sharp orientation towards the Mediterranean-type lands emerged. For example, in Sa'ir herd-raising fell from an estimated 15,000 head in 1937 to 3,000 head in 1967, and the number of shepherds decreased accordingly. More profitable income opportunities, increased access to centers of employment, contracted pasture lands, the changing image of herd-raising in the eyes of the younger generation, and many years of drought during the past two decades, have all joined forces to weaken the importance of herd raising in the frontier's rural economy. A reduction in grazing areas alone resulted from several factors: firstly, in the Judean hills several areas that were previously used for pasture were adapted for cultivating plantations. Secondly, at the close of the Ottoman regime, and during Mandatory rule, the frontier inhabitants used to migrate during summer or during years of drought to alternative pasture grounds located in the "Shfela" and along the coast. However, after 1949 this was no longer possible due to the establishment of the Israeli–Jordanian border. Thirdly, from 1967 onwards security measures prevented grazing in the desert since the area was used by terrorists as a transit zone.

Two major phenomena characterized the desert frontier during the 1950s and 1960s. The first, as previously mentioned, was intensive agricultural utilization of the Mediterranean parts of the area. Together with ex-rural employment this meant that the frontier was neglected to a certain extent. The second phenomena is reflected by the persistence of a small group who remained in the desert frontier. This group started to settle permanently in the *khirba*s and constructed buildings. This form of settlement came about owing to the difficulty of keeping herds close to the plantations and secondly, because of the relative proximity of the *khirba*s to the pasture lands. Another contributing factor was that the structure of land ownership in the *khirba*s enabled flock owners to build large houses inexpensively since the prices of land in the village itself had gone up considerably. This pattern of settlement was particularly evident in villages such as Samoa, Yatta, Sa'ir and Beit Fajar at that time. The village of Dura, in the western frontier, underwent a similar process.

During the 1970s, the process of recapturing the desert by the Mediterranean cultural group, had intensified. This was expressed by the rebuilding of *khirba*s and further construction in other places in the frontier.[9] Since by this time all the Mediterranean-type lands belonging to the villages had been fully utilized, the only direction left extending plantations was to the east.

Money for investments in plantations and construction was obtained from those who were employed outside the villages, both in Israel and in the oil producing countries. The improvement of the security situation enabled expansion in the frontier. Similarly, increased agro-technical information brought about a considerable extension of cultivated areas — fruit trees, wheat, barley and plantations — thus enabling them to utilize the desert frontier more extensively.

The Bedouin Settlement in the Desert Frontier

The Ta'amra, 'Ubadiya and Sawahra tribes sedentarized spontaneously since the end of the 1920s in the area lying between Abu Dis and Tekoa and have even infiltrated the Mediterranean-type area. For example, the Sawahra's settlements at the entrance to Jerusalem (near the High Commissioner's Palace); part of the 'Ubadiya tribe settled close to Sur Bahir; and the Ta'amra tribes can be found at the entrance to Bethlehem, Beit Sahur and close to the hills of Bethlehem–Beit Fajar vicinity. Some of these places were founded as "common" villages serving both Bedouin and fellahin, each group having its own defined territory (Marah-Rabah, Ma'asara and Abu Nujeim).

During the 1970s tents ceased to dominate this area, and houses became the order of the day. At the turn of the decade, the small tribe of Rashayda from southeast of Tekoa sedentarized with aid from the authorities. The desert frontier was transformed into an area of settlement, cultivated patches and a number of plantations. Several tribal members moved to the nearby towns and fellahin villages, and a few emigrated to the East Bank and the oil producing countries. The concentration (over 2,000 people) of many members of the Ta'amra tribe in Bethlehem has left its imprint on the cultural landscape. Several members of this tribe have settled in Beit Safafa (close to Jerusalem) and Khirbat Safa near Gush Etzion. These occurrences and good access between Bedouin settlements and nearby towns and villages combined to strengthen the interaction between Bedouin who had undergone sedentarization, and the villagers and townspeople. This brought about a small but nonetheless significant increase in intermarriages.

The pattern of Bedouin settlement is different in the southern part of the frontier in the area lying between Tekoa and Samoa. Up until the 1970s no Bedouin tribes had undergone sedentarization in this area, in contrast to what had occurred along the northern front. Those in the south had drier lands and consequently average density per kilometer was smaller. Here the tribes' strength against their rural neighbors was less than that in the Bethlehem frontier. Consequently, the villagers managed to maintain their cultivated patches and pasture lands in the desert frontier and, as previously mentioned, even in the desert itself.

During British Mandatory times, the location southeast of the Hebron Hills was barely accessible, and far from the main centers of development and employment in the Holy Land. Several villagers here raised herds and practised dry farming. The Bedouin were unable to participate in the local system of hired labor, a situation that did not hold for tribes close to Bethlehem and Jerusalem. During Jordanian rule the region of

Hebron constituted a marginal region of the kingdom and no development projects were carried out here. Inhabitants migrated to the Jerusalem area, East Jordan and the oil producing countries. With the establishment of the Israeli–Jordanian borderline in 1949, the Bedouin (the Jahalin tribe) of the region southeast of the Hebron Hills lost some of their pasture lands and water sources.

The new situation created after 1949 resulted in the concentration of the Jahalin, Ka'abneh and Sarai'a tribes in comparatively small areas (*dira*). These were restricted units offering no economic alternatives other than animal rearing (camels, sheep and goats). During the 1950s shepherds from Ka'abneh left the area and settled in the northern frontier lying between Taiyiba, Ramalla and Wadi Kelt, whereas many members of the tribe migrated to Khan al Ahmar on the Jerusalem–Jericho road. After the Six Day War when pasture land was reduced owing to security measures, the Jahalin moved to Za'atara near Mount Hordos (Herodion) and to 'Azaria on the Jerusalem–Jericho road, while the Ka'abneh moved to the Jericho road. In 1975 there were 1,930 nomads and a herd of 13,650 head in the southeast region of the Hebron Hills.[10] Those who remained in the area included members of the two Ka'abneh tribes and both the Sarai'a tribes.

During both the British Mandatory period and Jordanian rule, Bedouin of the region of the southeast Hebron Hills had no recourse to services, and especially educational services from which Bedouin in the Bethlehem–Jerusalem vicinity benefited. This state of affairs had serious social and economic repercussions: an increase in the number of school pupils usually results in a far smaller group willing to practise dry farming and grazing. The inhabitants of the southeast Hebron region had gained a notorious reputation as smugglers (mainly hashish) and constituted an important link in the Jordan–Israeli Negev–Egyptian route, but this "traditional" source of income slackened after the Six Day War.

After the Six Day War, the tribes of the southeast Hebron region underwent a process similar to that experienced by tribes of the Bethlehem–Jerusalem vicinity during British Mandatory rule (i.e., integration in external economic frameworks). This included an expansion of agricultural lands including even marginal areas, and an increase in the number of workers hired out for construction programs in Israel and the Hebron region. The authorities introduced several services including water pipes and clinics. Education and transport services improved (the Jordanians laid a road leading to Umm Heil and founded a school there) relative to the pre-Six Day War situation. By the 1970s all these factors resulted in more camps of permanent tents belonging to the Bedouin of southeast Hebron region, and eventually led to the foundation of a defined settlement.

CONCLUSIONS

Up until the Arab occupation, the Judean desert frontier functioned as a geographic and settlement unit that bridged the gap between the Judean Mount and the Judean desert. Its inhabitants practised diversified economic activities and exploited resources and physical features of the surrounding sub-units to the full. Differences between farmers and shepherds were apparent although they never reached the stage of physical confrontation based on two different societies or cultures.

The traditional division of the Judean Desert into sub-areas comprising narrow strips running from east to west, and naming them after Judean towns in the desert frontier (e.g., the Ma'on Desert, 'Zif Desert — excluding the Ein Gedi desert which is not in the frontier), indicate both economic and settlement integration in the frontier.

The location of the Judean desert, external to the world's great desert belt, and close to the Mediterranean-type region of Judea (the desert does not exceed 20 kms in width east of the Bethel-Hebron line), and the Dead Sea barrier in the east, have isolated the desert and the frontier from waves of nomad invasions which were so characteristic of other areas in the vicinity, including the Negev.

When the kingdoms of Edom and Moab were functioning in an organized fashion, they acted as a barrier against nomads from the Arabian Desert. In those times the Judean desert frontier, in common with the desert itself, was an integral part of the state, representing the eastwards expansion of permanent settlements. The relative importance of desert-oasis toparchies and the frontier in the administrative system of the Second Temple (as Klein confirmed) reinforces the previously mentioned view concerning the positive functioning of the Judean desert frontier and the desert as part of a political and economical state unit, in historical times. But from the beginning of the Arab period up until British Mandatory rule, the Judean Desert and its frontier underwent a massive process of nomadization.

During the latter half of the 1970s, the Judean border frontier is similar to that which existed prior to nomadic invasions. Public security, settlements, plantations and dry farming in the frontier have all expanded. Integration of the frontier's settlements in the economics and services of a far wider region has resulted in the modernization of these areas. One clear indication is in the agro-technical field even though traditional agriculture is practised as concerns grazing, dry farming and plantations. The nomads are being incorporated in industrial economy, and the fellahin are expanding their fields and settlements eastwards.

In terms of basic patterns, the Judean Desert frontier, historically, is not representative of desert frontiers in the Fertile Crescent. However, as concerns the processes which the frontier has experienced over the past few decades, this area can be viewed as a micro unit representative of a macro-phenomenon in the Fertile Crescent, as exemplified in Jordan and Syria. Lewis clearly shows the materialization of these processes to be in an area corresponding approximately to the Hejazi Railway in Jordan and east of the Aleppo–Damascus Railway (Lewis 1955, p. 49).

NOTES

1. Aharoni (1962) argues that the desert border changes from generation to generation depending on the extent of settlement-expansion.
2. Damascus is representative of a city where trade took place between nomads and permanent settlement, and also served as a station along international caravan routes.
3. Shalem (1974, p. 119) argues that the Judean Desert includes three strips representative of the Fertile Crescent — on a micro-scale: the Mediterranean Strip, the Irano–Turanian Strip and the Desert Strip.
4. Harel (1977) surveyed twenty-four roads and passes (Israelite, Roman and Byzantine) in the Judean Desert, nineteen of which are in the hills of the Dead Sea. I was informed of trade connections between Trans-Jordan and Hebron during the Ottoman Regime and British Mandatory rule, in an interview given in 1968 by a former Mayor of Hebron, Sheikh ‘Ali Muhammad Ja’abari.
5. For example, the conflict over pasture lands between the inhabitants of Yatta and the Jahalin tribe, and the war against the Zullam tribes and inhabitants of Dura against the Yatta villagers (Shalem 1968, p. 143).
6. Shalem argues that the area south of Ein Rogel (near Jerusalem) had been abandoned prior to the First World War, and since the 1930s had undergone cultivation. Shalem contends that the area indicates the situation of the desert's border (Shalem 1974, p. 400).
7. Conroyer in his book mentions a tradition whereby the "Qais" of Hebron overcame the Ta'amra tribe, and forced them to retreat into the desert. This throws light on the villagers' strength.
8. According to the 1922 Census the tribes in the Bethlehem–Jerusalem vicinity (Ta'amra, 'Ubadiya, Sawahra and Rashayda) numbered 10,250 whereas the tribes of South Hebron (Jahalin, Ka'abneh and Sarai'a) included 1,243 people. In the subdistrict of Bethlehem the tribes comprised one-third of the population whereas the tribes of southeast Hebron region numbered less than the inhabitants of Yatta. Shalem (1968) argues that the inhabitants of Yatta and Beni Na'im repelled the Jahalin tribe and purchased land from them.
9. Inhabitants of Sa'ir founded a small village and cultivated plantations there, and also built groups of houses in other *khirba*s. The plantations stretched

eastwards and included the area of Wadi Sa'ir. Yatta's built-up area expanded and its plantations extended eastwards towards Khirbat Carmel which eventually became a permanent settlement. In the Yatta–Tel Zif vicinity, new houses were built and plantations were developed. The built-up area eventually spread eastwards from Tel Zif towards the desert.

10. According to Sharon (1977) and Shalem (1968) several members of the Ka'abneh tribe migrated to the Jordan Valley during the British Mandatory period.

The Islamization of the Bedouin Family in the Judean Desert, as Reflected in the *Sijill* of the *Sharī'a* Court

Aharon Layish

This paper attempts to analyze the Islamization of an increasingly sedentary Bedouin society using the records of the *Sharī'a* Court.[1] Discussions will focus upon the tribes of al-Sawāḥra, al-'Ubaydiyya, and especially the al-Ta'āmra, in the Jerusalem-Bethlehem area. Some of these Bedouin, who claim Ḥijāzi and Najdi origin, appeared in the region from the sixteenth century and absorbed local *fallāḥī* elements. Their settlement has almost been completed, the process having been speeded up by proximity to economic and administrative centers. A large number of the Bedouin have settled in villages and even on the outskirts of Bethlehem. Many others have migrated to various places on the West Bank, and even to the Kingdom of Jordan (the East Bank) and the oil countries. In the wake of sedentarization, the tribe tends to break up into its constituent clans (Layish and Shmeuli 1979, p. 29).

The Islamization of the nomadic Bedouin is an ongoing process. At the present time the traditional popular Bedouin religion, practised as both a philosophy, worship and customary law, still reigns supreme. Orthodox Islam with its system of beliefs and institutions has only been superficially adopted. However, it has been observed that the sedentarization of Bedouin in modern times brings them into closer contact with this orthodox Islam. It is gradually becoming a binding norm for them in worship and observance, and their attachment to Muslim institutions and to religious functionaries, the organs and exponents of the *sharī'a*, is increasing (Baer 1964, p. 132 and 1969, pp. 13, 14). There are many reasons for this, such as the spread of education (both religious and secular), the influence of the mass media, and the strengthening of economic, social and cultural contacts with Muslim townspeople as a result of urbanization of commuting labor. One of the main reasons influencing the trend towards Islam is the abolition of tribal courts and the application of *shar'ī* justice to the Bedouin by legislative and administrative measures. But above all what brings the Bedouin closer to orthodox Islam are the exigencies of a modern state, especially licensing. For example, the performance of a marriage by the *ma'dhūn* — the authorized agent of the *qāḍī* — or the confirmation by the *Sharī'a* Court of a customary marriage is required before a change of marital status is entered in the Population Register; while a succession order from the *Sharī'a* Court is a condition of transfer to the Land Register.[2]

Relationships between the *sharī'a* applying in the court and that of custom obtaining among the Bedouin varies according to the stages of transition from a semi-nomadic to a sedentary society. At one extreme custom prevails, uncontrolled by the *sharī'a*. A recent study based on legal documents of the said tribes (Layish and Shmueli 1979, pp. 32-41), shows that custom still enjoys wide autonomy in matters of personal status. Present-day Bedouin customary law, as far as it can be isolated from the influences of Islamic law, derives from Jāhilī Arab customary law. Among the Bedouin, many terms and institutions of substantive law adopted by Islam have preserved their old customary connotations. There are many instances of intimate, informal customary arbitration being preferred to institutionalized, formalistic *shar'ī* jurisdiction (governed by the Ḥanafī doctrine), which for their taste is too rigid.

The other extreme reflects the assimilative power of the *sharī'a* with regard to custom. There is an increasing number of significant indications that custom is being superseded by the *sharī'a* in its own domain, namely arbitration. Expressions of a belief in the oneness of God and the mission of his prophet Muḥammad, and Qur'ānic passages, are liberally interspersed in the arbitral awards; *shar'ī* elements penetrate into customary substantive law; customary legal terms acquire a *shar'ī* connotation, and the arbitrators themselves may refer the parties to the *Sharī'a* Court for completion of a proceeding begun before them. *Sharī'a* justice is required by the Bedouin for reasons of legal security. The arbitrator's ability to compete with the *qāḍī* is diminishing, because the latter relies on sanctions provided by the state and his judgments are enforceable. Paradoxically, in the modern state where the *sharī'a* has lost its supremacy and parliament limits its application, the *Sharī'a* Court resorts to the long arm of the secular administration in order to enforce the *Sharī'a* (Bousquet 1960, pp. 170-71; Layish 1978, p. 272).

Islamization reaches its peak and completion in the *Sharī'a* Court. In the process of applying the *sharī'a* to a Bedouin society undergoing sedentarization, the *qāḍī* plays the main role. The *Sharī'a* Court is the meeting-place par excellence of *sharī'a* and custom. The *qāḍī* is constantly confronted with a population attuned to custom and is required to provide practical solutions for day-to-day social problems. How does the court respond to this challenge? To what extent is it alive to the need for completing the Islamization of the Bedouin, and what is its role in this process? We shall try to answer these questions on the strength of and on the basis of decisions and orders of the *Sharī'a* Courts of Jerusalem and Bethlehem, collected from Bedouin in the Judean Desert. We shall also avail ourselves of material from the *sijill* of the *Sharī'a* Court of Bethlehem throughout the last twenty years,[3] and of interviews with the *qāḍīs*.

ACQUIESCENCE IN THE EXISTENCE OF CUSTOM

The outcome of the confrontation between *sharī'a* and custom depends on the degree of orthodoxy of the *qāḍīs*, their religious and secular education, their social philosophy and, above all, their understanding of the Islamization processes of a tribal society undergoing sedentarization. Two definite, mutually exclusive attitudes of the *qāḍīs* towards custom can be distinguished: on the one hand, acquiescence in its existence while trying to fuse it with the *sharī'a*; and on the other hand, enforcement of the *sharī'a* as remodelled by the Jordanian Family Rights Law of 1951, while rejecting custom absolutely.

The principal means of introducing a customary norm into court decisions is by voluntary agreement between the parties. A tendency has long been observed among the *qāḍīs* to settle disputes between spouses peaceably, while drawing support from their official authority. This method dispenses with the application of the *sharī'a* and thus avoids its distortion.[4] The *Qāḍī* of Bethlehem, Shaykh 'Abd al-Qādir 'Abd al-Muḥsin 'Ābidīn, said in an interview: "Since reconciliation is stronger than the *qāḍī (al-ṣulḥ yuqawwī al-qāḍī)*, because it is based on agreement between the parties, it affects the *shar'ī* decision." He also attests that an arrangement by mutual agreement (*bi'l-tarāḍī*) is frequently achieved with the help of tribal notables (*wujūh al-'ashā'ir*) and that, moreover, when a *qāḍī* is unable to solve a particular problem, he refers the parties to an arbitrator.[5] The author was present at a meeting in court between this *qāḍī* and a tribal arbitrator, who discussed ways of settling a family dispute which was to have been heard in court. Shaykh Muḥammad Sa'īd Jamāl al-Rifā'ī, *Wakīl Qāḍī* of Bethlehem, is bolder in his readiness for concessions to custom. In his opinion, "custom (*'urf, 'āda*) is binding law (*ḥukm mulzam*), provided that it does not conflict with an express provision (*naṣṣ*) of the Qur'ān and the *sunna*." This recognition of custom as a source of law is contrary to the classical legal theory of Islam.[6]

The most significant criterion of the *qāḍī*s' attitude towards custom is, of course, their judicial practice. Indeed, the *sijill* attests to their inclination to compromise with custom and link it to the *sharīʻa*. The courts give retroactive effect to customary marriages of Bedouin not performed by a *sharʻī ma'dhūn*, and accept the testimony of Bedouin shaykhs' signatories to petitions (*maḍbaṭa*) certifying that the marriage, as stated in one case, was performed by a valid (*ṣaḥīḥ*) *sharʻī* union "in accordance with the custom of ʻArab al-Sawāḥra." The shaykhs' familiarity with the *sharīʻa* is doubtful, but this does not prevent the *qāḍī*s from legalizing the marriages, probably out of regard for the common good and especially for the offpsring of these unions. In one such case, the parties said they had not known that a marriage must be solemnized by the *ma'dhūn*.[7] Israeli *qāḍī*s are divided on this point: some confirm customary marriages ex post facto for the same reasons as their Bethlehem colleagues. Others, taking a formalistic view, do not see their way clear to confirm these marriages as they do not meet *sharʻī* requirements; they order separation (*tafrīq*) and the performance of a *sharʻī* marriage (Layish 1974, pp. 398-99, 402-3).

It is very usual to perform renunciation (*ibrā'*) and compensation (*khulʻ*) divorces in court for reasons of legal security, in view of the property relationships involved. Arrangements like this are sometimes determined by arbitrators preparatory to court proceedings (Layish and Shmueli 1979, p. 44). The principle guiding arbitrators in setting down any financial consequences is the measure of responsibility of each of the parties for the dissolution. They proceed in accordance with the customary concept of marriage (dominion (*baʻal*) marriage), by which the wife is not a party but the object of transaction. If the husband is at fault he loses his right to compensation, and if the wife is to blame *her guardian* is required to return the dower and reimburse the expenses of the wedding. The court accepts the agreed financial arrangements, but formulates them in a manner consistent with the *sharīʻa* and gives them the force of judgment. For example, the court is at pains to note that the *wife*, not her guardian, in return for the divorce, renounces the right to prompt and deferred dower and some *sharʻī* rights not usually exercised among the Bedouin, such as waiting-period maintenance. In other words, the arbitrator provides the substance and the *qāḍī* the form.[8] According to the evidence of the *Wakīl Qāḍī*, Shaykh al-Rifāʻī, the court sometimes avails itself of traditional kinds of security usual in arbitration, such as a fine (*gharāma*) and guarantor (*kafīl*), in case the wife goes back on her agreement of renunciation. In Israel, too, it has been observed that *qāḍī*s do not interfere in the financial arrangements of divorce by agreement and give them the force of judgment.[9]

REJECTION OF CUSTOM AND ENFORCEMENT OF THE SHARĪ‘A

In the absence of agreement between the parties, the *qāḍī*s carefully apply the *sharī‘a* according to the Ḥanafī school and the Jordanian Family Rights Law No. 92 (1951). The latter embodies far-reaching reforms in women's liberation as influenced by Ottoman and Egyptian legislation which, in turn, was based on the *takhayyur*-and-*talfīq* method, that is the adoption of elements of the non-Ḥanafī doctrine to back up the reforms, in addition to the authorative Ḥanafī position.[10]

It seems that marriage before the *ma'dhūn* (the person authorized to perform marriages who acts on behalf of the *qāḍī*) is today the commonest form of marriage among the Bedouin of the Judean Desert. Shaykh Mūsā ‘Awdat Allāh al-‘Ubaydiyya and Shaykh Sulaymān Sālim Muḥammad ‘Ashīrat Ṣalāḥ al-Ta‘āmra have confirmed that the development, which has brought about the present situation, began in the early days of the British Mandate and was greatly furthered under Jordanian rule by the imposition of sanctions against the celebration of marriages other than before the *ma'dhūn*. Sanctions include fines and the refusal of exit permits for the pilgrimage (*ḥajj*) to Mecca. In the absence of a *ma'dhūn* the parties must apply directly to the court for the solemnization of marriages.[11]

The *ma'dhūn*, who is a person with some religious education, either a townsman or a villager, is an important instrument in the *shar‘ī* indoctrination of the Bedouin. The marriage contracts drawn up by him appear to comply with the meticulous requirements of Islamic law and the modifications necessitated by secular legislation, absence of *shar‘ī* or secular legal bar to marriage, such as the woman being in her waiting-period after divorce or the death of a former husband, and the age of competence for marriage. According to Jordanian law the age of competence is seventeen for the bride and eighteen for the groom, but the *qāḍī* may permit the marriage if they are at least fifteen (instead of nine and twelve, respectively, according to the authoritative Ḥanafī doctrine), provided he considers them physically fit and the bride's guardian consents (Anderson 1952, p. 191).

There have been instances of Bedouin applying to the court for permission for the marriage of a girl of fifteen.[12] Shaykh ‘Ābidīn states that if the *qāḍī* feels that the boy or the girl is not mature, he reports to the *Qāḍī al-Quḍāt* in Amman who, in turn, directs all the courts in the kingdom to refrain from marrying them. Permission is also required where the groom is twenty years or more older than the bride. In such a case the *qāḍī* may permit the marriage according to article 6 after satisfying himself that the girl consents of her own accord and that the marriage is in her interest (*maṣlaḥa*). Shaykh ʻĀbidīn says that the latter is the case where the girl has no other supporter or suitor.[13] It should, of course, be taken into account that the *ma'dhūn* receives the relevant information from the tribal *mukhtār*s, who are not as a rule punctilious in the matter of impediments to marriage. The *ma'dhūn* solemnizes the union while all the essentials of a valid *sharʻī* marriage are brought into play: offer and acceptance (*ījāb wa-qabūl*), the use of explicit marriage terms (*zawwajtuka wa-ankaḥtuka*) and the presence of witnesses. The parties are properly identified (*taʻrīf*) and must be fully competent, of age (*bāligh*) and sane (*ʻāqil*).[14]

Moreover, marriage contracts frequently indicate that the wife takes possession (*qabḍ*) of the whole of the prompt dower. Instances of this practice are also recorded in the *sijill*. Thus, in one case, it is said that a woman of the Taʻāmra tribe was married with a prompt dower of fifty Palestine pounds, "took possession of it (*istalamathu bi-yadihā*) and acknowledged receipt." In another case, a woman of the ʻUbaydiyya tribe alleged that her husband owed her sixteen dinars which she had lent him out of her prompt dower, but she had no witnesses and the *qāḍī* decided that the matter came under the jurisdiction of a civil court.[15]

Furthermore, there are instances of Bedouin women stipulating in the marriage contract that the deferred dower be paid along with prompt dower *li-aqrab al-ajalayn*, that is the part realizable in the event of divorce or the death of one of the parties, whichever should occur first. The amount is usually trifling but may reach one third of the total dower. Shaykh Sulaymān Sālim Muḥammad ʻAshīrat Ṣalāḥ al-Taʻāmra says that the deferred dower was small under the Mandate and is larger today.[16] Although the division of dower into prompt and deferred is a matter of custom, not of law, its mention as a condition in the marriage contract is significant from a *sharʻī* point of view. The increase in the amount of the deferred dower seems to be due to the influence of urban society. Even if marriage contracts are drawn up by the *ma'dhūn* in a routine manner, and Bedouin women do not actually enjoy their right to prompt dower (which is paid to the marriage-guardian) any more than to deferred dower, the *ma'dhūn* plays an important part by introducing the *sharʻī* norm under which the wife is a party to the marriage contract and competent to dispose of property, into a society attuned to tribal custom (Layish 1975, p. 51 *seq.*; 1974, pp. 403-4).

The Jordanian Family Rights Law contains the innovative provision that if the marriage contract stipulates a condition in favor of one of the parties (for example, that the wife may repudiate herself, that the husband must not transfer their residence to a locality other than that agreed upon at the time of the marriage or that he must not take an additional wife), this condition must be respected, provided that it is expressly stated. An infringement of such a condition is a ground for an action for the dissolution of the marriage by the wife (article 21). Except for conditions as to the division of dower into prompt and deferred, which are considered legitimate according to the authoritative Ḥanafī doctrine, this reform is not applied in Bedouin society, although the *qāḍī*s are prepared to respect conditions so long as they are not inconsistent with the nature of marriage; this attests to the inferior status of women.[17]

The court awards maintenance (*nafaqa*) to a Bedouin woman, on her application, at the rate agreed by the parties or, in the absence of agreement, in reliance on an opinion by experts (*mukhbir*) under article 56 of the Jordanian law. The most frequent ground for a maintenance claim is lack of a "legal dwelling (*maskan shar'ī*)" as defined by religious law. Maintenance of the wife includes medical expenses, which is an innovation over the authoritative position of all the orthodox Sunnī schools (article 65).[18] The *qāḍī* permits the wife to borrow money (*istidāna*) for her upkeep when the husband leaves her "without maintenance and without a supporter," and the debt is collected from the husband under article 59. In one case, the court awarded maintenance to a woman of the 'Ubaydiyya tribe whose husband was in Kuwait — apparently in reliance on article 60 of the Jordanian law which enables the court to do so when the husband has absented himself to a nearby or distant place, or is missing, leaving the wife without maintenance.[19]

The court also awards maintenance to minors and to parents. The latter signifies an impressive change in the position of Bedouin women. Thus, in one case, a woman of the Ta'āmra tribe claimed maintenance from her three children on the ground that she was "poor and her children had means and earned more than they required, and she had no one else who owed her maintenance." In another case, a Bedouin of the same tribe claimed maintenance from his sons who were serving in the army and the National Guard. It seems that the Bedouin are encouraged to apply to the court in matters of maintenance in view of the fact that, unlike arbitrators, it can enforce its decisions.[20]

Bedouin also apply to the court in matters of obedience. It appears that the traditional, conventional means of returning the wife to the husband's house, namely the good services of mediators and the persuasive powers of her father, no longer satisfy them. They are drawn to the court by its ability to carry out its judgments through execution proceedings (i.e., through the police). Article 33 of the Family Rights Law provides that: "The wife shall be compelled (*tujbar*), immediately after receipt of the prompt dower, to stay in the husband's legal dwelling and to follow him wherever he chooses to go...." Shaykh 'Abd al-Qādir 'Abd al-Muḥsin 'Ābidīn, the *Qāḍī* of Bethlehem, interprets this article as a *bayt al-ṭā'a*, that is, an enforceable judgment for obedience. Shaykh Muḥammad Sa'īd Jamāl al-Rifā'ī, the *Wakīl Qāḍī*, finds support for this interpretation in other Sunnī doctrines. There is no *bayt al-ṭā'a* in the Ottoman Family Rights Law of 1917, which is still in force in Israel. Anyhow, the *Sharī'a* Court of Bethlehem awards *ṭā'a jabran*, enforced obedience, in reliance on the said article.[21]

The Jordanian Family Rights Law provides that suspended repudiation designed to cause the wife, by way of a threat, to do or refrain from doing some particular act, is invalid (article 70). The Bedouin have quickly learnt to use this as a defense against dissolution. Thus, in one case a woman of the Ta'āmra tribe alleging that her husband had three times said to her: "Go [you are] divorced," applied for confirmation of triple repudiation. The husband contended that he had said: "*'Alayya al-ṭalāq* [oath of repudiation] you shall not sleep at the house of your relatives tonight," meaning thereby to get her to admit to taking his watch which had disappeared. The *qāḍī* dismissed her application on the ground that she had not succeeded in proving her allegation, and that in any case suspended repudiation without intent to divorce was invalid under article 70. In a further case, a woman, also of the Ta'āmra tribe, alleged that her husband had told her: "You are irrevocably divorced by triple repudiation if you do not prepare supper for me; I shall kill you if you do not." She had refused to prepare supper and fled to the house of her relatives after being soundly beaten by him. The husband confirmed that he had sworn to divorce her but pleaded in his defense that he had intended to compel her to prepare supper, not to divorce her. The court dismissed her application — again, it seems, in reliance on article 70.[22] The Bedouin apparently obtain advice as to how they can extricate themselves from such awkward situations without dissolving the marriage, and the *qāḍī*s may have something to do with it. At any rate, they can accommodate the Bedouin in this matter without falling foul of the *sharī'a*.

It seems that Bedouin women have learnt to use the new grounds for dissolution provided them by the Jordanian legislator. The Family Rights Law prescribes that a wife may demand dissolution by reason of damage (*ḍarar*) done to her through at least one year's unjustified physical severance from the husband, even if his whereabouts are known and he has property from which maintenance may be derived (articles 89 and 90). In one case, a woman of the Ta'āmra tribe proved to the satisfaction of the *qāḍī* that her husband had been absent without just cause for six years, that all trace of him was lost and that damage had been done to her through their severance. The court pronounced dissolution in reliance on the said articles.[23]

As stated elsewhere, the Bedouin in "the period of the goat's hair tents (*yawm buyūt al-sha'r*)," that is before sedentarization, were not strict in regard to revocable divorce (*ṭalāq raj'ī*) and the waiting-period (*'idda*) (Layish and Shmueli 1979, pp. 38-39). On the other hand, the *sijill* records many instances of apparent recourse to revocable divorce in court and the reinstatement of the divorced wife during the waiting-period in accordance with the *shar'ī* norm. Thus, in one case, a Bedouin of the Ta'āmra tribe declared before the *qāḍī*: "My wife by a valid marriage which has been consummated, who is absent from the session of the court ... is divorced from my protection (*'iṣma*) and from marriage to me by one revocable divorce (*ṭalqa wāḥida raj'iyya*)." The *qāḍī* pronounced as follows: "We have declared to him that she is divorced from him by one revocable divorce, that she must observe the waiting-period from this date, that he may reinstate her during her waiting-period and that there is no bar to her marriage after the expiration of the waiting-period [unless she is reinstated during that period]." In another case, a Bedouin woman proved to the *qāḍī* that her husband had "divorced her by two revocable divorces ... and she confirmed that he had taken her again under his protection." The *qāḍī*, after having the parties swear to the truth of their statements, decided that there had been "two revocable divorces and valid reinstatement (*murāja'a*) of the wife and that a third divorce is left [to the husband] with regard to her."[24] It should, of course, be taken into account that it is very difficult for the *qāḍī* to control the application of religious law to matters of divorce among the Bedouin because he must accept the testimony of the parties unless some moral blemish is found in them. But as far as indoctrination is concerned the ceremonial display of the *shar'ī* norm by a religious-legal authority is in itself significant.

The Jordanian Family Rights Law further provides that a divorce accompanied by a number — either by word or sign — shall count only as a single and therefore revocable divorce (article 72). This far-reaching reform has already come to the notice of the customary arbitrators. Shaykh 'Abd Allāh al-Dar'āwī 'Ashīrat al-Shawāwra al-Ta'āmra reports that the *Sharī'a* Court does not confirm a triple repudiation and awards one divorce instead.[25] Indeed, the small sample of divorce decrees seen by the author includes no triple repudiation (performed on a single occasion), although there were many applications by women for confirmation of such a repudiation. In all these cases the court dismissed the application either because the wife had not succeeded in proving her allegation or for some other reason, but not on the strength of article 72. As we have seen above, the *qāḍī* counts the accumulated divorces and tells the husband how many divorces there are still to go before the duty of intermediate marriage applies to the wife. Although the wife obtains no relief, her very application to the court in this matter is an indication of an increasing attachment of the Bedouin to the *Sharī'a* Court. The general public seems unaware of the reform as to triple repudiation. Those who wish to restore their marriage after triple repudiation seek remedies out of court, as we shall see below. It seems that the *qāḍī*, Shaykh 'Abd al-Qādir 'Abd al-Muḥsin 'Ābidīn, does not endorse this reform. He has expressed the opinion that a man who takes back, without intermediate marriage, a wife divorced by a triple repudiation "angers Allāh, who will punish him for it."[26]

Bedouin also resort to the court in matters of *wiṣāya* and *wilāya* (executorship for property inherited by minors and guardianship over their persons). There is evidence of this as early as the end of the Ottoman period. Obviously, in matters of property, considerable importance attaches to legal safeguards and enforcement measures, and only the court can provide these. The *qāḍī* usually appoints male agnates (*'aṣabāt*) as executors or guardians, in the order of entitlement prescribed by the *sharī'a* but which conforms also with customary law. One case is recorded in Bedouin documents in which a man of the Ta'āmra tribe willed some property to his minor son with the guarantee of two well-known arbitrators, Shaykh Muḥammad Sālim al-Dhuwayb and Shaykh Muḥammad Aḥmad Abū 'Āmriyya, both of 'Ashīrat al-Sharay'a al-Ta'āmra. He entrusted the minor son to them as a deposit (*amāna*), that is he made them executors for the property.[27] The *sijill* records instances of the appointment or dismissal of the paternal grandfather, a paternal uncle, or a brother, as guardian of a minor and executor for his property in the Ta'āmra and 'Ubaydiyya tribes.[28]

However, and this is an innovation in the application of the *shar'ī* norm, there are also instances of the appointment of women as *shar'ī* executors for the property of minors in cases where the father has died without having designated an "elected executor" (*waṣī mukhtār*) in his will, and there is no paternal grandfather and no elected executor on his behalf.[29] The court may appoint an agnate as guardian and the minor's mother as supervisor (*mushrifa*) as well. Thus, in one case, the court appointed the paternal cousin of a girl minor as guardian and her mother as supervisor. Shaykh 'Abd al-Qādir 'Abd al-Muḥsin 'Ābidīn explained the division of responsibility between them as follows: the mother has custody of the daughter (*ḥāḍina*) and the cousin looks after property matters and contacts with outside agencies. Supervision by the mother is essential because there is no religious-legal ban (incest prohibition) on cousin marriages. The agnate-mother combination is a sort of compromise between the customary and the *shar'ī* norm.[30] Moreover, there were cases where the court, through the *mudīr al-aytām* (director of the orphans' fund), took control of the moneys of orphans of the Ta'āmra tribe whose paternal uncle had abused his position as guardian.[31]

Bedouin resort rather frequently to the *Sharī'a* Court for the issue of succession orders, which attests to the increasing importance of land as an economic factor as sedentarization progresses. Land is becoming an object of transactions outside the family, hence the growing need for succession orders as legal proof of rights in property. The court apportions the estate among the legal heirs according to a mixed religious-secular system of succession: *mulk* and movables according to the *sharī'a* (*al-mas'ala al-shar'iyya*) which generally gives a woman half the share of a man of the same class and degree of relationship to the deceased while cognates (*dhawū al-arḥām*) are last in the line of heirs; and *mīrī* according to the Ottoman Law of Succession of 1913 (*al-mas'ala al-intiqāliyya*), which allots to a woman the same share as to a man and does not discriminate against cognates.[32]

Needless to say a reference to the *shar'ī* or legal share of a woman in a succession order does not prove that she will actually inherit. There are various ways of excluding her from the succession: renunciation, gift, distribution of the property in the deceased's lifetime etc., but there can be no doubt that a *shar'ī* order of succession of the court, even if not implemented, has a normative value in a society attuned to tribal custom. Moreover, documents and other sources show that Bedouin society is also adopting, albeit very slowly, the *shar'ī* norm of succession in respect of women. Thus, in one case, a woman renounced her share in her father's estate in favor of her brother, except for one item of immovable property which she actually took.[33] Shaykh Ibrāhīm 'Abd Allāh al-Dar'āwī 'Ashīrat al-Shawāwra al-Ta'āmra and Shaykh Sulaymān Sālim Muḥammad 'Ashīrat Ṣalāḥ al-Ta'āmra say that in the past a daughter would renounce her share in her father's estate upon her marriage to prevent fragmentation of the family property, but that she does not do so now because "the *sharī'a* has become stronger than custom (*far'*)." According to them, the deceased's widow takes an equal share with the sons although it passes to the sons upon her death. Similarly, it is usual for Druzes to will living quarters and income-producing property to the wife and to unmarried or "severed" (divorced or widowed) daughters on condition that these assets revert to the family upon their death.[34] Some distribute property among their daughters in their lifetime. Under custom, as we have seen elsewhere, a daughter only inherits in the absence of sons.[35]

A grandson whose father predeceased his grandfather is superseded by the sons of the deceased in the *Sharīʿa* Court as well — according to the *sharʿī* distribution — but the grandson takes his share under the Ottoman Law of Succession.[36] The absence of representation in Islamic law originates from patrilineal customary law, so that there can be no question here of the *qāḍī* compromising with tribal custom. The Muslims of Bethlehem and its surroundings overcome the absence of representation by willing to grandsons "what would have been their father's share had he been alive." Such a will is valid to the extent of one third of the estate. Shaykh Muḥammad Sālim al-Dhuwayb and Shaykh Sulaymān Sālim Muḥammad say that this practice obtains among the Bedouin as well, who resort to the court in this matter because a *sharʿī* will is "stronger" than a customary one. They note in this connection that when sons are disinherited, or consider themselves unjustly disadvantaged by one heir being given preference in their father's customary will, they claim their *sharʿī* right in the *Sharīʿa* Court after the father's death, and the court sets aside the will.[37] Wills in favor of an orphaned grandson, without quantitative limitation, have also been encountered among the Israeli Druzes. Their religious law allows complete freedom of testation, although the Druze Law of Personal Status of 1948, which has been adopted by the Druzes, recognizes the principle of representation (Layish 1976, pp. 104, 111; 1982, pp. 322-23; Coulson 1971, p. 143).

BEDOUIN HAVING RECOURSE TO RELIGIOUS-LEGAL OPINION

Another impressive manifestation of recourse to the *sharīʿa* by Bedouin is their seeking a religious-legal opinion from an *ʿālim* to solve a distressing problem. The subject in every instance encountered was triple repudiation pronounced in anger. To permit a thrice-divorced wife to return to her husband she must, under Islamic law, have first been validly married to another man. The new husband must consummate the marriage (although the Qur'ān, Sūra II:230, does not expressly require this), and only when he has divorced her or has died is she again permitted to return to the first husband after the expiration of the waiting-period. All the Sunnī schools hold, as a matter of principle, that the intermediate marriage must be bona fide. The Shāfi'ī, Mālikī and Ḥanbalī schools say that if it has been expressly stipulated by the parties that the second husband shall marry the woman "in order that she may again be permitted (*bi-qaṣd al-taḥlīl*)," then this marriage is void because it is tantamount to a temporary (*mut'a*) marriage and thus does not meet the requirements of an intermediate marriage. Abū Ḥanīfa, on the other hand, whose opinion is accepted by his school, holds that such a stipulation is void but that the marriage is valid, though religiously reprehensible (*makrūh*), and that the woman is permitted to return to her first husband. Where the second husband marries the woman "so that she may again be permitted to return," but without this having been expressly agreed and stipulated between the parties, all the schools except the Ḥanbalī hold that the intermediate marriage is valid though reprehensible. The Jordanian Family Rights Law of 1951 follows the innovation of the Ottoman Family Rights Law, based on the positions of the Māliki and Ḥanbalī schools, by laying down that the woman shall be permitted to return to her first husband after a consummated intermediate marriage, provided it was not concluded with even the unexpressed intention of making her again lawful to him (article 82). This is a notable deviation from the authoritative doctrine of Abū Ḥanīfa (Linant de Bellefonds 1965, pp. 413-17; Anderson 1952, p. 202 and 1951, p. 277; Abū Zahra, p. 270).

According to Bedouin concepts, of course, an intermediate marriage is a very severe sanction in terms of female chastity. A self-respecting Bedouin who wishes to live in conformity with religious law finds it difficult to meet this harsh requirement. The remedy for this predicament, as illustrated by a few instances in the documents of the Bedouin and the *sijill* of the *Sharī'a* Court, is to seek the opinion of an *'ālim* which will show him a way out. Thus, in one case, a respected shaykh of the Ḥamūlat al-Radayda al-'Ubaydiyya conducted negotiations for the marriage of his brother. It seems that some difficulties cropped up in these negotiations, for the shaykh "behaved foolishly and his foolishness got the better of him and great anger filled him against the father of the bride," whereupon he pronounced the words: "I swear that my wife shall be divorced (*'alayya al-ḥarām* lit.: 'a ban on me') if my brother marries that man's daughter (*yataḥallal* lit. 'makes her lawful to himself')." Some people who were there tried to calm and stop him after the first repudiation, but, as was to be expected, their intervention only made matters worse. He repeated the repudiation formula several times, swearing that the girl would never set foot on his doorstep. His oaths apparently served their purpose: the difficulties vanished, the marriage was celebrated and the bride moved into his house. But then his attention was drawn to the fact that his own wife was divorced. He thereupon applied to a Shāfi'ī *'ālim* in Bethlehem for a religious-legal opinion (*mā qawlukum dām faḍlukum* "what is your decision, may your honor endure?") as to how he could reinstate his wife without an intermediate marriage.

The *muftī* proposed two alternative solutions:

(1) The oath formula (*'alayya al-ḥarām*) is merely a declaration made implicitly or by allusion (*kināya*), which must be clarified by intent (*niyya*) as to divorce (*qaṭ' al-'iṣma*). If the husband pronounces the repudiation formula three times while intending to divorce the wife, then a *muḥallil* (intermediate husband) is required, but if he does not pronounce three repudiations, he may reinstate her before the expiration of the waiting-period, without a new dower and even without her consent, as in the case of a revocable divorce, which does not terminate the marital union. If the waiting-period has expired, he may only take her back by a new marriage and a new dower, and with her consent. The upshot of all this is that in the absence of intent to divorce the repudiation is not effective.

(2) The other solution is indirect. It challenges the *shar'ī* validity of the customary marriage, which requires elements such as offer and acceptance, explicit marriage formulas and the presence of two witnesses. The *muftī* declared that the duty of *taḥlīl*, of an intermediate marriage, only applied where the marriage was valid (*ṣaḥīḥ*); if one of its elements was missing, it was irregular (*fāsid*) and the Shāfi'ī Imām [Muḥammad ibn Idrīs] ordered its termination and the conclusion of a new, valid marriage with a dower. We may assume that the *muftī* knew that Bedouin marriages were customary, not *shar'ī*, and, therefore, if the man had intended to divorce his wife he could argue that his marriage was irregular and that a new marriage was required. This was unpleasant but not disastrous for it meant that an intermediate marriage was unnecessary.[38]

In one case, a woman of the Ta'āmra tribe ingenuously reported in the *Sharī'a* Court that her husband had divorced her by triple suspended repudiation: "[You are divorced by] triple repudiation (*ṭalāq bi'l-thalāth*), absolutely, if you do not prepare my supper...." and that he had said this four times. The wife had refused to comply and sought refuge with her relatives. She had stayed with them for a fortnight until he fetched her back to his house through mediators (*wusaṭā'*) after informing her that he had obtained a legal opinion (*fatwā*) declaring the divorce invalid, and she had resumed married life with him. The contents of the *fatwā* and identity of its author are not recorded, but he was clearly not a *qāḍī* and probably not a Ḥanafī *'ālim*, for the Ḥanafī doctrine, which prevails in the *Sharī'a* Court, is characterized by a formalistic attitude and, as already stated, attaches no importance to the element of intent. He was probably a Shāfi'ī *'ālim* for the Shāfi'ī school is dominant in the West Bank.[39] Shaykh Ibrāhīm 'Abd Allāh al-Dar'āwī says that when a Bedouin has divorced his wife by *barrānī* (i.e., out-of-court) triple repudiation, they may go to a *ma'dhūn* or a religious (*dīnī*) shaykh and ask for a *fatwā*. They will tell him "exactly" what happened, and he, for a few dinars paid to him "out of appreciation and respect," will pronounce the *ṭalāq* to have been a single repudiation. They will not go to the *qāḍī*. Shaykh Sulaymān Sālim Muḥammad says that a religious functionary in Bethlehem gives absolving *fatwā*s on the ground that there has been a "divorce in anger (*za'al*)," without intent (*niyya*) and he orders the husband to give alms (*kaffāra*) to the poor. The practice of seeking a *fatwā* to enable the reinstatement of a divorced wife has also been observed in Israel. In North Africa, *fatwā*s for reinstatement after triple repudiation are obtained on the plea that the husband was insane at the time.[40]

To sum up, the very fact that the question of reinstatement preoccupies the Bedouin, is a notable landmark in the Islamization process. They tell revealing stories about the *muḥallil*. When a man who has divorced his wife by triple repudiation has regrets, he is advised to choose a trustworthy *muḥallil* who will undertake to divorce the woman after a night against payment of a few dinars. For safety's sake, the *muḥallil* is given some wine to drink — in contravention of a religious prohibition — lest he feel tempted to consummate the marriage. In fact, it has happened quite frequently that the *muḥallil* refused to divorce the woman. Resort to the *muḥallil* and especially the *muftī* or *'ālim*, and various other devices to restore the marriage, are significant evidence of the establishment of the *shar'ī* norm among the Bedouin. Resort to the *muftī* is voluntary for he is not part of the court system. He, too, makes concessions, though ostensibly he does not have to deviate from religious law to facilitate reinstatement of a divorced Bedouin wife. He is thus an important instrument to impart the *shar'ī* norm to Bedouin society. It seems that not all the Bedouin are aware of article 72 of the Jordanian Family Rights Law which, as stated, provides that a divorce accompanied by a number shall count as a single and therefore revocable divorce. If they were aware, they would seek relief in court rather than use the services of the *muftī*.

Ḥājj Mūsā Muḥammad 'Īd al-Sharāy'a, of Za'tara, reports that in one case a man divorced his wife by saying: "You are divorced according to the three schools (*madhāhib*): no Chrsitian, no Muslim and no Jew will bring you back." This was a "rhetorical flourish," intended to express his determination not to restore his marriage under any circumstances; though, here, too, there is a suggestion of Muslim consciousness. Yet we may doubt whether the Bedouin are aware of the legal differences between the three religions. In fact they are not even aware of the differences between the Islamic schools of law. Shaykh Ibrāhīm 'Abd Allāh al-Dar'āwī and Shaykh Sulaymān Sālim Muḥammad declared in an interview that they were all the same to them, that they did not consider themselves bound by any particular school but acted on the principle of expediency (*maṣlaḥa*) according to the circumstances of the case. They probably discovered the advantage of the Shāfi'ī over the Ḥanafī school in the matter of reinstatement quite empirically — after failing to obtain relief in the *Sharī'a* Court where the Ḥanafī doctrine prevails. The authority of Bedouin arbitrataors is not limited to reconciliation between the spouses; if they consider dissolution unavoidable, they may pronounce it even without having received permission from the latter in accordance with Ḥanafī requirements. Such wide authority is in keeping with the Mālikī doctrine but we doubt whether the Bedouin are aware of this. Shaykh Ibrāhīm 'Abd Allāh al-Dar'āwī says that there is no connection between tribal arbitration and the Mālikī school.[41]

SUMMARY

The Islamization process is thus at its most intense in the *Sharī'a* Court. The *qāḍī* plays a central role in controlling custom and linking the Bedouin to the *sharī'a*. We have seen that custom, as expressed in the voluntary agreement, even if contrary to the *sharī'a* in substance and spirit, is "stronger than the *qāḍī*" and is legitimized by him. The question may be asked to what extent is there a similarity here to the role played by the *qāḍī*s in the formative period of Islamic law or to *'amal*, the practice of *qāḍī*s in North Africa?

Before the doctrines of the religious-legal schools (*madhāhib*) had crystallized, the *qāḍī*s acted as legislators, in a way similar to the arbitrators who formulated custom in the pre-Islamic period. They combined customary practice (which sometimes ran counter to Qur'ānic precepts) with "Islamic law" by unfettered individual reasoning (*ra'y*) and with a distinct tendency towards Islamization of the legal matter. But this contribution of the *qāḍī*s was not embraced in the theory of Islamic law (*uṣūl al-fiqh*), which does not recognize case-law or precedent, any more than custom, as legal and binding. The task of developing the legal system soon devolved on the *muftī*s (Coulson 1959, p. 20 and 1964, p. 28; Schacht 1964, p. 25).

On the other hand, the judicial practice which developed in North Africa, and especially in Morocco in the late fifteenth century, acquired a recognized status among the local *fuqahā'*. The *qāḍī*s realized that if they tried to strictly apply the Mālikī doctrine to a custom-oriented society they would completely estrange the latter from the *sharī'a*, and custom would reign absolute. They therefore preferred to compromise with it while linking it to the *sharī'a*. For this purpose they created what Schacht calls "a kind of protective zone around the *sharī'a*," that is to say an area in which the *sharī'a* met custom half-way without nominally giving up its supremacy. They did so having regard to the public interest (*maṣlaḥa*) by pragmatically applying "weak" (*ḍa'īfa*) or "irregular" (*shādhdha*) elements of the extensive Mālikī legal heritage which were compatible with custom. These traditional mechanisms provided *shar'ī* legitimization for innovative legal practice. Although the *qāḍī*s' solutions were ad hoc, their successors in office recognized them as binding; in Milliot's words: "La règle de droit, originairement fondée sur la coutume, s'appuie désormais sur le précédent judiciaire; une modification de la coutume primitive n'entraînerait pas sa revision" (1953, p. 176). The element of continuity creates a dimension of positive law. Some define *'amal* as a "realistic" type of law, as distinct from the theoretical type represented by Islamic legal doctrine (Berque 1960, pp. 427-28; Coulson 1959, pp. 21-23 and 1964, pp. 143-47; Milliot 1953, pp. 167-78; Schacht 1964, pp. 61-64, 84).

There is no similarity between the decisions and orders of the *qāḍī*s, charged with applying the *shar'īa* among the Judean Desert Bedouin, and the practice of the early *qāḍī*s or the Mālikī *'amal*. This is as far as we can judge from the small sample of decisions and orders, in spite of the readiness of the present day *qāḍī*s to meet custom half-way. For one thing, that readiness is usually limited to cases where there is agreement between the parties; where there is not the *qāḍī*s strictly apply the *shar'ī* norm which, as they know but do not openly admit, Bedouin society cannot always live with. In fact, as we have shown elsewhere, Bedouin may prefer tribal arbitration even after proceedings before the *qāḍī* have already begun (Layish and Shmueli 1979, p. 35), and the *qāḍī* himself sometimes refers the parties to arbitrators when he realizes that the case cannot be satisfactorily disposed of by letting *shar'ī* justice take its course. A systematic tendency of the *qāḍī*s to use unfettered discretion, or the *maṣlaḥa* principle, and traditional mechanisms likely to facilitate the assimilation and adaptation of custom, has not been observed. Despite the existence of a court of appeal and a uniform material law, the system of binding precedent has not yet been consolidated in *shar'ī* justice, and there is consequently no continuity in the judicial practice.

On the other hand, the Shāfi'ī *muftī* tends to a certain sophistication designed to facilitate the adoption of the *sharī'a* as a way of life for Bedouin by taking the sting out of it in serious cases, that is by compromise with custom. But this has not developed into a permanent systematic method such as the *ḥiyal* (legal devices), which have been an important instrument of the Islamization of custom.

In Israel, too, the Islamization of the Bedouin is in full swing. Some of the *qāḍī*s are more or less consciously guided by *maṣlaḥa* or even by a need to adapt the legal norm to the requirements of a Bedouin society in process of sedentarization. That is, they compromise with custom while linking it to the *sharī'a*. But social motivation is not sufficient. There is need for a theoretical infrastructure and more refined legal tools to legitimize the decisions of the *qāḍī*s, and for this purpose an extra-judicial religious-legal authority would seem to be required. The ability of the *sharī'a* to control custom and draw it into its orbit is also diminished by the secularization which Islamic law is undergoing in a non-Muslim state (Bousquet 1960, p. 171; Layish 1974, pp. 407-9 and 1975, p. 334).

NOTES

1. The paper is based on legal documents obtained from the *Sharī'a* Court of Bethlehem and from Bedouin in the Jerusalem–Bethlehem region. It is part of a comprehensive study of custom and *sharī'a* among the Bedouin settled in that area being prepared by the author, with collaboration of the late Dr. Avshalom Shmueli, under the auspices of the Middle East Research Unit of the Harry S. Truman Research Institute in the Hebrew University of Jerusalem. The author thanks the Institute for its assistance. The collection of the documentary material would have been impossible without the whole-hearted cooperation of Shaykh 'Abd al-Qādir 'Abd al-Muḥsin 'Ābidīn and Shaykh Muḥammad Jamāl al-Rifā'ī, *Qāḍī* and *Wakīl Qāḍī*, respectively, of the *Sharī'a* Court of Bethlehem; of arbitrators, *mukhtār*s and other Bedouin, and of the Military Government. To all these and many others the author expresses his gratitude.

2. According to Shaykh 'Abd al-Qādir 'Abd al-Muḥsin 'Ābidīn, the *Qāḍī* of the *Sharī'a* Court of Bethlehem at the time when this paper was prepared, Bedouin resort to the court is motivated more strongly by those exigencies than by increased Muslim orthodoxy (interview of 21 April 1975).

3. The data are based on a sample taken at random but still representative of all matters of personal status and succession of Bedouin in the *Sharī'a* Court. The sample includes also Bedouin who have settled in Bethlehem and the neighboring villages.

4. Layish (1975, pp. 106, 111, 180-181, 206-9, 252-53) and the sources indicated there. This inclination has also been noticed among the Druze *qāḍī*s. See Layish (1982, pp. 375-76).

5. Interview with the *Qāḍī* on 21 April 1975. This statement was confirmed to

the author by Ḥājj Mūsā Muḥammad 'Īd al-Sharāy'a of Za'tara on 3 June 1976. See Layish (1974, p. 400).

6. Interview with the *Wakīl Qāḍī* on 5 May 1975. See Schacht (1964, p. 62).

7. *Sharī'a* Court of Jerusalem, Confirmation of Marriage, 4 August 1956 (Muḥammad Sharārī al-A'raj al-Sawāḥra); *Sharī'a* Court of Bethlehem, Sijill Ḥujaj 'Āmma, No. V, p. 7 no. 1, p. 12 no. 12, p. 22 no. 1.

8. *Sharī'a* Court of Bethlehem, Sijill Ṭalāq No. III p. 8 no. 21, p. 30 no. 4, p. 41 no. 35. p. 176 no. 13; Sijill Ṭalāq No. XII, p. 7 no. 19/2, p. 16 no. 40/1.

9. Interview with the *Wākīl Qāḍī* on 5 May 1975. See Layish (1974, pp. 400-1 and 1975, p. 198).

10. Official Gazette, No. 1081 of 16 August 1951, p. 1272. See Anderson (1952, pp. 190-206).

11. Interview with them on 6 October 1975. See Chelhod (1971, p. 103).

12. For example, *Sharī'a* Court of Bethlehem, Contract of Marriage, no. 79393 of 13 April 1958.

13. Interview with him on 21 April 1975 and 6 July 1975. Cf. Anderson (1952, p. 192).

14. *Sharī'a* Court of Bethlehem, Contracts of Marriage no. 79393 of 24 April 1958, and no. 38426 of 29 October 1935; Mūsā 'Awdat Allāh al-'Ubaydiyya, Confirmation of Marriage for Registration in the *Sharī'a* Court, n.d.

15. *Sharī'a* Court of Bethlehem, Contract of Marriage, no. 79393 of 24 April 1958; Sijill Ḥujuj 'Āmma, No. V, p. 12 no. 12; Sijill al-Aḥkām, No. IX, p. 97 no. 211/61.

16. *Sharī'a* Court of Bethlehem, Contracts of Marriage, no. 38426 of 29 October 1935 (20 pounds prompt dower and 10 pounds deferred dower); Bayt Sāḥūr, no. 79393 of 24 April 1958 (45 pounds and 5 pounds, respectively); Bethlehem, Mūsā 'Awdat Allāh al-'Ubaydiyya, Confirmation of marriage for Registration in the *Sharī'a* Court, n.d. (95 pounds and 9 pounds, respectively); Sulaymān Sālim Muḥammad 'Ashīrat Ṣalāḥ al-Ta'āmra, Arbitration — Family Dispute (Impotence), n.d. (60 dinars and 10 dinars, respectively); interview with Shaykh Sulaymān Sālim Muḥammad 'Ashīrat Ṣalāḥ al-Ta'āmra on 6 October 1975.

17. Interview with Shaykh Muḥammad Sa'īd Jamāl al-Rifā'ī on 5 May 1975. See Anderson (1952, pp. 193-94); Layish (1974, p. 403 and 1975, p. 30 *et seq.*).

18. For example, *Sharī'a* Court of Bethlehem, Sijill al-Aḥkām, No. IX, p. 25 File 163/60, p. 58 File 79/61, p. 99 File 210/61, p. 370 File 71/71. See Anderson (1952, p. 200).

19. *Sharī'a* Court of Bethlehem, Sijill al-Aḥkām, No. IX, p. 2 File 60/60 and File 11/63, respectively. See also p. 1 File 56/60.

20. *Sharī'a* Court of Bethlehem, Sijill al-Aḥkām, No. IX p. 163 File 139/62 and p. 10 File 75/60, respectively. See also *ibid.*, p. 57 File 57/61, p. 71 File 116/61. Cf.Layish (1975, pp. 104-5).

21. For example, *Sharī'a* Court of Bethlehem, Sijill al-Aḥkām, No. IX, p. 28 File 162/60 and File 168/60, p. 43 File 25/61, p. 16 File 127/60; interview with the *Qāḍī* on 29 April 1975 and with the *Wakīl Qāḍī* of 16 October 1975. See Layish (1975, p. 101).

22. *Sharī'a* Court of Bethlehem, Sijill al-Aḥkām, No. IX, p. 165 File 19/63 and p. 370 File 82/71, respectively. See Anderson (1952, p. 201); and Layish (1975, pp. 156-57, 189-90).

23. *Sharī'a* Court of Bethlehem, Sijill al-Aḥkām, No. IX, p. 129 File 180/62

(the Court of Appeal did not confirm the decision). See Anderson (1952, p. 202).

24. *Sharī'a* Court of Bethlehem, Sijill Ṭalāq, No. XII, p. 2 no. 5/2 and Sijill al-Aḥkām No. IX, p. 1 File 42/59, respectively.

25. Interview with him on 14 and 19 November 1975. See Anderson (1952, p. 201).

26. For example, *Sharī'a* Court of Bethlehem, Sijill al-Aḥkām, No. IX, p. 1 File 42/59, p. 165 File 19/63. Interview with the *Qāḍī* on 21 April 1975.

27. Muḥammad Sālim al-Dhuwayb 'Ashīrat al-Sharay'a, Will of 29 June 1956.

28. For example, *Sharī'a* Court of Bethlehem, Sijill Ḥujuj 'Āmma, No. V, p. 5 nos. 7 and 9, p. 6 no. 10, p. 14 no. 9, p. 15 no. 12, p. 16 nos. 13 and 14; Salāma Ismā'īl Ḥamdān 'Ashīrat al-Shwāwra al-Ta'āmra, Executorship of 8 Sha'bān 1322H. See Layish (1975, p. 263 *et seq.*).

29. For example, *Sharī'a* Court of Bethlehem, Sijill Ḥujaj 'Āmma, No. V, p. 5 no. 8, p. 6 no. 11, p. 15 nos. 10 and 11. See Marx (1967, p. 185).

30. *Sharī'a* Court of Bethlehem, Sijill Ḥujaj 'Āmma, No. V, p. 14 no. 7; interview with the *Qāḍī* of 21 April 1975. See Layish (1975, p. 265 *et seq.*).

31. *Sharī'a* Court of Bethlehem, Sijill al-Aḥkām, No. IX, p. 127 File 31/62.

32. For example, *Sharī'a* Court of Bethlehem, Sijill Wirātha, No. II, p. 1 nos. 1 and 3, p. 2 nos 4 and 5. See Layish (1975, p. 307 *et seq.*).

33. Sharārī Muḥammad al-A'raj (Abū Qā'id) al-Sawāḥra, *Waṣl Tanāzul* of 29 May 1956.

34. Interview with them on 22 June 1975. See Layish (1976, pp. 113-14 and 1982, p. 337 *et seq.*).

35. Rizq al-Sa'īd Rizq 'Ashīrat al-Shawāwra al-Ta'āmra, *Maḍbaṭat Ḥaṣr Irth* of 18 November 1954; Layish and Shmueli (1979, pp. 39-40).

36. For example, *Sharī'a* Court of Bethlehem, Sijill Wirāthāt, No. II, p. 33 no. 9/3.

37. For example, *Sharī'a* Court of Bethlehem, Sijill Ḥujaj 'Āmma, No. XV, p. 75 no. 30/2, p. 176 no. 36/2. See Coulson (1971, pp. 52-53); interview with Shaykh Muḥammad Sālim al-Dhuwayb and Shaykh Sulaymān Sālim Muḥammad on 29 December 1975.

38. 'Alī Muḥammad Ḥasan Ḥamūlat al-Radāyda al-'Ubaydiyya, *Fatwā* (reinstating a divorced wife), n.d.

39. *Sharī'a* Court of Bethlehem, Sijill al-Aḥkām, No. IX, p. 370 File 82/71.

40. Interview with Shaykh Ibrāhim 'Abd Allāh al-Dar'āwī on 14 November 1975 and with Shaykh Sulaymān Sālim Muḥammad of 3 June 1976; Layish (1975, p. 176); Linant de Bellefonds (1965, p. 411, note 1) and the source indicated there.

41. Interview with Shaykh Ibrāhīm 'Abd Allāh al-Dar'āwī and Shaykh Sulaymān Sālim Muḥammad on 5 August 1975, 6 October 1975 and 14 November 1975, with Ḥājj Mūsā Muḥammad 'Īd al-Sharāy'a al-Ta'āmra of Za'tara on 3 June 1976, with Shaykh Muḥammad Sa'īd Jamāl al-Rifā'ī on 16 October 1975; Nimr 'Awda al-Mubarrak 'Ashīrat al-Nabāhīn al-Ta'āmra, *Ṣakk Taḥkīm* of 29 September 1963. See Tyan (1960a, p. 48 *et seq.* and 1960b, p. 72).

Blood Revenge in Bedouin Society

Joseph Ginat

Instances of murder among the Bedouin who live within the borders of Israel, and those in other Arab countries, are fairly frequent.[1] The Bedouin themselves often explain after such incidents that the killer did not have homicidal intentions but was carried away by the heat of an argument: the consequences were not intended, and neither was the act premeditated. One example of a cause for squabbling is over who should go first when shepherds meet at a well to water their flocks. Even so small a controversy may lead to homicide. While the first killing may occur on the spur of the moment and without prior planning, this is not, of course, the case when a murder takes place for revenge. The very idea of retribution — in this case putting to death someone who has killed another — is intentional and premeditated. The Bedouin themselves explain blood revenge by arguing that if a man has been slain, there must be one grave opposite the other grave. Despite this apparently simple explanation its realization is hardly satisfactory. A Bedouin may sometimes shrug off the importance of one human life but if such an attitude were deeply anchored in the thought and feeling of the community no blood revenge would follow. Revenge is in essence a rebellion against the shedding of blood — a reaction that expresses outrage that this should have happened. I shall investigate in this paper those instances in which blood revenge is preferred, and those in which blood money is paid.

Sometimes the word "feud" is incorrectly used in place of blood revenge. Feud refers to prolonged hostility leading to repeated murders, on a mutual basis, between the rival groups. I claim that feud does not exist in Bedouin society, only blood revenge or the payment of blood money. The terms feud and blood revenge are not interchangeable. Furthermore, wars and raids between rival tribes and groups do occur in Bedouin society but this is not blood revenge, nor is it for that matter feud.[2] Blood revenge refers to a single killing to avenge a murder that has taken place. In this paper I shall only be concerned with blood revenge.

Bedouin society is organized in such a way that collective responsibility within the group significantly influences the pattern of life. Each member of a co-liable group[3] knows that if he murders someone, or even if he kills him unintentionally without any premeditation he creates a conflict with the injured co-liable group that can last for many years and might lead to blood revenge. In many cases of blood revenge it is not the individual who caused the murder upon whom revenge is taken. It can be, and there are many occasions when it is, a member of the murderer's co-liable group — somebody who is completely innocent and apart from the original argument is murdered in revenge because of collective responsibility. Although any member of the group can be killed as a revenge, according to the principle of collective responsibility the members of the injured group will usually try to kill a close relative of the murderer.

An important distinction in blood dispute in Bedouin society is whether the killer and his victim are members of different co-liable groups, or whether they both belong to the same co-liable group. Different norms and procedures apply according to whether the killer and his victim are in any way related or not.

KILLER AND VICTIM FROM DIFFERENT CO-LIABLE GROUPS

As a reaction to the killing of a member of a certain corporate group, a single retaliation will follow — the murder of one member of the murderer's co-liable group, or the payment of blood money (*diyya*) following negotiations through the services of a mediator.[4] Blood revenge or the payment of blood money is usually supposed to stop the cycle of hostile relations between two groups. Until revenge has been taken or until a cease-fire (*'atwa*) has been concluded, every member of the murderer's co-liable group lives in constant fear of death. The time period during which *'atwa* is effective is not clearly defined, though it is usually valid for at least one month. There is, however, no obligation whatsoever to prolong the agreement.

The custom regarding *'atwa* among the Bedouin in the Negev differs from that in the north of the country. *Ṣulḥa* (peace settlement) negotiations in the Negev are opened before the end of the year following the murder. Sometimes an *'atwa* will be agreed upon for several years, until a peace agreement is concluded. In the Negev, the party who has inflicted injury hopes that *'atwa* will be followed in due course by peace. Yet there is no binding obligation on the part of the injured party. The party responsible for the murder is not required to pay any sum to the mediators or to the representatives of the injured party. However, it is often the case that mediators receive a remuneration. Among the Bedouin of the Galilee, on the other hand, the notables who organize the mediation ceremony stipulate what is to be paid to the injured group by the party responsible for the murder. When the *ṣulḥa* ceremony is arranged, the sum handed over on the occasion of the *'atwa* is deducted from the total amount agreed as compensation.[5] When a group in the Negev accepts blood money, an interim agreement is reached. It covers the period between the conclusion of *'atwa* and the *ṣulḥa*. This contract is called *jira* (based on payment of money or the handing over of a bill). At the *jira* ceremony, the amount of money paid by the party responsible for the murder is announced ('Āref al-'Āref 1933, p. 90). The money is entrusted to the mediators until the final sum is paid as blood money at the time of the *ṣulḥa* ceremony.

The ethnographic data presented in the following case histories refers to killing for blood revenge and also to the payment of blood money for manslaughter. These particulars throw light on the conditions in which an injured group will oppose a cease-fire (*'atwa*), and insist on murder as the only possible form of revenge, as well as conditions whereby an injured group will conclude a *ṣulḥa* after payment of blood money. By describing various case histories an attempt will be made to find a general explanation for the reactions of the injured group.

In analyzing blood disputes it is important to recognize the significance of the effects of violent death on those emotionally close to the victim. It is true that a man's feelings are often akin to those in his group, whose members are linked to him through bonds of blood relationship. But there may also be especial relations of friendship or good comradeship.

Collective responsibility does not mean that everyone relates to everyone else within the group in the same way or that sympathies and antipathies cannot develop on an individual basis. Although an individual will formally react the same way as other members of his group concerning the death of a member of the co-liable group, the deceased may or may not be strongly motivated in promoting revenge. Although the individual acts according to prescribed norms, he may urge normative action more passionately and more convincingly when his feelings are roused. A man whose feelings are hurt may refuse blood money and insist on physical revenge. When he is indifferent he may wait for others to advocate revenge.

Students of society must bear in mind that human beings are not only part of economic, social and political structures, but are also individuals who react to the same challenge in unique ways — even if they live in an identical or nearly identical manner. Their duties and privileges may be the same, and their patterns of behavior dictated by custom, but even within this sytem there is still room for a variety of emotions and reactions. Sometimes a person's strong emotional reaction may result in an outburst which presents a dramatization of the incident, arousing feelings of empathy and compliance. An individual who feels personally injured may not acquiesce when blood money is accepted for a murdered relative to whom he has been close. He may resort to action without the consent of the group.

KILLER AND VICTIM MEMBERS OF SAME CO-LIABLE GROUP

Where the corporate group functions well, a way is usually found to appease and compensate the injured family without recourse to blood revenge or blood money. Peters says that revenge is not taken within the group (nor when persons live at a great distance from the group as stated in the previous section). Clearly, if revenge is taken within the group, the loss to the group will be twice as great. Dispute in the case of murder within the group is resolved through the murderer's exile or the expulsion of the person who killed without premeditation, for a period of several years (1967, pp. 264-65).

However, if the immediate family demands revenge or blood money this indicates that the group is not functioning well. Where revenge and payment of blood money takes place within the group the same conditions apply as when the killer and victim are members of different co-liable groups.

Where the killer and his victim are members of the same co-liable group, it is the Bedouin norm that the group should resolve the crisis with the least disruptions to the group's activities. This is achieved (providing of course that the injured party is not bent on revenge) by (1) the murderer going into self-exile for an undetermined time period; and (2) the murderer giving his closest unmarried female relative to the closest male kin of the victim.

The time period of the self-exile is determined by the elders of the co-liable group shortly after the exile (which has to be out of the area where the co-liable group lives) takes place. The decision regarding the length of the exile depends on the circumstances that led to the homicide. Clearly, a premeditated murder will be viewed differently than an accidental death caused by an individual. Many times the exiled person will enlist the services of a mediator to help reduce the period of exile. There are cases where the closest relatives of the victim initiate the return of the exiled individual back to the fold of the group; as well as cases where the exiled individual feels that he has been unfairly treated by his group and builds himself a new life attached to a different group.

When the murderer goes into exile he gives his closest unmarried female relative to the closest kin of the person who was killed (i.e., his daughter or sister to the deceased's father, brother or son). The girl who lives in such a relationship is called a *ghura*. The *ghura* lives with this person until she gives birth to a male offspring. This act is done in order to compensate the family for their loss. After giving birth the woman may return to her natal family. However, in most cases, if the relationship was satisfactory, a marriage is arranged. The bride price is usually about half of the regular price. This is because the woman is no longer a virgin, even though it was the husband who deflowered her. When the marriage takes place the exile of the murderer is terminated, if not before. There is a paradox in this Bedouin norm for both the family to which the murderer belongs and the injured family may be brought closer — through a marriage union.

FACTORS AFFECTING REVENGE OR SETTLEMENT

When the economy of a group is based on wage labor, this group will be anxious to resolve the quarrel quickly because their daily and regular trips to their places of work will make them vulnerable to the revenging group. When the economy of the group is based on the raising of herds, the movements of group members are not regular and violent revenge more easily avoided. When groups lived in the desert in tents it did not present a problem to repitch the tents of one group at some distance from another group in case of a dispute. However, when the Bedouin live in houses, daily interaction between the two groups is unavoidable. The sedentarized Bedouin are thus anxious to solve the dispute quickly.

More and more Bedouin are now entering the wage labor market on a permanent basis. In undertaking such work the Bedouin accepts a certain responsibility to attend work regularly. If for reasons of a blood dispute he decides one morning that it is unsafe for him to attend, it is highly likely that his job will not be waiting for him when he decides that it is safe to attend. The wish to keep one's job and the benefits accruing to this, is a strong reason to make sure that blood disputes are settled quickly. It is important to remember that this reason is multiplied by all those group members who partake in wage labor. Many of the Bedouin who are not already engaged in wage labor, practise intensive cultivation techniques not just for their own use but for sale on the market. Intensive cultivation requires regularly daily looking after. This regularity and the danger inherent in it makes it important to negotiate a quick settlement.

The economic factors outlined above usually underly any analysis of a blood dispute. However the principal reasons for motivating the injured group's choice is in the main political. It must be understood that the Bedouin are highly politicized. The conduct of their daily life and the main topic of their daily conversation is related to political activity and intrigues within their society. A man's political standing is akin to his honor — to be safeguarded and if possible increased. Marx (1973) gives an example of how circumcision ceremonies are used to promote the political and economic standing of the father and the co-liable group.

There are other factors which also must be considered. The outraged individual of the injured group may well refrain from taking revenge if prolonged imprisonment would result. Marx refers to such a case where the potential avenger would have had to go to prison for a long time if he had acted out his revenge (1967, pp. 193-94). After the initial cease-fire, when the heat of the moment for revenge may have subsided somewhat, economic and political considerations often guide the decision of how the injured group reacts. For example, imprisonment might not only take away the breadwinner of the family but also weaken the group if this individual has a high political standing. Consequently, it often happens that revenge is abandoned, especially in cases where the murderer lives at a great distance and where the group of the murdered man has no economic, political or other relations with the group which infliected injury on one of its members. But this is avoidance of the norm.[6]

Collective responsibility is a heavy burden. Each member of a group knows that if he murders or kills unintentionally, the *khams* may have to go into exile for several years. If no *'atwa* is reached, another member of the family, not necessarily the murderer, is likely to be killed. When members of the co-liable group understand that one of its members acted without due consideration of collective responsibility he is likely to be expelled from the group.[7] This turns him into a *meshamas*. *Shamas* means "sun" in Arabic and a *meshamas* is one who is exposed to the sun or who is exposed publicly.

Where the perpetrator of violence is a *meshamas* and continues to live in the same area, the avenging group cannot renounce its duty of blood revenge. Blood money will not be received by an injured group from any individual pronounced a *meshamas*. No *'atwa* can be arranged, and not even the compulsory three-day term of *'atwa* may be imposed on the injured group. Because no negotiations can be held (in cases of blood dispute) with a person unattached to any group, the avenging group is left with no alternative but to try to kill him in revenge. There may be additional members in the group of the murderer who are not of the *khams* but such persons are not forced into exile after a murder. They do not participate in the payment of blood money, nor do they receive a share of any blood money paid to the group which they have joined. However, it is customary for every male member of the group who is not of the *khams* to give the family of the murdered man a camel or its value in money. This payment is called the "camel of sleep" (*be'ir al-nom*) and once it is accepted the giver can sleep in his tent without fear. The payment is really an "insurance policy," a wise precaution that prevents a possibly hasty act. 'Āref al-'Āref (1933. pp. 78-79) points out that members of the sixth and seventh generations, as well as those who have joined the group, pay for the *be'ir al-nom.* This observation indicates that collective responsibility is only up to the fifth generation.

One major factor affecting revenge or settlement is the political condition of the injured group. Where a leader sees the need to bring cohesiveness to his group, he will use a blood dispute case for encouraging revenge rather than peaceful settlement. All of the following case histories will indicate that the decision to seek revenge or agree to a settlement is in some way economic and/or political.

CASE HISTORY I

Some groups whose members are of peasant origin originally from the area in which the fortress (*qal'a*) of Khan Yunis is located, live among the Bedouin of the Negev and are called Qla'iyya (Marx 1967, p. 197). Until 1968, they did not possess any tribe of their own but were subject to the authority of three tribes in the Ẓullām sub-federation, and the tribe of Quderat al-San'a. The Qla'iyya and other peasant groups had previously owned no land where they originally resided. They migrated to regions inhabited by Bedouin, particularly the lowland of Beersheva-Arad. The dispersion of the Qla'iyya among the Bedouin tribes is indicated in figure 1. The situation of the Qla'iyya is well described by Marx:

> The peasants acquired land wherever and whenever they were able to obtain it, and then remained under the protection of the tribe from which the land had been bought. Thus one now finds that the members of many peasant

> groups are formally divided up among three or four tribes though other groups will be concentrated in one tribe (1967, p. 77).

Despite the formal membership of co-liable groups with several tribes, the Qla'iyya pitched their tents together and in this way succeeded in creating their own political framework. As early as the 1950s, the head of the Qla'iyya groups asked the authorities to recognize the groups as an independent tribe, a resolution reflected in the 1959 Knesset election campaign. In 1968 the head of the largest co-liable group was finally nominated head of the tribe and awarded the coveted seal of the Sheikh.

In 1970, a group within the newly formed tribe (A) seceded from the tribe. This group convinced the authorities that its members had nothing in common with the other group except their peasant origin. The head of the seceding group (B) was appointed head of a tribe, being permitted to use the Sheikh's seal as a symbol of his position, as well as to carry a pistol. In the fall of 1971, yet another group (C) seceded from the first tribe (A) and also tried to be recognized as an independent tribe,[8]

Figure 1

Dispersion of the Qla'iyya among the Bedouin tribes

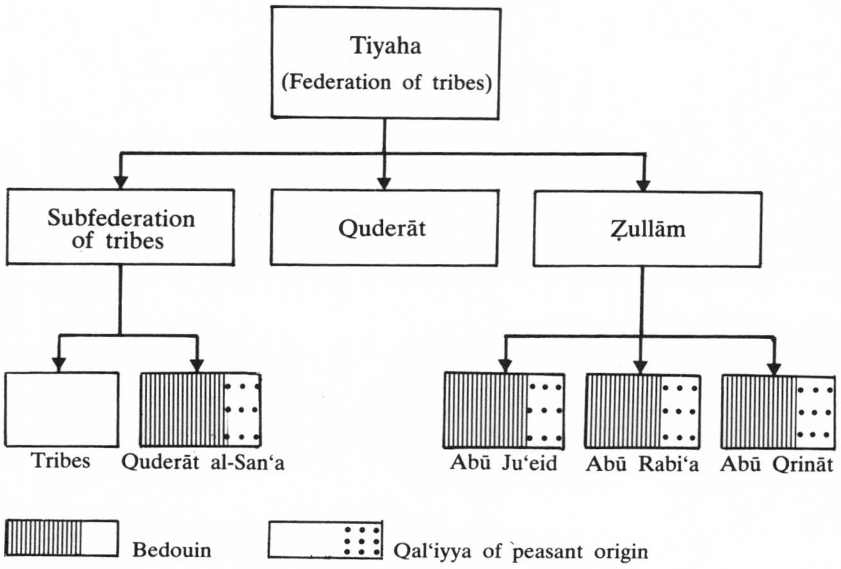

although its head had not yet won recognition at this time. The split in the Qla'iyya after recognition by the authorities as a tribe is set out in figure 2.

The head of tribe B did his best to persuade members of group C to join his tribe. Verbal clashes between tribe B and group C created tension which focused on pasture and the right to draw water from certain wells. (Prior to the political maneuvering of the involved parties in attempting to gain recognition as independent tribes, there had been

Figure 2

The split in the Qla'iyya after recognition by authorities as a tribe

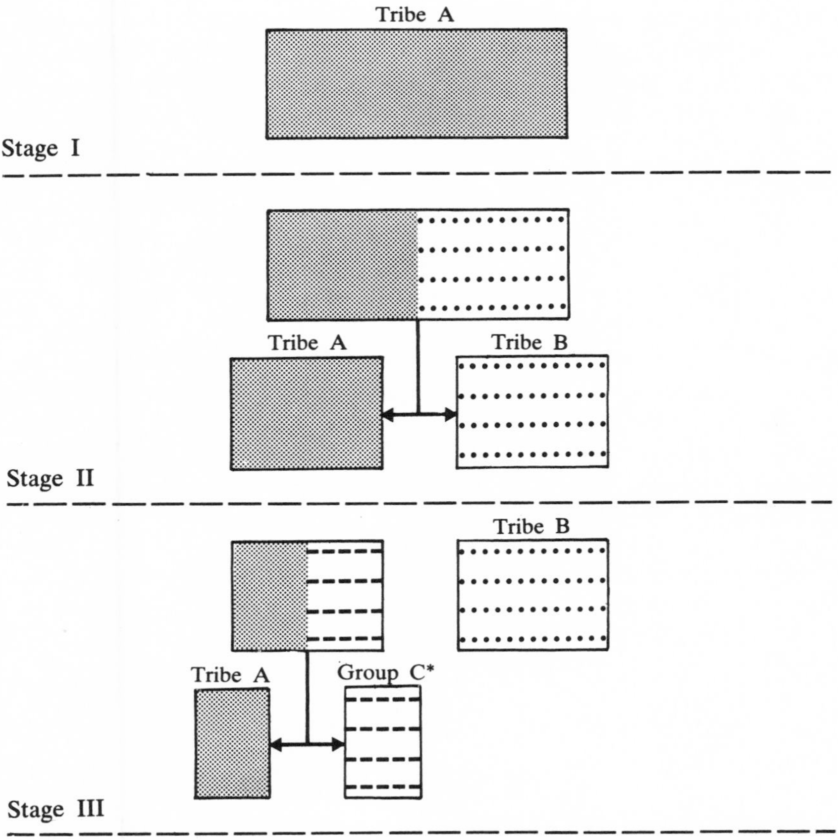

* Group C seceded from tribe A but had not yet been recognized as a tribe.

no conflict over the shared use of these scarce resources.) Finally, a murder took place. On 25 May 1972 members of tribe B ambushed members of group C close to Beersheva and in the fight a member of tribe B was killed.

Those attacked belonged to the same co-liable group, whereas the ambushers came from three different co-liable groups, all of whom were members of tribe B. Police investigations did not establish the identity of the murderer and the incident was defined as a mass quarrel. Immediately after the murder had taken place, several notables of various tribes turned to the leader of the injured group and declared a state of *'atwa mafrūda* (an enforced cease-fire).[9] The head of the injured group turned a deaf ear to every suggestion of peace and only submitted *nolens volens* (willingly or unwillingly) to *'atwa*, which lasts three and a third days as custom prescribes. An enforced cease-fire enables the co-liable groups (one of whose members killed a man) to find shelter in the encampment of another tribe.[10] Such a cease-fire takes place irrespective of the wishes of the injured group. If they do not submit willingly to a cease-fire, then they must accept it unwillingly, but accept it they must.

The elders of the tribe experienced in the handling of blood disputes assembled to deal with the situation. It is customary to arrange a cease-fire to last for a year, if agreed to by the injured party, during which time it is hoped that the tempers and frustrations of the injured group will have died down somewhat, and then to try and arrange a lasting peace treaty with a negotiated compensation in the form of blood money. However, custom did not prevail on this occasion.

The head of group C and group members argued that the head of tribe B was preventing the head of the co-liable group from concluding a peace agreement. The head of tribe B, however, maintained that it was not for him to decide but depended on the members of the injured group, who were not prepared to accept blood money. After several meetings with the members of the co-liable group in the Sheikh's tent, one of the elders said that there was no hope of reaching an agreement, and that the members of the co-liable group were determined to murder a member of the attacker's group. Other notables supported this view, and it was therefore suggested that a *ṣulḥa* committee be set up. This is not the custom in the Negev, although it is common in the north of the country. In *ṣulḥa* committees, members are chosen from the ranks of Bedouin leaders and representatives of the administration. In this instance, the governor of the district, a representative of the Prime Minister's Office, and a representative of the Police, in addition to the sheikhs, served on the committee, but their efforts proved futile.

Pressure was exerted by the authorities on the leader of tribe B by confiscating his revolver and suspending him from office. Talks were held with the leader of the co-liable group (one of whose members was murdered), and he received certain promises and assurances in the event he would accept blood money. However, these actions were to no avail and at the end of May 1973, one year after the murder, the members of the co-liable group of tribe B avenged the death of their member by murdering the brother of the head of group C. Three of the members of the avenging group were found guilty of murder and sentenced to life imprisonment in January 1974. Figure 3 shows the relations, within the same co-liable group, between the man who was killed and his avenger. The avengers accused of murder were his uncle and two of his cousins.

The Qla'iyya number about 1,800 while there are about 7,000 Bedouin of the Ẓullām tribes. The tracts of land owned by the Qla'iyya peasants and acquired from the Bedouin are in the district between Tel al-Milḥ and Tel 'Arad.[11] The camps of the Qla'iyya are concentrated between

Figure 3

The killed man and his avengers

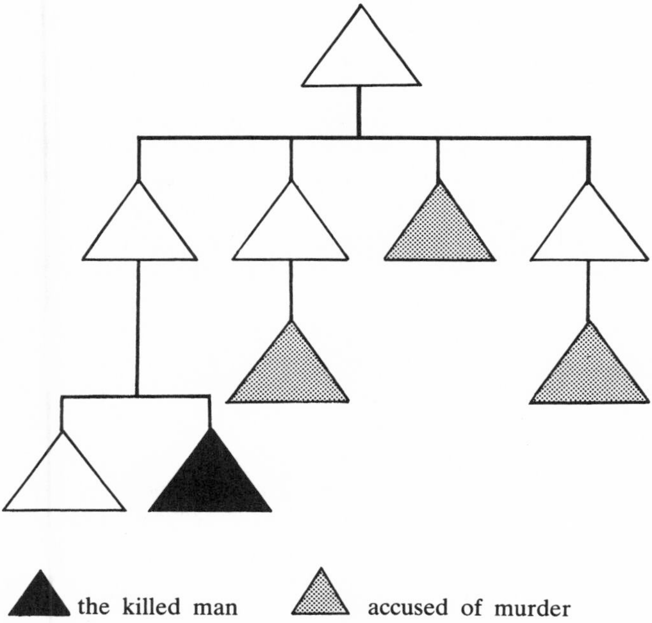

the school of Kuseifa and Tel al-Milḥ. The encampment of tribe B is the most southern of all and is located next to Tel al-Milḥ. Tribe A is located in the center, whereas the members of group C are settled at the northern-most end of Kuseifa (which is intended as a permanent settlement for the Bedouin of the district). Marx points out that:

> Even though the peasant group own some land, it would still be true if one called them "landless", for the land is never sufficeint for their requirements, and they still have to obtain the larger part in share-cropping arrangements, wherever available. There is, of course, some connection between the source of a man's land and his political allegiance, so that the peasants are in many ways politically tied to their Bedouin landowners. But this economic and political dependence on the Bedouin does not in any way detract from the peasants' allegiance to their own co-liable groups (1967, p. 78).

This condition prevailed until the end of the 1960s. In recent years the economic and political dependence of the peasants on the Bedouin has decreased. Although the Qla'iyya lease land from the Ministry of Agriculture, it is not enough for their subsistence. Many young men have become wage earners and commute long distances to work.

Well before the antagonism between the parties, one of the leaders of the four co-liable groups of tribe B moved close to Lud where he bought a stone dwelling house, and in 1967 he became a member of the committee of Trustees of the Muslim Waqf in Lud. Some families from two co-liable groups, one from that of the injured group that had taken revenge and others from the Sheikh's group, pitched their tents close to one of the Arab villages in the Triangle[12] and lived there all year round. They are employed in Jewish agricultural settlements, or grow vegetables on land leased from Arab villagers, utilizing modern systems of cultivation, including irrigation and plastic covers during the winter season. The fourth group possesses flocks and has grazed them for several years in the area between Beit Shemesh and Ramle. Since they do not keep black goats, they do not encounter much difficulty in obtaining pasture permits.[13] Most members of the group stay with their flocks during the lambing and milking season, from October to April, selling their dairy products chiefly in Ramalla district. Thus at various seasons of the year, a considerable part of the tribe is found outside of the Negev encampment. The cultivation of the land near the encampment requires no more than several weeks work each year.

After the murder of a member of his tribe the leader of tribe B saw a chance of uniting the whole tribe. As a pretext he assembled the males of the tribes for consultations. They went to the Negev, concentrating in one encampment close to Tel al-Milḥ. Blood disputes do not often occur, but mutual responsibility "constitutes the ultimate obligation of members of a co-liable group" (Marx 1973, p. 241). Had the members of tribe B agreed to *'atwa*, tension would have abated. Not only would the members of other co-liable groups have returned to their habitual occupation in the north of the Negev but also the members of the injured co-liable group would have left the Negev to return to the place which they have inhabited for the last decade, the Triangle and Ramle-Lud. The leader of tribe B set up a large guest tent (*shiq*) which was crowded all hours of day. The Sheikh even asked the Ministry of Education to add further classes to the school attached to the tribe in order to accomodate the children of the assembled families. The Sheikh fully understood that his suspension from office was temporary, a ruse in order to exert pressure and make him agree to *'atwa*. In his eyes the consolidation of the tribe was of the greatest significance. The fact that the tribe had been split in the past had weakened its organizational structure. The blood dispute offered an opportunity for strengthening his position. The appearance of Sheikhs and other notables in his tent for consultations clearly added to his status. Usually unity is achieved by decreasing tension in the group, but in this case unity was achieved by increasing tension.[14] This was possible because only the injured party is in a position to agree or not to agree to *'atwa*.

The Sheikh of tribe B understood that an agreement of *'atwa* even if it was not subsequently renewed, is an indication of a lessening of tension, and would have an adverse effect on his aim of consolidating his tribe. The political factor was decisive when the leader of tribe B incited the injured co-liable group to revenge. The murder of the brother of the leader of group C, who was ambitious for official recognition as Sheikh, is also politically significant. The revenge could have been implemented through the killing of any member of the co-liable group, but the intention was to injure the leader.

CASE HISTORY II

Marx (1967, p. 241) describes the case of Jedū'a Abu Ṣulb who was expelled from his co-liable group by his agnates.[15] He "was persecuted by bad luck" or "began everything the wrong way" say the Bedouin, and became involved in a number of blood disputes. In 1951 he wounded a member of another section of the tribe, but the members of his group were able to resolve this blood dispute. Two years later, while hunting, he accidentally shot and wounded a shepherdess. The dispute following this incident was prolonged since the sounded shepherdess subsequently died from gangrene. Jedū'a's group ended this dispute, but he was proclaimed *meshamas* and expelled from his *khams*.[16] No one could now hold the former group responsible for his actions. Some time after this he crossed the border (between Israel and Egypt) into the Sinai Desert, and again got into trouble. When the Egyptians discovered his illegal presence he tried to escape, injuring a Bedouin during the shooting that occurred. Jedū'a returned to Israel and was employed as a watchman by an agricultural company, whose fields bordered on those of the al-Huzayel tribe. Several young men of the Tawara group (whose origin is from southern Sinai) conspired against him, claiming that they had priority in employment in this region because they were of local origin. Jedū'a was attacked and in the ensuing fight a man was killed. In the subsequent trial Jedū'a pleaded self-defense. The Tawara knew that he was expelled from his *khams* and decided to kill him at once, so before the trial opened several young men of the Tawara group staged a fight close to the prison. One of them insulted a policeman and made several derogatory remarks about the State of Israel. He was arrested and found to be in possession of a knife which he had hidden in his shoe, and which was clearly intended to be used in order to kill Jedū'a. The court sentenced Jedū'a to three years imprisonment but he was released after two years.

Jedū'a asked the military governor to find shelter for him at some distance from the Negev, and in the winter of 1960 he went to live with a Bedouin tribe in the north of the country. His hosts refused to accept payment from him, although he himself received wages for his labors during his stay with them. Despite the kindness he received from the Bedouin in the north, he could not forsake the Negev and in the summer he returned to work as a watchman in the United Jewish Fund forests close to Dimona. At night he slept in different creeks, never remaining in one place all night. In 1962 he married and had a son but in the spring of 1964 fate caught up with him and he was killed in a fight by two men from a different co-liable group than whom he was in dispute.

Members of the Tawara still claim that the blood dispute between Jedū'a and themselves is not yet at an end and that his son will be murdered when he grows up. They believe that even after he was expelled from his co-liable group, agnates kept in contact with him and that the expulsion from his group, made known to all tribes prior to the last quarrel, was a fake (Marx 1967, p. 24-42). This, however, is not the end of the story. For Jedū'a's son claims that he too will revenge his father's death.

CASE III

In the spring of 1975, a thirty-year-old Bedouin, a contractor, of the Abu Raqaiq tribe, was killed by his father's brother's son (*ibn 'amm*). The father of the murderer and the father of the victim both used to be herders. At this time, the father of the victim, although financially supported by his sons, possessed herds for which he leased a certain pasture. Members of his brother's nuclear family invaded the pasture and there followed verbal insults that led to physical violence in which one of the sons (the contractor) of the man who had leased the pasture was stabbed in his arm. The event led to tension between the two families. Several years later, another fight took place in which the man who had previously been stabbed in the arm (son of the man who had leased land), was attacked and killed by a paternal cousin. The court sentenced the accused man to four years imprisonment. His father and brothers went into exile as the accused man would have done had he not been incarcerated (Hardy 1963, p. 92). The exiled father and brother decided to live with the al-Huzayel tribe at a distance of about twenty kilometers west of their own residence. Although they had formerly lived in shacks, they now pitched tents which they attached to one of the co-liable groups of the host tribe.[17]

The victim's brother maintained that revenge would be taken, and several notables among the Bedouin of the Negev did their best to bring about an *'atwa*. They were, however, unsuccessful in their attempts. The head of the co-liable group in whose vicinity the victim's relatives now resided, explained that the reason for the unsuccessful attempts at promoting an *'atwa* was that for several years before there had been no cooperation between the two families. This was largely due to the fact that the sons supported their respective families by a non-agricultural livelihood. As a result, there was little interaction between the two families, and a corresponding loss of mutual cooperation which is necessary where close families are engaged in full-time agriculture or herding.

Coincidentally, the wealthiest among the sons of both families was the victim. When sons derive their livelihood from sources other than the land or herds there is a separation of interests, and envy and rivalry are often the consequence. The men in this case history were no longer dependent only on their ascribed status, which was identical because of their close blood relationship. That the victim had succeeded most among the descendants of the two families clearly created a difference between the achieved status of the individuals. This distinction must have been a source of tension between them. Where one's livelihood is largely dependent on the cooperation of other family members, such as in tilling the land or minding flocks, disputes do not usually develop.

Neighbors of the victim's nuclear family were convinced that there had been a premeditated deliberate killing and not a spontaneous flare-up of passion, during which a man had hit out blindly and had accidentally caused death, as often happens according to Bedouin evidence. They explained that in the first fight the stabbing had been carefully planned and was only the first phase of premeditated murder. The decision of the father and brother of the murderer to live outside the camp, but still to remain in the region, was unsatisfactory to the family of the victim. The need for revenge might have been obviated if the family of the murderer had moved to the north of the country instead of remaining on the periphery. The fact that there was a necessity to ask for *'atwa* is proof of the disfunction of the group even before the murder. Such an action is not customary within the co-liable group. This case history illustrates that cleavage within the co-liable group may result when there is no economic cooperation between close relatives and eventually this may impede the group's effectiveness.

CASE HISTORY IV

Bedouin who are employed as teachers or clerks often express their fear of verbal clashes between members of their group and another group, knowing that such clashes may eventually involve them in a blood dispute. One Bedouin, referred to here as Ḥassan, wished to leave his group to avoid being involved in any blood dispute that might arise. He learned, however, that this cannot easily be effected. He feared that he might be cut-off from his extra-tribal source of income as a result of tribal affairs in which he no longer had an interest, and he anxiously watched his group for potential disputes with other groups. To him, group membership had become a burden since he was not in need of economic cooperation or group protection. In other words, the justification for the existence of co-liable groups may diminish where socioeconomic changes have taken place. It was true, he admitted, that revenge usually focused on the person himself and his close relatives when injury was inflicted, but this was not always the case. Thus all members of a co-liable group are not really safe until *'atwa* is conducted, a situation which he, for obvious reasons, feared and resented.

Since he himself could not de facto give up membership in his co-liable group, he took other measures to safeguard his security and those close to him. He persuaded the heads of several nuclear families in his group to expel a cousin whose conduct was likely to involve the group in disputes. The cousin was duly pronounced a *meshamas*. However, in

September 1977 Ḥassan's fears were justified. A fight occurred between a number of teenagers belonging to Ḥassan's group, and others from a different group and another tribe. There were casualties on both sides. The notables of the respective tribes attempted to solve the dispute internally by telling the police that the culprits could not be found. However, this reconciliation attempt was unsuccessful and the culprits were handed over to the authorities.

Tension mounted sharply after the incident, both groups making mutual accusations and each group disclaiming responsibility. Ḥassan was deeply worried and when he realized that he could not effectively leave the group, he argued in favor of a modification of the norms of collective responsibility. He felt that these norms should not now be strictly adhered to when the Bedouin were living in a world so dramatically changed from when the norms were first promulgated. This is certainly possible, as representatives of the Bedouin in the Negev discovered in Jordan (on a visit of condolence to King Hussein after his wife's death). The Bedouin of Jordan restrict blood revenge to just three generations instead of five in the case of co-liable groups. This is a good example of how customs function within changing socioeconomic conditions. Once the conditions surrounding the customs no longer prevail, they are likely to be relinquished.

CASE HISTORY V

In 1974 bloodshed occurred in the tribe of Ḥujerat, which was settled at Bir al-Maksur in the district of Shfaram. The owner of a combine harvester started to harvest the field of a member of another co-liable group of his tribe. The son of the owner of the field appeared and demanded that the man leave the field immediately, whereupon the owner of the combine went home carrying a sack of grains he had already harvested. The son of the owner of the field came afterwards to demand the grain but the combine owner said he wanted his payment first. The dispute escalated from words to blows, and the combine owner knocked his opponent out by hitting him on the head with a rock. The man died and the combine owner was arrested.

The head of the tribe, who usually acted as judge and mediator in blood disputes among the Bedouin and the villagers of Galilee, immediately secured a cease-fire agreement. Fifteen days later the *ṣulḥa* took place even before the trial opened. Police charged the man with manslaughter in self-defense and agreed to release him on bail prior to the opening of the trial, in which he was later pronounced innocent.[18] According to the *ṣulḥa* agreement he had to pay a sum of Il. 70,000

(Israeli Lirot) to the family of the dead man as compensation and to exile himself to the Negev for seven years. Even though the members of the tribe knew that he had acted in self-defense it was still necessary for an *'atwa.* Even if a killing is accidental and recognized as such by those involved, it is still necessary to secure a *ṣulḥa* agreement. There have been cases where revenge has been taken even though the first death was accidental.

The incident related above occurred in a permanent settlement of the tribe where field cultivation is a minor livelihood and most of the tribe are permanently employed outside the settlement. These circumstances and the fact that the shepherds of the tribe do not have close grazing areas for their flocks (and would thus be in greater danger from the injured group because of the distance from the camp) were compelling reasons to negotiate a quick peace agreement.

It was the responsibility of the head of the tribe, a well-known mediator in murder cases among Israeli Arabs, to decide whether the injured group should accept *'atwa* and blood money. Where the group is not bent on revenge, as in this case, the mediator may often shorten the negotiations.[19] His suggestion that the murderer be exiled for seven years, despite the recognition that he had acted in self-defense, made the arrangement of the *ṣulḥa* possible. Since the beginning of 1977 the exiled man has pleaded, through various people, with the head of the tribe for permission to return. He argues that the conditions of the *ṣulḥa* were stipulated in his absence while he was still under arrest and before the court found he had acted in self-defense. The head of the tribe, the mediator, thinks the request premature. The exiled man, together with his family, thus cannot return, but the members of his co-liable group who have remained where they live and work, do have social contact with the murderer's family.

In this case the fact that both groups were sedentarized and lived in the same settlement, was important in securing a quick *ṣulḥa* agreement. The head of the tribe wished to make sure that no dispute threatened their economic livelihood. The change in the economic and social structure of Bedouin tribes explains the difference in the handling of blood disputes like this. In this case it was recognized that the victim was largely responsible for his own death.

CASE HISTORY VI

In 1966 a wedding ceremony took place amongst settled Bedouin approximately fifty kilometers north of Beersheva. At weddings and other happy events it is customary to fire pistol shots in the air as a manifestation of joy.[20] During this particular festivity, however, a Bedouin was killed and the Sheikh of one of the tribes was arrested and accused of murder. Although the fatal shot was proved to have come from his revolver, the Sheikh was pronounced innocent for lack of evidence. The man killed was a member of a co-liable group of a tribe living in the vicinity of the Sheikh's tribe. There were ambiguous facts regarding the circumstances of the shooting. Several Bedouin mentioned an exchange of insults between the Sheikh and the murdered Bedouin, several minutes after both had left the guest-tent. A shot was heard and the Bedouin was found dead, lying in a pool of blood. Others testified that the killing had been unintentional. In the course of the police investigation, *'atwa* was agreed upon by the two co-liable groups involved. Discreet negotiations were held to prolong the period of *'atwa* until the end of the trial, because it was feared that the true state of affairs might come to light.

About one year after the incident, the members of the injured co-liable group accepted a proposal of *jira*. In the discussions regarding the blood price they defined the killing as murder. The negotiations led to a compromise which made an immediate arrangement of the *ṣulḥa* possible. The injured co-liable group was relatively small, being a section of the tribe that was not strongly organized. Several of the sections of the tribe had more than once turned to the authorities asking to be permitted to sever their links with the tribe and to be recognized as independent tribes.[21] The Sheikh who paid the blood money (thus confessing to the manslaughter) was the head of his tribe and his status among the tribes was high. He was also popular with the representatives of the government, and was frequently consulted by them. The members of the injured group were of low socioeconomic status, and a peace agreement with the co-liable group of the Sheikh was considered most desirable, promising many economic and political advantages.

Another case history involving groups of dissimilar strength is found in the tribe of al-Huzayel. In 1966 a member of the Sheikh's co-liable group unintentionally killed a member of the same tribe of the Abu-Ghani group. A stray bullet escaped from his rifle while he was cleaning it. Not only was *'atwa* granted immediately, but representatives of the injured group argued that there was no need for blood money.[22] A member of the Sheikh's co-liable group repeatedly offered to make payment, but was met with a firm refusal.

The family of the murdered man did not enjoy high status in the group, partly the result of the family having separated several years previously, some of its members having moved to the Ramle region. The reason for the refusal of blood money is to be found in the different status of the involved parties. The Sheikh enjoyed much higher status than the group whose relative was accidentally killed. The weaker group sought to create a relationship in which the stronger group was indebted to it by refusing to let the latter pay their debt. Had the injured group accepted blood money, the matter would have been closed and the status quo preserved; by not accepting indemnity, the imbalance between the two groups was reduced. The stronger group would now be obliged to the weaker one. This obligation would most probably be effected through some form of economic help, and under certain circumstances it would mean having to support or defend the weaker group. The just claim (with respect to receiving a blood payment) of the weaker group was thus put to their material and political advantage. These shifts were perhaps never spelled out in so many words, but members of both groups were conscious of the state of affairs. The stronger group repeatedly tried to pay its debt being aware of the implications that the refusal implied.

CONCLUDING REMARKS

The ethnographic data presented in this paper indicates that blood disputes rarely last for many years.[23] Some disputes, of course, cannot be resolved quickly. When the outcome of a dispute is still in the balance, the field work of the anthropologist is greatly helped by the fact that the parties involved will tend to mention and elaborate other instances of murder which occurred in the not too distant past. In the *'atwa* negotiations, or in the preliminary phases, the participants also describe other instances as models for decreasing tension in the current case. If one interviews the mediator and those involved in the dispute, some of these persons were probably involved in earlier blood disputes already concluded. This provides additional factual knowledge and a basis for comparison.

In this paper I investigated those instances in which blood revenge is preferred, and those in which blood money is paid. A distinction was made between where the killer and victim belong to different co-liable groups, and where they belong to the same co-liable group. In the former case, in order to ensure greater cohesion within the group, the leader will try to use the murder of one of its members as a basis for unification. Tension will be artificially intensified to make members feel they have to stand together, the leader hoping that the solidarity formed within the group will outlast the blood dispute. The refusal of *'atwa* may lead to the murder of a member of the group who inflicted the injury. If a man expelled from his group or even someone who joined a certain co-liable group becomes a murderer, there will not as a rule be a peace agreement. The members of the injured group will attempt to murder him if he remains in the area.

Socioeconomic and political variables are usually the main determinants in the reaction to blood disputes. The political factor should be examined on two different levels: the political relationship of the two groups involved in the blood dispute and the political structure of the injured group itself. On the evidence and analyses of the case studies presented here, it may be said that solutions are structured by the situation in which they occur. One should not assume that because two co-liable groups have the same physical environment, and the same economic basic and structure, that they will react in the same manner to the murder of one of their members, particularly when the internal political organization of the two groups are different.

Where the killer and his victim belong to the same co-liable group and the group is not organized, acts of revenge may be expectd within the group. Sedentarized organized groups whose members are not employed seasonally, but who hold permanent jobs, will try to resolve disputes by paying blood money and arranging for *ṣulḥa.*

NOTES

1. The thesis in this paper and part of the ethnographic data were presented at a lecture held at the Annual Meeting of the Israeli Anthropological Society, held in Jerusalem in March 1977. The analyses are taken from a wide-ranging study of Bedouin and rural societies including the Christian and Druze communities. I thank Emanuel Marx, Tel-Aviv University, and Philip Carl Salzman of McGill University, for their helpful comments.

2. The term feud is generally applied to all types of hostility. Peters (1967, p. 269) distinguishes between types of feud that should follow from the segmentation model developed by Evans-Pritchard. According to Peters, revenge is impossible within a tertiary group (parallel to the co-liable group in the Negev). Between two different tertiary groups, blood revenge or payment of blood money may take place. At the level of secondary sections (parallel to the sub-tribe in the Negev — a co-liable group with some individuals or families who for one reason or another left their original group and joined the tribe), there is feud; while at the level of primary sections (practically the same as any tribe in the Negev), there exists a reciprocity of hostilities leading to raids. Hostility at the level of tribes (which are very similar to sub-federations of tribes or a federation in the Negev), generally expresses itself in warfare. Black, Michaud has this to say about feud: "Since feud is an essentially diachronic phenomenon it is usually impossible to observe a whole feud at first hand. Much of the material on feud presented by anthropologists has consequently been gleaned from conversations with tribesmen from stories told about great deeds in the past.

Such material is naturally wrought with contradictions stemming from the desire of the opposed individuals and groups to exonerate and justify their position in a feuding relationship. But in the absence of written records this is the only possible method of investigating feud" (1975, pp. 234-35). Regarding wars and raids see Sweet (1965) and Musil (1928).

3. The term "co-liable group" was coined by Marx in *Bedouin of the Negev* (1967). It refers to the *khams*, that is the group formed by all descendants of one ancestor to the fifth generation.

4. For a full explanation of the role of the mediator, see Ginat, "The Role of the Mediator: With Special Reference to Blood Disputes."

5. There are instances when the injured party among the Bedouin of the Galilee refuse to accept money during the *'atwa* ceremony. It is possible that the custom of giving money became a norm among Bedouin of the Galilee under the influence of villagers. The ceremony of *'atwa* among those living in the Triangle (see note 12) villages resembles the one held among the Negev Bedouin. No money changes hands during the *'atwa* which is termed *'atwat sharaf*, an agreement of honor. The Bedouin claim that it is easier to violate an agreement based on payment of money than one that effects a man's honor.

6. Avshalom Shmueli, in a personal communication to me, relates an instance of a formal settlement of blood disputes between distant groups. He states that there was a formal settlement between the Ta'amra tribe and a group in Nablus. Such a settlement may perhaps be partly explained by the fact that in dry seasons and drought years Bedouin of the Ta'amra region need to graze their herds and flocks on the eastern slopes of the Samarian mountains, not far away from Nablus.

7. For a full exposition of the outcast in Bedouin society, see Ginat, "Meshamas — The Outcast in Bedouin Society."

8. This group was recognized as an independent tribe by the authorities in 1979.

9. According to 'Āref al-'Āref, two versions exist regarding enforced cease-fires. One version claims that it lasts one day, another version that it lasts three days (1933, p. 180). All my informants claim that the period is three days and three nights, and one-third of a day (*Thalāthat aylām wa-thalāthat layael wa-thilth yōm*).

10. Every members of a group that is granted shelter is called *ṭanib*. *Ṭanab* literally means the cord of the tent connected to a peg. Those seeking the protection of the tent-dwellers pitch their tents by continuing the line of tents of the group that is to play host to the refugee. The cords of the first tent of those asking for shelter are tied to the last tent of those who offer shelter. When anyone comes to ask for shelter for himself this is called *dakhil*. He holds on to the central pole of the tent and asks for asylum. (The verb *dakhal* means to enter.) The person seeking asylum only for himself is seated in the *shiq* (that part preserved for hospitality) and there he spends the night. He is thus taken into the host's home and enjoys his protection. Robertson-Smith (1966, pp. 48-49) provides additional information regarding *dakhil* and *ṭanib*.

11. The Qla'iyya marriage patterns are distinct from those of the Ẓullām Bedouin. The percentage of in-group marriages among the Ẓullām amount to 70 percent, while the corresponding figure is 30 percent for the Bedouin (Marx 1967, p. 112). The Bedouin of the Ẓullām tribe endeavor to establish as many relations as possible through marriage among the groups of the three tribes

residing in the district (Marx 1967, p. 143); the Qla'iyya, on the other hand, try to cope with their landless situation through marriage within the group (Marx 1967, p. 223-24).

12. The Triangle is actually a strip of territory of Arab villages that were under Jordanian control after the War of Independence, 1948. This area was given to Israel in exchange for other territory in the Rhodes cease-fire agreement, 1949, between Israel and Jordan. The strip of land itself does not form a triangle, but the three major cities in the Samarian region of the West Bank form a triangle, of which this strip of land is a part.

13. Black goats are rather destructive animals. The authorities will thus only permit Bedouin to graze them in areas where they can do no harm to the local flora.

14. See Coser (1956, chap. 7) for the theoretical basis of this remark.

15. The names in all the case histories presented here have been changed except for the case of Jedū'a Abu Ṣulb. Marx, in his discussion on the Abu Ṣulb group, refers to the case using the real name. See Marx, *Bedouin of the Negev*, pp. 238-42.

16. See note 7.

17. See note 10.

18. In Israel, arrest follows murder if the suspect is known, and release against bail cannot be arranged until the termination of the trial. The court, according to the law, cannot but impose sentence for life on anyone found guilty of murder.

19. In the present case it was in the mediator's interest to accelerate the process of negotiation. but frequently he may prefer to let it drag over a prolonged period. See Ginat, "The Role of the Mediator — With Special Reference to Blood Revenge" for case histories where the mediator prolongs the negotiations on purpose. The status of the mediator fits the definition and analysis of George Simmel (1971, pp. 145-8) in his study on the subject of the "Stranger." "He is objective and both sides trust him. He is both close and distant at the same time, and therefore helps reduce tension." According to Coser, the main function of the mediator is to reduce tension and the level of aggression. It is his task to propose formulae which will be adopted and will lead to an end of the dispute (1956, p. 50).

20. During wedding and circumcision ceremonies the Bedouin customarily fire shots into the air while singing and dancing takes place. They explain that this is a way of expressing joy. The sound of a shooting whips up enthusiasm, and many more people feel impelled to join the circles of the singers and dancers. Sometimes, a man holding a license to keep a weapon may permit relatives or friends to use it in order to fire some shots on such an occasion.

21. The sections who now wish to secede from the tribe under discussion belonged, in the past, to other tribes. In the War of Independence, 1948, the majority of several tribes chose to move into Jordanian territory. Those sections remaining in Israel were annexed by a tribe to which the co-liable group of the victim belonged.

22. In general, when a certain group renounces payment of blood money, it does not divulge this intention beforehand. After the sum stipulated as blood money has been handed over, and at the end of the *ṣulḥa* ceremony, the head of the group declares that the peace concluded is a true one, but payment of money is renounced. In the presence of the guests he returns the money to the representative of the family, a member of which was responsible for the injury.

Recently it has become customary to give the money in a transparent plastic bag in order to let those invited see the money.

23. Professional literature abounds with analysis of blood disputes by various scholars, among them Robertson-Smith (1966), Kennett (1925), Hardy (1963), Peters (1967), and Black-Michaud (1975). In addition, many travelogues refer to such disputes and text books have at least partly dealt with some of the issues. Investigation has focused on procedure rather than on ethnographic findings. Only Marx (1967) and Colson (1953, 1962) have presented field data as the basis of their analysis. A great deal has been written on *'atwa* and how it has to be negotiated, on the roles of mediators and judges, on the amount of blood money to be paid, and on other developments in the procedure of the handling of blood disputes. As often as not, the term "feud" slips in. Where there is feud there is a chain of reciprocal murders, one following the other. Revenge for the first killing, which terminates the process of disputes, cannot be defined as feud.

The Exercise of Power by Bedouin Women in the Negev

Gillian Lewando-Hundt

This analysis deals with the dynamics of power and influence between men and women in a society where sex roles are highly differentiated. Its particular focus is the basis and exercise of power by women among the Negev Bedouin. The private female domestic sphere will be viewed as a power base for women.

In the course of this analysis, the family will be conceived of as a power system whose members have different degrees of access to resources which form the basis of power. Women occupy a variety of roles during their life cycle, some of which are of longer duration than others. At one time or another they are daughters, sisters, brides, daughters-in-law, mothers and mothers-in-law. These different roles give them access to a number of resources such as certain kinds of information, certain persons, the control of certain economic resources, or certain kinds of authority. Women employ these resources in various ways in order to increase their power and influence. Their deployment of these resources will be referred to as strategies (Lamphere 1974, p. 99). This analysis will focus on the resources and strategies that women use, and will involve a discussion of domestic disputes.

> Because women are confined to the domestic sphere, their efforts to achieve power necessarily bring them into competition with close kin and affines: with those to whom they are bound by moral and ethical ties... Women in such household may ostensibly fight over trivialities, but the real stakes are political — the capacity to determine the actions of others (Fishburne Collier 1974, p. 91).

Two central theses will be discussed. The first is that the power of the Negev Bedouin women is based in, and exercised from, the domestic sphere, but influences events and persons beyond this sphere. The second is related to the effects of settlement and wage labor on the power of Bedouin women. (Negev Bedouin society is in the process of transition from semi-nomadism based on flocks and land, to settlement based on wage labor.) This second thesis states that settlement accompanied by wage labor results in increased sexual segregation of women from men, and also increases access of women to other women, thus widening their sphere of personal freedom and mobility. The first part of this article examines the first thesis (the extent and limits of women's power as exercised from and extending beyond the domestic sphere); the second part presents a description and explanation of the effects of settlement and wage labor on women's social lives. Paradoxically, settlement increases access to other women but wage labor, through increased segregation from men, limits the extent of their power and influence.

FIELDWORK

The fieldwork upon which this analysis is based was carried out intensively from January 1972–May 1973 and also from 1974–78, in the Negev, the southern part of Israel. The researcher lived with two families. One was a settled tent dwelling family from the Abu Rgaig tribe who lived near Tel Sheva, a planned village, 10 kilometers northeast of Beersheva. The other was a semi-nomadic family from the 'Azazmeh tribe, 20 kilometers southeast of Beersheva.

There are close to 40,000 Bedouin in the Negev (38,600: Statistical Abstract, 1976). A few are semi-nomadic, living in tents, moving with their flocks of sheep and goats in search of pasture and water, and growing wheat and barley using rainfall.[1] Owing to the increasing industrialization of the area, however, the number of Negev Bedouin that can be regarded as semi-nomadic is rapidly decreasing. Some continue to live as semi-nomads but also have an additional irregular source of income from wage labor. Others are settled and live in tents pitched permanently in one spot or in huts or houses. Their income is either from wage labor and land, or entirely from wage labor. Thus the following combination of economic resources can be found in the Negev:

- I Flocks and Land
- II Flocks, Land and Wage Labor
- III Land and Wage Labor
- IV Wage Labor

A fundamental dividing principle can be distinguished between the first two and the latter two types: the former are associated with semi-nomadism, the latter with settlement. The presence of a flock involves the former, while its absence involves the latter. The combination of economic resources used by a family has major implications regarding family structure, the division of labor in the family, consumption patterns and women's power. The above classification will facilitate the analysis of Negev Bedouin society. Three ideal types will be used: Semi-nomadic (Type I), Mixed (Type II), and Settled (Type III and IV).

REVIEW OF THE LITERATURE

In recent years a growing amount of literature has been published on the subject of women's position, power and influence in Mediterranean and Middle Eastern societies (Nelson 1972; Sweet 1967; Friedl 1967; Aswad 1967; Riegelhaupt 1967). Some of the issues and problems raised in this literature will be discussed in the course of the present analysis of the power and authority of Negev Bedouin women.

Anthropologists who have studied Middle Eastern nomadic societies argue unequivocally that two social worlds exist: "The private sphere of the tent (the woman's world) and the public sphere of the camp 'the man's world'" (Nelson 1972, p. 46). Cunnison exemplifies this approach and states that:

> In day to day life the woman's place is at the tents, and the man's place is at the tree. This division of the camp, where people spend most of their lives, into a female sector and a male sector is representative of the division of functions of the two sexes. Women's life is private life. Men have their private hours but their life is by and large public (1966, p. 116).

Cunnison not only emphasizes the separateness of these two worlds, but also concludes that women play no formal part in political activities and have a "socially and legally inferior position" (p. 116). Marx writes that "While the rights of women are fully recognized in the domestic sphere, Bedouin are quite explicit that only men take part in political action in any form" (1967, p. 186).

Many ethnographers present Middle Eastern nomadic societies as consisting of two separate social worlds: a male world which is public and political, and a female world which is private and domestic. Nonetheless it is unclear how meaningful or accurate is this division of Bedouin social life into two worlds. The ethnographers who have assumed the existence of two separate worlds have often hinted that the private female world is not purely domestic but bears political dimensions. This lack of consensus amongst ethnographers concerning the degree of active political power and influence of women has been noted by Nelson (1972, p. 44). There is, however, general agreement that women have a passive political role. Agnates arrange the marriages of their women, and women's marriages create affinal links which are economically, socially and politically important. Women are the means for the creation of these links. Marx (1967, p. 157) and Peters (1967, p. 57) argue that women convey information and mediate between their male kin and their husband's family.

There is disagreement over women's share in domestic and political decision making. Barth maintains that there is a bilateral pattern of decision making with women playing an active part in decisions on domestic, family and economic matters (1961, pp. 15-16). On the other hand, Asad maintains that it is the male household head who makes the final decisions on all household matters (1970, p. 37).

Ethnographers have neglected the informal political transactions between men and women in the family, and thus the political aspects of much that occurs in the domestic sphere. Whereas the formal political organization of the tribe has been extensively explored, relatively little has been written about the micro level of Bedouin social organization such as the family and the household. Barth (1961) and Pehrson (1966) regard the household as the smallest unit in tribal structure. Asad (1970) analyzes how the formation of camps is influenced by the family's labor needs. Peters' article (1965) discusses the effect of a son's marriage on his natal family and, in particular, on his relationship with his father. Asad's analysis (1970, chapter 4) of the sources of domestic power in the household is an exception to the general tendency to regard the household and family as merely an economic unit or as a segment of tribal structure.

THEORETICAL APPROACH

A specific theoretical approach to the concepts of power and authority, based on the writings of Weber and others, will be adopted in this analysis. Weber defines power as follows: "'Power' (Macht) is the probability that one actor within a social relationship will be in a position to carry out his own will despite resistance, regardless of the basis on which this probability rests" (1968, p. 53). Weber also defines in some detail the nature of "peaceful conflict" as a means to attaining power:

> A social relationship will be referred to as "conflict"

> (Kampf) insofar as action is oriented intentionally to carrying out the actor's own will against the resistance of other parties. The term "peaceful conflict" will be applied to cases in which actual physical violence is not employed. A peaceful conflict is "competition" insofar as it consists in a formally peaceful attempt to attain control over opportunities and advantages which are also desired by others. A competitive process is "regulated" competition to the extent that its ends and means are oriented to an order (p. 38).

Bailey is also concerned with regulated competition for power. He conceives of politics on all levels as a game with teams, rules and prizes. The participants may be states, governments or individuals, all of whom make choices and adopt certain strategies for specific ends. Competitions take place according to certain rules and "the devices of confrontation and encounter... enable competitions to be settled without the destruction of resources on which the whole society, not merely the political structure, depends" (1969, pp. 29-30). This analysis will focus on the way semi-nomadic, mixed economy and settled women exercise power and influence within and beyond the domestic sphere. Just as there are resources and strategies universal to all Negev Bedouin women, there are others specific to particular constellations of economic resources or social relationships.

PART I: RESOURCES AND STRATEGIES IN THE FAMILY

As a woman passes through her life cycle she occupies various roles. Each role involves the woman in a different constellation of social relationships with the members of her family and household. In some roles, such as mother or mother-in-law, the woman has authority (legitimized power) over others in the family. In other roles, such as wife or daughter-in-law, the woman is subordinate to others in the family. While she may lack authority, she nevertheless has resources at her disposal for the exercise of power. The following analysis will examine the ways in which women exercise power both when they lack authority, and why they have it.

RESOURCES USED IN SUBORDINATE RELATIONSHIPS

Rights and obligations of role partners are defined by societal norms. Women in subordinate role relationships (wife, daughter-in-law) safeguard their rights by protesting against their more powerful role partners' deviance from these norms. Asad has pointed out that the norms defining relationships in the household and family reflect power relations. He writes:

> The possession of rights including those that define the authority of the household head, is not merely a matter of moral norms, but also of power relationships within a particular organizational framework. For although all members are held to be bound together by the norms of household reciprocity, those with greater power have a wider range of choice in the way such norms can be fulfilled, as well as a greater opportunity of manipulating or infringing them... *the inequality of power between men and women is permanent and inescapable. It is therefore characteristically women who accuse men of departing from norms of household reciprocity rather than the other way around* (emphasis added, 1972, p. 81).

There are certain norms which define marital relationships. The husband has certain rights, as does the wife. The husband has the exclusive right to his wife's sexual services, labor and obedience. His wife, in turn, has certain rights as defined by Moslem laws. Her husband is expected to provide her with a normal sexual life, accommodation and clothing, and accord her fair treatment. Mohsen (1970, pp. 225-29) describes at length the three customary rights of settled Bedouin women in Egypt, which are very similar to the norms prevailing in the Negev.

Case I: A Wife's Protest over her Husband's Use of Physical Violence in a Semi-Nomadic Family

A was married to B in a sister exchange marriage (B's elder brother C married A's younger sister D). Both couples (AB + CD) were semi-nomads from the 'Azazmeh tribe. Their agricultural land was in valleys parallel to one another. They therefore camped within walking distance of each other when they ploughed and sowed in November, and when they harvested in May. One morning, during the harvesting season, the following incident occurred. B spent the morning sitting in her tent spinning. Her husband A harvested all morning. He had expected her to harvest with him since all the family help in this strenuous activity. He returned home mid-morning and accused her of being lazy and disobedient. They argued and he beat her with a tent pole. She left home and walked to her brother's tent which was pitched some three kilometers distant. There she tearfully said that A had beaten her, and both her mother and brother were very angry. Her brother C promptly beat his wife D (A's sister) with a tent pole.[2] The two sisters-in-law sat together quietly sobbing and drinking tea. Some hours later A (B's husband and D's brother) arrived and sat in the guest section of the tent, waiting for his brother-in-law C who had returned to harvest. His mother-in-law proceeded to scold him energetically for beating her daughter. C came and A related to him how disobedient and lazy B had been. C decided that the whole dispute was six of one and half a dozen of the other and sent the rebuked young couple home.

This incident shows the contraventions of two well-established norms — obedience and fair treatment. Wife B was disobedient and her husband A beat her. The beating was in retaliation for the disobedience; however, beating is considered ill treatment. B protested by leaving her home and returning to her natal family. This served two purposes. By leaving she withdrew her domestic and sexual services from her husband. By returning to her natal family she made his offense public which gave her family the right to defend her and mediate the dispute. This strategy is to protect the infringement of the norm of fair treatment by withdrawing domestic servcices and submitting one's husband to sanctions from one's family. Thus every time a husband beats his wife, she leaves home and returns either to her natal family or to her agnates.

Another norm which is widely accepted and frequently contravened is the ideal norm stipulating equal treatment of co-wives. A husband is meant to give his wives gifts of equal value and to divide his nights equally between them. Men often deviate from the norm, for the position of the wives is usually not equal and, in addition, they have personal preferences. Women have recognized this issue. For example, one recently displaced first wife said "My husband scolds me about the sheep. But he doesn't scold my co-wife. She is dearer to him. She is still young. It's not good. He leaves the old one for the younger one." The husband in question described his two wives as follows: "The first is like a storeroom for children, the second is like a dove for the night and sleep." Despite this recognition that equal treatment does not exist, the principle is still upheld by women. For example, one young second wife came home to her brothers in anger because her husband had bought a new dress for her co-wife and nothing for her. Her husband's father negotiated with her eldest brother and it was agreed that her husband would buy her a new dress and then take her home. Her sisters commented: "Our sister is right. There must be equality for the two wives."

Some norms are ambiguous and are subject to interpretation by the women. As a result of the transition to settlement and wage labor, there arise new situations and requirements with regard to social behavior. Women demand different patterns of behavior, basing their claims on variations of accepted norms. This reformulation of norms contitutes a modification of the social structure. For example, one of the norms governing marital relationships is a right of the wife to adequate food, accommodation and clothing. Women's conceptions of what is adequate vary according to their social origin and their changing expectations. For example, a Bedouin in the Tel Sheva area took a second wife of village origin. She intensely disliked living in a tent. Shortly after the birth of her first child, she returned to her parents. She left the infant with the co-wife, refusing to return to her husband until he provided her with a home consisting of four walls and a roof. Her husband eventually built a hut for her and she returned to live with him.

In addition to the relationship between husbands and wives, another superordinate-subordinate relationship is that between mothers-in-law and their daughters-in-law. They have different and opposing interests. Daughters-in-law are interested in gaining influence over their husbands and building up an elementary family and household unit. Mothers-in-law are interested in retaining influence over their sons and in building up a uterine family upon which their security and status depend when they are divorced or widowed. They are related in different ways to the same man, over whom they compete for influence. In sedentarized families this conflict of interests is more overtly expressed than in semi-nomadic and mixed economy families.

The transition to wage labor has affected the structure of the Bedouin household.[3] Families which are semi-nomadic or depend on a mixed economy live in extended family households during the father's lifetime. Father and sons have joint economic interests in the flock and land. On the father's death, the sons split up to live in nuclear family households and they may or may not continue living in a residential cluster. In settled families a fission of the extended family household occurs during the father's lifetime. Sons live in a household with their father only during the first few years of their married life. They then live in nuclear family households, usually near their father and brothers. Only when the parents are economically dependent on the son does the extended family household exist until the father's death.

The following examples illustrate these different kinds of family households. One semi-nomadic extended family household of the 'Azazmeh tribe consisted of three tents. The father, his wife and two unmarried sons lived in one; each of his two married sons lived in their own tent with their respective wives and children. The livestock were herded as one flock and all the household ate together. On the father's death the extended family household broke up. The flock was divided between the two married sons. The widow and the unmarried sons camped with the eldest son, his wife and children. The younger son and his wife camped on their own. For another case, in a settled family of the Abu Rgaig tribe, each son lived with his parents in an extended family household immediately after his marriage and continued to do so until his younger brother married. The son and his wife had their own hut but they ate with the parents and their remaining unmarried siblings. Each son worked regularly for a salary. Their father did not work regularly. He had a small plot of agricultural land and practised folk medicine, and was partly dependent on his sons' wage earning capacity.

When a daughter-in-law lives in an extended family household with her husband's parents, she works under her mother-in-law's direction. She is expected to fulfill the role of the daughter, whom she has often replaced, by doing most of the physical labor and household chores, thereby leaving the mother-in-law with more leisure. She should do most of the breadmaking, fuel gathering, cooking, washing and water-fetching. Their days are spent together and only their nights are spent apart. Disputes centering around the daughter-in-law's demand for economic and residential independence occur frequently in settled families. In semi-nomadic and mixed economy families, the daughters-in-law and their children are vital members of the labor force. In settled families, the daughter-in-law is exclusively concerned with domestic activities such as caring for the children and the dwelling, and preparing food. Since the daughter-in-law in a settled family is no longer bound economically, she feels freer to express her desire for a nuclear family household. She may vie with her mother-in-law for control over her husband, or she may knowingly express desires and demands that her husband supports but is unable to express. The following incident is an example of where a daughter-in-law demands her own household.

Case II: Demand for Nuclear Family Household in a Settled Family

A and her husband and two children lived with her widowed mother-in-law in a tent outside the village of Tel Sheva. A's husband owned a house in the village but preferred living with his widowed mother whom he supported. A wanted to move to the house, her husband did not, and A angrily returned to her natal family. On her return, her husband moved back with her to their house in the village. A few months later, A began objecting to her mother-in-law buying food at the local store and charging it to her (A's) husband's account. The matter reached a head when A's husband bought a sheep which was slaughtered for guests of the family who were entertained by her mother-in-law. During the argument which ensured, A accused her mother-in-law of living off her husband's money and dominating her grandchildren.

This incident illustrates how a daughter-in-law resented her mother-in-law's influence. She demanded residential and economic independence. She gained the former but not the latter. The daughter-in-law's protest and demand for residential independence resulted in the fission of the household. The immediate cause and occasion of the fission was the daughter-in-law's protest. The underlying cause was the separation of economic interests accompanying wage labor. By convincing her natal family and her husband of her need and right to a nuclear family household, this daughter-in-law managed to achieve control of her own household. Thus, by means of protest, women safeguard their rights and occasionally reformulate norms in their favor.

Women's protests against deviance from norms have a certain regularity of form which utilizes two resources. The first resource is their control over their domestic and sexual services. By leaving their husbands' household and returning to their father's or brother's household, women withdraw their domestic services from their husbands. The sexual division of labor is such that their husbands are very dependent on their services and by leaving they severely disrupt the running of their households. Only the women cook and care for the children. When they leave, the children are left unattended, without food or supervision. If the family is settled, the husband is probably absent all day working outside. If the family is semi-nomadic or living from a mixed economy, the husband is more often at home in the daytime but still, the woman's absence deprives her husband of her labor which is valuable in the daily maintenance of the flock and the processing of products. By leaving they also withdraw their sexual services.

The husband is faced with a number of options when his wife leaves him. He may rely on a female relative such as his mother, sister-in-law or unmarried sister to help him with the children and the household, in this way managing during his wife's absence. Sooner or later, however, he will go to his wife's agnates and either try to persuade her to come home or demand a divorce. Some women exploit the clearly defined sexual division of labor to their advantage. Since they have a monopoly of many domestic tasks, the men are dependent on them. Women exploit this dependence by withdrawing their services until their demands are met. Their demands may vary from an apology, to a new dress, to an independent household. This was the case in the examples just cited.

The second resource a woman utilizes when she protests norm infringement and goes to her agnates, is her right to protection by her agnates. Whenever women protest over norm infringement they return to their agnates, taking with them infants that they are nursing. The term used to describe women who are staying with their agnates as a result of domestic conflicts is "*mahāwlah.*" A woman is entitled to help and protection from her agnates throughout her life. When a woman is married her agnates transfer their rights in her childbearing capacity and labor to her husband and his family, but they retain moral responsibility for her. Their honor is linked to her modesty. The norm is such that whenever she is ill-treated she may return to them, or whenever she misbehaves her husband may send her to them. Her agnates should give her shelter and food whenever she needs it, and should defend her interests and mediate between her and her husband. They should support her when she is divorced or if she is widowed with no adult sons.

Various explanations have been advanced concerning the agnates continued defense and protection of their women after their marriage. Rosenfeld maintains that a woman's agnates' home is always open to her if she forgoes her property rights. (According to Islamic law, women are entitled to one half of the amount of property inherited by their brothers.) Rosenfeld states that: "She is dependent on kinship, the major construct of her life, due to the determining factor in her life, her forfeiture of her claim to the property of her father's house. To take the claim is to forfeit the guarantees of kinship" (1960, p. 67). Mohsen also takes this view concerning women amongst the Awlad Ali, settled Bedouin in the Western Desert: "In forfeiting her rights of inheritance a woman secures for herself the continuous security and protection of her kin-family, and the protection of her rights" (1970, p. 233).

In the Negev Bedouin society, women do not inherit half their brother's share of property either in land or livestock. Women from semi-nomadic and mixed economy households are given a few head of livestock on marriage, as are their brothers. The women, however, do not inherit more livestock on their father's death nor do they inherit land. Settled Bedouin usually have little or no land nor flocks. Men have less to gain through inheritance and women have less to forfeit.

Peters takes a slightly different approach. He maintains that women not only renounce their rights of inheritance but also their rights to their bride-wealth. As a consequence of this renunciation, they can make claims on their agnates. The woman's husband continues to pay the bride-wealth to her family, in installments, after the marriage takes place. These installments are often paid in resolution of a marital dispute. Peters states that: "What they do is to force claims which they support with their rights. Their claims are not arbitrary; they are commensurate with their rights, otherwise they could not be sustained" (1976, p. 31).

In the Negev, however, the total amount of bride-wealth is paid prior to the actual marriage and not after the marriage as in Cyrenaica. Negev women do receive a small proportion of their bride-wealth in the form of gold jewelry and household goods. In the past such items were purchased by the groom's family, but are now increasingly being purchased by the bride's family. One settled informant was given gold jewelry valued IL 2,000 by the groom's mother and household goods by her mother valuing IL 1,000. The rest of the bride-wealth — IL 16,000 — was put in a closed bank account. It will be used for the bride-wealth of her younger brother's bride.

It is perhaps erroneous to view a woman's right to protection from her agnates as a result of forfeiture of her rights to her father's property and her bride-wealth. Negev Bedouin women are still protectd by their agnates even though they receive part of their bride-wealth. Because of the Bedouin inheritance traditions explained above, it is also possibly erroneous to view Islamic laws of inheritance as a relevant point of reference for the Bedouin themselves. There are other factors which explain a woman's continued use of her agnates' home. A woman is perceived by others and herself as an individual who belongs to her natal family as well as to her marital family. She is a member of a certain sub-tribe; she is her father's daughter and her brother's sister, as well as her husband's wife and her son's mother. She does not change her name on marriage, and retains her link with the natal family throughout her married life. She visits them on special occasions such as religious holidays and mediates the relationships between the two families (Marx 1967, p. 104). Therefore, her agnates tend to encourage the stability of her marriage and concern themselves with her interests.

In the context of domestic disputes a woman's agnates perform a very particular function. They provide the means of limiting, institutionalizing and resolving conflicts. When a dispute flares up, a woman knows she can return to her agnates. They will protect her and mediate between her and her husband. By going to her agnates she makes the issue in dispute public and involves her family in the process of mediation. A woman's family are obligated to defend her interests. They *biyhmuha*. This word has the same root as the word for lawyer *muḥamee*. Although a woman's agnates are always ready to defend her interests, they usually oppose the break up of her marriage unless she has been wronged continuously over a long period. They may, therefore, persuade both the parties involved to compromise over the issue in dispute and encourage their kinswoman to return to her husband.

If the husband is clearly in the wrong, as when a well established norm has been contravened, the woman's agnates demand an apology and a fine which he pays to his wife. If their kinswoman is in the wrong, they soundly berate her. Her family is less likely to support her demands when they involve the reformulation of norms. Although a woman's agnates usually encourage her to return home to her husband, the actual decision to go home is the woman's own. She may refuse to return to her husband until he apologizes or agrees to set up an independent household. If, however, her family does not support her position, she has to withstand their pressure. Women often use return to their agnates as a bargaining base. The following case history illustrates this.

Case III: The Natal Family as a Bargaining Base

A married and lived with her widowed mother-in-law for a year and a half until after the birth of her first child. A relates that her mother-in-law would not give her anything — tea, coffee, bread or sugar. She would go visiting and leave A to do the household chores all day. A wanted her own tent and told her husband. But her husband was young and weak, and would not breach the matter with his mother. After a quarrel between the two women over a minor issue, A returned to her family with her baby and stayed there three months. She refused to return until she had her own tent. Her husband capitulated, and since then she has never lived with her mother-in-law.

A, by withdrawing to her family, manipulated her husband and mother-in-law into giving her her own tent. Another aspect of the strategy of returning to one's agnates is that it enforces a physical distance between the antagonists, thus limiting the conflict between them. In all the case histories cited here, the women have left home after an argument involving an exchange of words or blows. Women choose whether to protest over norm infringement or whether to remain silent. Their choice is based on a calculation of the positive and negative consequences of their protest as a strategy. A daughter-in-law in a settled extended family household is more likely to demand her own household than her semi-nomadic or mixed economy counterpart.

WIVES AND CHILDREN — PASSIVITY AND MILITANCY

According to Bedouin custom and Moslem law, divorce by one's husband results in separation from one's children as they belong to the father and his lineage. The bride-wealth paid by the groom's family to the bride's family not only compensates them for the loss of a daughter but also for the rights to the children from her womb. When a woman is divorced she leaves her children with her husband's family. If the children are very young she may keep them with her whilst she lives with her natal family. If she remarries, however, her first husband's family claim the children.

Women greatly fear being separated from their children through divorce. The desire to stay with their children increases their tolerance of norm infringement by their husband and his family. Once they have children, they weigh the consequences of initiating disputes over norm infringement. One informant reminisced about the stormy days of her early married life: "Then I was newly married. Now I no longer get angry and run home — for my children's sake. My husband can take them. When you have children things are different." Several years later, this same informant's husband took a second wife. The girl said to me at the wedding of her co-wife: "I am not angry for my children's sake. I am singing. No one can see into my heart." An older woman commented on her behavior: "She is clever. A crying, troublesome first wife is often divorced." Thus, too vigorous defense of their rights can result in divorce and the loss of their children. This encourages women to be passive or to argue between themselves rather than directly confront their husbands or sons.

Occasionally a woman makes a calculated provocative gesture which upsets the status quo and forces a change in the constellation of relationships around her. These incidents occur when a woman can no longer tolerate her situation. Then she makes a dramatic, catalytic gesture, which sometimes may have an element of self-immolation. For example, one woman could not bear the prospect of her husband acquiring a second wife from Gaza and marrying their daughter to a man there. She deliberately set herself alight with the primus stove in his presence and survived, though badly scarred. Her husband dropped his plans. The following incident is another example of this type of behavior.

Case IV: Catalytic Gesture which Induced Separation

A husband took a third wife. His first wife was separated from him and lived with her married son. His second wife was living with him. At the time of his marriage to his third wife, he gave his second wife some money and told her, "I want a holiday from you for two months." During the first few weeks after the marriage, he lived with his new wife in a tent adjacent to his second wife's tent and the latter became very jealous. Then he decided to move away with his new wife and packed up their belongings. They were about to leave when the second wife appeared at the entrance of her tent. She was adorned in her best clothes and jewelry, and brandishing her husband's gun. She threatened to kill him, his wife and herself. In her own words, "I had gone mad with jealousy." From that day she has been separated from her husband, and went to live with her adult sons. The second wife related this story to me when she came to visit her husband shortly before his death. She said: "I don't love him anymore. Then I loved him. I haven't visited him since that time, but I've come now because he is so ill."

According to Bedouin custom, only men have the right to formally initiate separation or divorce their wives. Women, however, can force them to do so. In this case the second wife found her position unbearable. By her action, she put her husband in a position where he had no choice but to separate from her or divorce her. Thus, women can choose whether to protest or not.

USE OF LAW AND CUSTOM

Another resource that women use for the extension of their power and influence is Israeli civil law and Moslem religious law. Both these legal codes define women's rights more liberally than Bedouin custom. Israeli civil law prohibits polygamy and both legal codes define women's rights to maintenance and custody of children more generously than Bedouin custom. The difference between the two legal codes and Bedouin custom is put to use by both men and women, although in different ways. Settled husbands and wives are more likely to utilize the legal codes than semi-nomadic or mixed economy Bedouin. This is partly because they have more knowledge of them, and also because the men have generally registered their marriages at the Moslem Court and the Ministry of the Interior in order to receive their social benefits from their employers and the state.

According to Israeli civil law, polygynists are liable for prosecution and are fined heavily. Men have developed various strategies for circumventing the law. The most common device used is the performance of only one of the marriages both according to custom and with legal registration, and the performance of any succeeding marriages according to custom but without legal registration. Both Bedouin custom and Islamic law permit polygyny, and if a marriage is unregistered the authorities are unaware that it has taken place. Another method of circumvention is to divorce one wife legally and register the marriage of the second wife, but to continue living as if married to both. Layish (1975, p. 73) presents various other ways men circumvent this law prohibiting polygyny.

Women have begun to press for the application of the civil law prohibiting polygyny. For example, one first wife objected to her husband taking a second wife. She went to the local police station, lodged a complaint against him for having two wives, and the husband was prosecuted. There was a lengthy investigation and litigation process, and finally he was fined IL 2,500. He did not, however, divorce his second wife as a result of the court case. The first wife continued to employ a number of other strategies to cast the second wife aside. She poisoned the second wife's turkeys and frequently insulted her. The second wife kept returning to her agnates and finally her husband divorced her at her family's request. The first wife's use of the law was one of a number of strategies she used to rid herself of the co-wife.

Islamic religious law gives women more rights to the custody of their children and maintenance than Bedouin custom. According to Layish, Islamic law contends that the mother has the best title to custody of her children providing she is sane, responsible, does not remarry a stranger, and can maintain them. He writes:

> The mother's right is independent of the legal relationship between the parents; it does not lapse on her divorce. But if after her divorce she marries a stranger ... she is denied the right to *hādana* (custody) so long as the marriage exists. The period of *hādana* ends when the child is seven in the case of a son and nine in the case of a daughter, whereupon the child passes into the care of the father. The custody of the children in no way affects the father's natural guardianship over these persons. He owes them maintenance during the *hādana* period (1975, p. 246).

Bedouin custom is variable but generally custody is given to the husband's family either as soon as the parents are divorced or when the mother remarries.

One informant became aware of her rights according to Islamic law when her husband divorced her in accordance with the law in order to marry a second wife legally. The husband was using the divorce as a constitutional device. He intended to go on living with his first wife and her six children. The informant decided that she would claim her lawful rights attached to her legal divorce. She put in a claim for custody and maintenance; the Moslem judge granted her custody of the children and told the husband to record the ownership of the house the family lived in, in his first wife's name. Rather than do this the husband sold the house and built two huts. The informant manipulated the law just as her husband did. It did not enable her to keep possession of the house, but she did get legal custody of the children. Thus, both men and women use the legal codes to their own advantage. The men seem to derive more profit from it than the women for they can continue being polygynous. The women cannot prevent polygyny by using the law. They can, however, use the law to obtain custody of their children or to make trouble for their husbands.

Women in subordinate relationships utilize the limited means at their disposal to the fullest in safeguarding their rights. Women choose whether and when to make an issue out of norm infringement, and whether to use the law. For example, when remaining with their children is more important to them than altering their husband's behavior, they may feel that they can best safeguard their interests by being passive. Women's protests over norm infringement may safeguard their interests or extend their power and influence when a husband apologizes for mistreating his wife. On the other hand, their protests may fail to alter an existing unsatisfactory situation and thus may simply be expressive of discontent. Protesting norm infringement is thus a strategy which has its uses but also has its limits.

RESOURCES USED IN SUPERORDINATE RELATIONSHIPS

Bedouin women gain increasing authority as they become older, marry and become wives, mothers, grandmothers, mothers-in-law and widows. Bedouin women derive much of their authority and social status from their menfolk — their fathers, husbands and sons. Teknonymy is practised. Women are always referred to as X's daughter, Y's wife and Z's mother. They are never acknowledged by their personal name in public outside their immediate family. Their status is largely derived from their position as wife and mother. Bedouin women also have increasing social freedom and status as they grow older and approach and pass menopause. Once they are past childbearing age, they are considered more neuter than female and may associate relatively freely with unrelated men, travel to the market unaccompanied and sit in the guest section of the tent.

One of the principal resources of Bedouin mothers is their children. As elsewhere, they use their children as information gatherers and messengers. Both boys and girls prior to puberty have a degree of physical and social freedom which women do not have. Their mothers utilize this: they send the children to female neighbors with requests, invitations or information. Children are sent to pick up material from their aunt, to tell their married sister that their mother is ill or that certain guests are expected. Mothers also keep themselves informed about the identity of guests and topics of conversation in the guest section by sending their young children to fetch and carry, and at the same time observe and report on who has arrived and what is going on. Thus, mothers utilize their children to keep in contact with each other and are informed about events occurring beyond the confines of their domestic sphere.

Mothers are also responsible for the care of their young children. In semi-nomadic and mixed economy families the menfolk are frequently around the home during the day and participate in taking care of the children. In settled families the men are wage earners and the women are solely responsible for the running of the home and the care of the children during the day.

Motherhood gives women not only authority and influence over their children when they are young and dependent, but also when they are adult and acquire affiliations of their own. All Bedouin women have their say in the choice of brides for their sons and their influence is partly derived from their position as wife and mother. It is also derived from the social segregation of the sexes in Bedouin society. Since men have little access to unrelated women and even less to unmarried girls, they are dependent on their wives and mothers for information about them. When a son wishes to marry, he usually tells his mother first. She and her husband then discuss the various possibilities. The mother then goes to visit the women of the families mooted. She quietly observes the daughter's looks, behavior and interaction with those around her. She then returns home and reports her findings to her husband. A mother may favor a certain girl as her prospective daughter-in-law or a relative from her own husband's family. She can sometimes influence her husband's political outlook and preferences by coloring her account of the various girls she has seen. Thus, through her husband's dependence on her information, she is extremely influential in the preliminary stages of choosing a bride for her son. She plays no overt part, however, in the formal negotiations that follow.

A Negev Bedouin mother also has some degree of influence over her daughter's marriage although her husband needs no information from her about available men. One informant related that her husband arranged the marriage of their eldest daughter to his father's brother's son and only told her when the bride-wealth had already been agreed upon. The informant was very upset. She insisted that the marriage could not take place for at least a year since her daughter was so young, and her request was granted. Thus, although she could not influence the choice of a groom she managed to influence the timing. Some mothers are more involved over the choice of a husband for their daughters. This occurs when a woman comes to visit her home in order to find out if her daughter is available or eligible. In these instances the mother discusses the visit with her husband.

Both Cunnison and Asad emphasize the role of the mother in negotiations for the marriage of daughters. Asad writes that although the Kababish father has the right of consent to the groom, the Kababish mother has the right to her daughter's bride-wealth since she is losing her daughter's services. She also has the right to grant permission for her daughter's departure and usually tries to delay it (1972, p. 63). Cunnison writes that amongst the Baggara the bride's mother receives part of the bride-wealth and that there is often an argument about the amount to be paid between the men of both families. The bride's mother is invariably supported by other women in this respect (1966, p. 95).

In Negev Bedouin society the bride's mother plays no part in the formal negotiations over her daughter's bride-wealth. She may tell the mother of the groom at an early stage that it would be worthwhile for his father to come and formally request the hand of her daughter, but frequently these preliminary enquiries are carried out by men. She does receive part of the bride-wealth but never receives all of it. For example, the bride-wealth of an informant married in 1968 totalled IL 5,000. Her mother and grandmother were each given IL 500. Informants explain that the mother's share of the bride-wealth (*razwah*) represents recognition of the fact that the mother suckled, weaned and cared for the daughter. The Negev Bedouin mother, like the Kababish mother, sorely misses her daughter's domestic services when she marries, and thus tries to postpone her marriage. An unmarried daughter does most of the daily household tasks, leaving her mother free to visit other women. One weary mother related how since her youngest daughter's marriage, she has been working like a young girl in her own home. Negev Bedouin mothers also influence their married children's behavior in order to further their own or their family's interests. The following case history illustrates this.

Case V: A Mother's Influence Over Her Married Daughter

H and his sister were partners to exchange marriages. The sister was the second wife of an elderly man. His first wife was the eldest daughter of this man. The first wife was very upset at having a co-wife. She told her daughter to make trouble with her husband H so that he would divorce her and thereby force her own husband to divorce H's sister. (In an exchange marriage, when one couple get divorced, the other couple often do so as well.) H found his young wife very unreasonable and argumentative, and eventually divorced her. The first wife's strategy only partly succeeded. She managed to end her daughter's marriage but she did not manage to get rid of her own co-wife, for his sister and her elderly husband seemed quite content with each other. H told his sister that she could stay with her husband and used the money to marry another woman who has since borne him eight children.

Besides motherhood, there is another role which sometimes gives women authority and power. This is widowhood. Widows are able to decide for themselves whether they will remarry and to whom, as well as the composition of their household. Every widow has the right of consent or refusal concerning her remarriage. She may choose to live with her agnates or she may decide to live alone with her dependent children. She may choose to remarry and live with or without her children, depending on whom she decides to marry. Not all widows decide to remarry. They remain single and live either with one of their married sons or alone with their dependent children. If the widow's late husband has few agnates, she is unlikely to remarry. If she has little property, her husband's agnates may be less anxious to marry her. If the widow is middle-aged, there is no pressure from her agnates or her affines for her to remarry. A widow who does not remarry has considerable influence within her married son's household and considerable authority as a household head if she lives on her own with her dependent children. It is *only* as a widow that a woman has an opportunity to be a household head and to manage property.

In the Tel Sheva area there are thirteen widows and not one of them lives with her agnates. Five of them are household heads, living with their dependent children. (Three of the five have no agnates in the country, but two of them do.) Six of the widows live in their married son's household. Three out of six have dependent children and three do not. There are two widows who live alone. One has agnates and no sons. The other has a son and agnates. These widows have chosen neither to live with their agnates nor to remarry. There are several factors encouraging them to live as household heads or with their married sons. One is that there are not so many of their husband's agnates available to remarry. Four of them were married to men who were brothers. There is only one surviving brother and he has not married any of his brothers' widows. Two of the widows were married to men who have no surviving brothers.

The availability of state benefits in the form of children's allowances, pensions and social welfare benefits makes it easier for a widow to live alone or with her dependent children. These benefits are particularly important to settled widows who do not have a flock they can live from and whose children are too young to work. One widow in the area has six children under the age of fourteen. Her husband's agnates are all dead. Her father lives a few kilometers from her. She has chosen to remain unmarried and live as a household head with her children. She continues renting the land her husband leased from the Land Administration and collects both a children's allowance and a social welfare benefit. Another woman has no sons and her husband had no livestock or land. Her agnates wanted her to come and live with them after her husband's death. She told them that she preferred to continue living alone and that she could support herself from her pension.

Previous fission of the extended family household also makes it more acceptable for a widow to live alone if she wishes to do so. For example, one widow has a married son. She and her son's wife quarreled many years previously, and her son and his wife set up their own household. She and her daughter lived from their flock and the daughter eventually got married. The widow continued living alone near her son but not as part of his household. Her flock was herded by her daughter's husband and she remained economically independent of her son. Widows often choose not to remarry. If their children are unmarried, they become household heads with full control over the economic resources of the household. It is one of the few positions of authority and control over economic resources that Bedouin women can assume. When their sons are married they may either live with them in their household or continue living alone. State benefits encourage widows to live as independent household heads both whilst their children are unmarried and later when they are married. The state benefits have made a traditional option easier and of longer duration.

The role of folk healer also gives women some independence. Women who become folk healers are usually past menopause and are often widows. Both men and women visit them with an assortment of problems. These range from the medical — failure to conceive, impotence — to those requiring divining ability — who stole my son's gold? When will I have a son? The folk healer prescribes herbs or amulets, or is asked to divine the cause and outcomes of problems. Women who are folk healers exercise both power and authority over unrelated and related men and women who visit her. They pay for her services and thus she also has an independent income.

UNIVERSAL RESOURCES

There is a certain resource and a number of strategies which all women use. Their use of them is independent of status or of particular stages in their life cycle. The resource is a woman's control over her own body and social relationships — her self-autonomy. The strategies are the use of illness and avoidance. Illness is used as strategy by many Bedouin women. It frequently expresses the unhappiness women feel about certain situations. It also may be used to attract attention and influence others.

Informants often say that the state of the body reflects the state of the mind. It is common for a first wife whose husband is about to take or has taken a second wife, to suffer from aches and pains. She then requests to be taken to the doctor. One first wife informant, who is neglected sexually and socially by her husband, often has general aches and pains and asks to be taken to the doctor, invariably in the middle of the night. Her mother-in-law is of the opinion that there is nothing wrong with her except her sadness and anger (*zacal*). Another informant related how when her first ex-husband came and took her son away from her to his family, she cried all that day and on the next day she went to the doctor since she was "ill from her sadness." Illness is often the last resort when all other resources and strategies have failed to alter an unsatisfactory and painful situation. It is a legitimate means of receiving attention and sympathy.

The sick role, however, is not only expressive of a painful situation. A "sick" woman can legitimately withdraw from normal social activities, behave strangely, and demand the attention and concern of her family. The following case history illustrates a mother's use of illness as a strategy to influence and control her sons.

Case VI: An Instance of a Mother's Influence Over Her Married Sons in a Settled Family

A is a widow, with two married sons, B and C, from her first marriage. C had been living separately from his wife and six children for two years.

He supported them but lived with his mother. C announced that he wished to take a second wife from Gaza. His mother and brother B both violently opposed the idea. His mother was not intrinsically opposed to his taking a second wife. She had been suggesting various of her own female relatives as possibilities. She was opposed to the particular girl he had in mind because she was of socially inferior status, being of peasant descent, whereas the family were of Bedouin descent. She had worked selling vegetables in the market which is something no Bedouin girl would do. She had met C there. She was quite old (in her mid 20's), not very pretty and very independent. C's elder brother B was also opposed to the idea of his brother's proposed marriage. He was opposed to this particular girl and opposed to the idea of a second marriage "on principle." He maintained that his brother did not earn enough money to pay the bride-wealth, and to support two wives and their children adequately. C, however, was determined to marry this girl whom he felt was educated and lovable. The two brothers argued over the matter and could not reach an agreement. B told C that if he went ahead with his plan to marry the girl, he would no longer consider him his brother. C returned home to his mother and told her of the argument and B's serious threat. His mother was appalled at the idea of lasting enmity between her sons. She became very angry, her heart started beating fast and she could barely breathe. She told C that she needed a doctor and because she was angry with C she was going to sleep at B's house. Whilst C telephoned his brother to come and get her and bring a doctor, his mother ran down to the road and started making her way laboriously on foot. B came to collect her and the doctor gave her two tranquilizing injections. The doctor then left for town to bring some medication. Whilst the doctor was away, the mother turned on her two sons and berated both of them soundly. The upshot of the discussion was that B declared that if his brother married the girl, he would on no account help him with the bride-wealth or the expenses, but that he would not sever his relations with him. C declared that he would not expect his brother to help him. Thus an agreement was reached. The mother A admitted to me afterwards that her hysterical fit had been contrived as a device to get them to come to some sort of agreement.

In this case the mother abandoned her opposition to her son's marriage when she saw that it could result in lasting enmity between her two sons. By throwing an hysterical fit she aroused their concern over her health and their guilt over the suffering they were causing her. She thus managed to renew amicable relations between her two sons. It was more important to her to retain fraternal amity than to prevent the marriage.

Avoidance as Strategy

Avoidance relationships exist in many societies. Radcliffe-Brown views both avoidance and joking relationships as means of maintaining equilibrium. He writes that: "Customs of avoidance or extreme respect towards the wife's parents, and of privileged 'joking' with the wife's brothers and sisters, can be regrded as the means of establishing and maintaining social equilibrium in a type of structural situation that results in many societies from marriage" (1953, p. 108).

Radcliffe-Brown thus describes a type of avoidance relationship which exists between a man and his in-laws in many cultures. Murphy calls this role "specific avoidance" (1970, p. 313). This differs from the type of avoidance relationship which exists amongst the Negev Bedouin. The form of avoidance practised between Bedouin women does not occur between every mother-in-law and daughter-in-law. It occurs between specific individuals who live together or near each other, and have some unresolved conflicts of interests between them. It is only instituted after an outbreak of conflict in order to limit further overt conflict. It signifies a state of siege and sometimes operates as a sanction. It is situational specific avoidance rather than role specific avoidance.

Avoidance is a strategy used by women either as a manipulating mechanism or as a sanction in a prolonged power struggle. Avoidance is instituted when a conflict is irresolvable. The annoyed woman may continue living with her husband and the other members of the household, but refuse to eat with or speak to her antagonist. The Arabic word for this state of avoidance is *aimharib*. Bedouin informants have explained that this form of avoidance only occurs between close relatives or people who live together. It may occur between two brothers, two co-wives, a mother-in-law and her daughter-in-law. Women frequently use this form of avoidance amongst themselves. I encountered only two cases of brothers, and one of husbands and wives, maintaining an avoidance relationship over a prolonged period of time, whereas it was a relatively common occurrence between co-wives, or mothers-in-law and their daughters-in-law. Brothers may decide to live apart and husbands and wives may get divorced. Women, however, do not choose their co-wives or their mothers-in-law, nor can they decide to live apart from them unless they want to end their marriage.

I would postulate that settled women utilize the maintenance of avoidance as a strategy more frequently than their semi-nomadic or mobile mixed economy counterparts. Settled women live in greater proximity with the other women in their husband's family. Huts and houses are permanent structures which cannot be moved at will. They are generally grouped in residential clusters based on the extended family. In addition, the daily activities of settled Bedouin are exclusively centered around and based in the home. Mobile, joint family households (semi-nomadic and mixed economy) on the other hand, can pitch their tents at some distance from each other, unless they live in one tent. Frequently they are separated by several kilometers as a result of the needs of the flock. They often spend many hours of the day apart for the flock has to be herded and water has to be collected. As mentioned above, avoidance may be used as a sanction in a prolonged power struggle. The following case history illustrates this.

Case VII: Use of Avoidance as a Sanction in a Settled Family

X was married to Y. They lived in a hut near the tent of Z, Y's mother. Z lived with her unmarried son and Y's son by his first wife whom he had divorced 14 years previously. X and Y lived with Z as one household. After being married for eighteen months, X asked Y if they could eat separately. Y was opposed to this and they started arguing. Z heard them and asked them if they were fighting. X then insulted Z. She called her, her mother and her grandmother prostitutes. Z and X were about to start fighting when Y separated them, put X in a taxi and sent her home to her parents. He went to fetch her after a week. From the time she returned, she and Y ate apart from Z. X apologized to Z for insulting her. Z refused to accept her apology and told her that she never wanted to speak to her again. For the last two years X and Z have not spoken to each other.

In this incident the daughter-in-law achieved her aim of the setting up of her own household, but at a price. Her mother-in-law expressed displeasure by instituting avoidance which operated as a sanction. The daughter-in-law was very isolated. Her husband was away at work all day and any guests were entertained in her mother-in-law's tent. The institution of social avoidance, in this case, also saved the mother-in-law from losing face for it diverted attention from the setting up of a separate household.

The maintenance of avoidance may simultaneously operate not only as a sanction but as a manipulating mechanism. It may control irresolvable conflict between two women and thus enable them to continue living together. The following case history illustrates this.

Case VIII: Avoidance as a Coping Mechanism in a Mixed-Economy Family

A is a widow in her 40's with three married sons, two married daughters and two unmarried daughters. Her husband had been much older than she. When her husband died in 1972 her elder son B vowed that she would always have a home with him for he dearly loves her. B's brothers live in a residential cluster with him. B is married through a sister exchange marriage with his first cousin. He and his wife C have five children. A and C have long-standing hostility between them. They did not speak to each other for 13 years and from 1972-1975 they lived in one tent. The tent was divided into three divisions: one for guests, one for A and her unmarried daughters, and one for B and C and their children — three divisions and three fireplaces. A described the situation as follows: "If my son didn't love me, he wouldn't have made me a home with him. As his wife married through sister exchanges, she can't leave him." Last year B took a second wife. His new wife shared the main tent with his mother and C moved to her own tent a few meters away. Avoidance between A and C was continued. Although they didn't talk to each other, they would cooperate passively. For example, on one occasion they both helped a neighbor set up a loom. A sat at one end arranging the threads and C sat at the other end. The neighbor unstrung the wool, walking in between them. In 1976 C gave birth to male twins. She was very overworked caring for them. In addition, her mother had a stroke and came to live with her. All the neighbors began pressuring A to help C. Finally she relented and sent her daughters to help her, and began talking with her.

This is a case where the two women had to continue living together. The wife wanted to continue her marriage, and the mother wanted to continue living with her sons. The maintenance of avoidance enabled them to continue living in one household. Relations were reestablished between them only when there was a possibility of maintaining physical distance.

SUMMARY

Bedouin women have a number of resources and strategies which they employ to influence other members of their households. The resources and strategies available to a woman reflect both universal, situational and role-specific elements of Negev Bedouin life. The determining variables are status within subordinate relationships: wife, sister, daughter, daughter-in-law; status within a superordinate relationship:

mother, mother-in-law, widow; and lifestyle: semi-nomadic, mixed-economy or settled. According to her particular situation a woman may: return to her agnates, thus withdrawing domestic services and enlisting familial support; use catalytic gestures; take advantage of the gap between law and custom; exercise influence over children; become ill; and institute avoidance.

Settlement increases the likelihood of conflict between mothers-in-law and daughters-in-law over the fission of the extended family. It also encourages the use of law, of avoidance and the social independence of the widow. All the other resources and strategies are used by all the women in the area whether they are semi-nomadic, living from a mixed-economy or settled.

PART II: SOCIAL AND ECONOMIC RESOURCES

There is strict sexual division of labor and a high degree of sexual differentiation amongst the Negev Bedouin which allows women to control the domstic sphere. They care for their children, their home and the processing of domestic products. Women are also socially restricted from unrelated men. Settlement and wage labor has resulted in a greater segregation of sex roles. Whereas in the semi-nomadic or mixed-economy the woman plays a vital part in helping her husband in the daily maintenance of the flock and the land (and thus has considerable power), settled women play a more limited productive role. They no longer herd. They occasionally harvest and weave, but primarily they have total responsibility for the home and their children whilst their hubands work away from home.

Yet, this greater segregation from their men is accompanied by increased accessibility to other women. This is because settlement has resulted in the development of residential clusters of related families within the general area inhabited by the sub-tribe.

VISITING PATTERNS

All Bedouin women visit the women of other families. The pattern and form of this visiting varies according to whether the women live in semi-nomadic or in settled families. Semi-nomadic families camp in nuclear or extended family household units and are generally isolated from other families. The women are busy helping with the flock and running the home. Their visits are of three sorts: they attend parties with their husbands to celebrate circumcisions and weddings, they visit their families, and they visit other related women after they have given birth. Notions of balanced reciprocity (Sahlins 1972, p. 194) underpin attendance at these parties and the gifts given by the male guestes to the host and by the female guests to the hostess. Party going is reciprocal and includes close kin, members of the same sub-tribe or tribe, and perhaps other tribes. Men may occasionally attend these parties alone, but women may not.

Once at the party, however, a woman has considerable independence in social activities. She spends her time in the women's section of the guest tent. She sings, dances, and may help to prepare the food. She has an opportunity to meet the other female guests, to renew old acquaintances and establish new ones, to catch up on the latest births, deaths and marriages. For the semi-nomadic woman these parties are the only occasions when she meets other women in large numbers. Besides attending parties, semi-nomadic women also visit their families. They visit them on the two main feast days of the year, and they visit them when their brothers marry, or their mothers or sisters give birth. They may visit them for no particular reason other than the feeling that they haven't seen them for some months. They also visit their fathers or brothers when they are angry and wish to avoid their husbands. They may visit their families alone or accompanied by their husband or mother-in-law.

Semi-nomadic women also visit their sisters and sisters-in-law, and perhaps other kin and affines, if they are camping nearby when such kin have given birth. These visits take place during the first forty days after birth and are solely among women. The new mother receives gifts in the form of money (*nūqūt*) from the women who visit her. She subsequently returns the visit and gift when her erstwhile guests give birth.

Semi-nomadic women have little opportunity for casual visiting when their camps are far from another. When they do camp close to another family whom they know, they may sit and chat together during the hours of leisure. Most semi-nomadic women have a daily routine of watering and herding, and baking. In the course of watering or herding, they may meet a female acquaintance and chat a while with her. For example, on one occasion whilst herding with an informant, we met her sister-in-law who was herding in the same area. We sat and chatted, drank tea and sewed for about fifteen minutes. On another occasion two flocks were being watered simultaneously from a cistern belonging to one family. The other family were affines and were sharing the cistern during that period. The women chatted together while they watered the animals. Women's encounters with other women whilst herding or watering occur without their husbands' knowledge or permission, as also do their visits home to their agnates when they are angry.

The visits made to other women at parties or at their homes are carried out with their husbands' knowledge and permission. For example, one informant went to visit her sister seven days after she had given birth. It is customary to prepare a special meal of thanksgiving (*fadū*) that the child is alive on the seventh day after its birth. The informant did not tell her husband that she was going on a visit. She walked to her sister's tent, which was pitched some five kilometers away, had lunch and came home at midday. Her husband expressed his anger when she came home. He had no objection to the visit itself, but he resented the fact that she had not asked his permission. On another occasion a wife wanted to visit her family but her husband told her that she could only do so when they had finished harvesting the barley crop.

The pattern and form of visiting amongst settled Bedouin women is rather different from that of their semi-nomadic counterparts. Since they live closer together, their visits occupy only part of the day and are of shorter duration. Like semi-nomadic women, settled women carry out the same three main types of visits — going to parties, to their kin and to women after childbirth. Settled women visit more women and visit them on a number of additional occasions. This is possible because wage labor has resulted in women spending more time at home without their husbands, while settlement has resulted in a greater residential density which gives women increased access to other women. Settled women live in residential clusters near their husbands', brothers' and cousins' households. If the women have married their cousins, they probably live near their mothers and sisters as well. Settled women thus have easy access to a number of women living near them. The proportion of these who are their affines or their kin depends on whether they married their cousins or unrelated men. For example, S of the Huzail tribe married P of the Abu Rgaig sub-tribe. S lives in a residential cluster of her husband's brothers. All the women around her are not her kin except for her sister who married a man from her husband's sub-tribe.

The greater residential density of settled Bedouin and the increased segregation of sex roles have affected women's visiting patterns in various ways. First, informal visiting often develops between the women living in one residential cluster and their neighboring residential cluster. For example, Family A lived in a tent pitched 50 meters from Family B's tents. They belonged to different sub-tribes of the same tribe. The women and girls of the two families would visit each other frequently — to sew together, or for a few glasses of tea — in between their domestic activities. The household head of Family A also utilized the guest tent of Family B during the summer months, for his summer tent had no guest section. In another case M married her first cousin (*ibn ʻamm*). She lives in a residential cluster with his brother, but she also lives within walking distance of her mother and two of her sisters who also married their cousins. She visited informally not only her husband's brother's wife but also the women of the adjacent residential cluster. They and their husbands were both her and her husband's first cousins. Her husband utilized the guest tent of his uncle which was nearby. There were various other related households living nearby which M visited only on formal occasions. M's residential cluster consisted of her half brother and widowed mother; the uncle's widow; the uncle's guest tent; a first cousin; other first cousins (in M's home); and yet more first cousins in her husband's brother's home. A pattern of casual visiting may thus develop between the women of separate households living in one residential cluster and the women of a neighboring residential cluster. These neighbors may be related or not.

A second consequence of greater residential density, and increased leisure and segregation of sex roles, is that settled Bedouin women visit more women than their semi-nomadic counterparts and they visit them at more crucial points in their life cycle. Settled women, like semi-nomadic women, visit others when they are newly married and after childbirth. They give them gifts of money (*nūqūt*). These gifts are eventually returned to them when they themselves give birth. The number of individual visits is greater so that each woman receives more gifts and incurs more social obligations. These visits usually occur during a short period after the event. Each day several women come to visit the woman in question. They arrive in the morning at about eight to nine o'clock. They sit and chat whilst drinking tea and coffee. After eating lunch they leave at about midday. These morning hours are the period when they are free to visit. Their children are at school and their husbands at work. They bring the children of pre-school age with them if they have no unmarried teenage daughter or sister-in-law who can look after them at home.

In addition, settled women visit each other whenever one of their children has been ill and has recovered, or when there has been a death in the family. The following incident is an example of visits made as a result of a child's ill health. Y, the son of X was hospitalized for nephritis for five days. Her sister-in-law and her eldest daughter cared for the younger children. For the ten days following Y's release from hospital, women came to Y's home daily in order to praise God that Y was healthy. Seven days after Y's release from hospital X's sister gave birth to a son. When she returned from the hospital her mother, sister and sister-in-law went to visit her. She lives about four kilometers away. X did not accompany them since she was still receiving visitors as a result of her son's illness.

Women also visit each other when there has been a death. They either visit during the days immediately after the death, or forty days after the death, or on the eve of the two main Moslem feast days. On the eve of the feasts the women visit the graves of the sub-tribe. They go in the early morning, pass amongst the graves, identify them, and distribute sweets to the children. They then repair to the home of a woman of their acquaintance whose husband or son has recently died. For example, in the Tel Sheva area, in 1972, women of the Abu Rgaig sub-tribe visited a family whose son had been killed in a motorcycle accident that year. In 1973 women who visited the graves adjourned to the home of a young woman who had been widowed recently. Not all the women of the sub-tribe came to visit the widow that morning. Eight women were present, all of whom had some link with the widow. Four of these women were also widows and in common with the young widow they had married into the sub-tribe. Two of them were of peasant origin like the young widow. Three of them had been widowed at an early age when all their children were young, as was this widow. The other four women present were wives of neighbors. Their husbands were related to each other and the dead man, and they lived in the same area. The visit to the young widow by this particular group of women would seem to be stressing agnatic solidarity. These women were unrelated to each other, other than through the men they married. They were all married to men of the Abu Rgaig sub-tribe. However, not all the women of the sub-tribe came. The ones who came were either neighbors who were married to close relatives of her late husband, or they were widows who like her were outsiders and widowed with young children. They were identifying with her plight and giving her support, as women and as stranger widows.

In addition to formal visiting at periods of rites of passage like marriage, and birth and death, settled women also have certain activities which they do in groups. They may go out together in groups of two or three to collect wood. This involves walking quite far away from the home, as the area around a permanent residential cluster is generally overgrazed and denuded. They also help each other set up their looms for weaving. These activities turn into social events. On one occasion a loom was set up at an informant's tent with the help of her sister, her mother and the mother-in-law, and her daughter-in-law from the neighboring household. The two older women gave instructions and advice to the younger woman, all of whom said that they had been learning to weave gradually since their marriage. Once the loom was set up a special meal of rice was cooked in honor of the occasion.

The absence of men at home during the day, coupled with the increased access to other women and the availability of bus services, has not only encouraged morning visits but has also encouraged the development of another type of activity. Groups of women venture into what were formerly exclusively male spheres. They go to Beersheva together and visit the market, and visit the hospital, the bank and the post office. Semi-nomadic women visit these places only with a male chaperon, either their husbands, fathers or sons. Their menfolk are at home and available. These visits to town are brought about by economic necessity. Women claim their pensions and their children's allowances every two months, and they have to collect them themselves. Although their husbands or sons could stay home from work and take them to town, it is becoming more customary that women go to town together by bus or by taxi. For example, two sisters and their sister-in-law went to town to collect their children's allowances. They subsequently bought food, dress material and jewelry at the market. On another occasion, a widow and her uncle's wife and married daughter went to the market, and then went to visit a niece in the hospital. Thus, several women together are able to do things that cannot be performed individually.

Settled Bedouin women meet each other more frequently than their semi-nomadic and mixed-economy counterparts. They are, therefore, well informed about the activities and health of members of their sub-tribe. Whereas semi-nomadic women often hear information second or third-hand from their husbands when they return home from the market, settled men often hear information from their wives when they return from work in the evenings. In the semi-nomadic context, women remain more isolated in the home and men roam the market place reactivating contacts with members of their family and tribe. In the settled context, women remain at home but have more ample opportunities and time for visiting. The men spend their daylight hours in a work situation which socially and spatially separate them from their home and sub-tribes. When they return home, men spend their afternoons and evenings in their own home or in the guest section of a relative's home. They no longer have the time nor the energy for extensive visiting. Their wives, however, do have the time. They visit women whose husbands have died, or women after childbirth, or women whose sons are getting circumcised or married. Whereas husbands only come to the circumcision party on the Saturday morning, women attend during the mornings of the preceding week. They are more closely involved in the sub-tribal social life than their husbands.

Settled women's visiting patterns partly reflect their husbands' political interests and kinship links. Most of their visiting is among the women married to male members of their husband's family and sub-tribe. They also visit neighbors and offer hospitality to their husbands. If their husbands have argued with certain individuals or families, their wives do not visit the women of these individuals or families. For example, the Abu Rgaig men do not visit the Abu Taha men in Tel Sheva. Similarly, the women of the two groups do not visit each other. An example on the level of individuals is an informant who quarreled with his half brother. He did not speak to him or visit him for two years. His wife's sister was married to his half brother. The women were forbidden to visit each other.

Women's visiting patterns are not, however, totally shaped by their husband's interests. They also reflect their own interests and relationships. Women are ideally meant to ask their husband's permission to go visiting and often do so. But they also often visit others without informing him. They are able to do this because the men are absent from home and the women form a conspiracy of silence amongst themselves. The following two examples illustrate this. The aforementioned sisters who were forbidden to visit each other owing to their husbands' quarrel used to meet secretly at regular intervals. Whenever the older sister brought her children to the Tel Sheva village clinic, she would visit her sister who lived in the village. When she gave birth in the hospital, her younger sister came to visit her. Whenever she went home to visit her parents and siblings, her younger sister would arrange to return home at the same time. In another case an informant was divorced and remarried shortly afterward. Her two year-old-son by her first marriage was kept by her first husband's family. Her second husband's family lived approximately three kilometers away from them. Her former mother-in-law was very fond of her and knew how much she missed her son. One day when her husband and son were not at home, she told her children that she was going to visit the local dervish and came to visit the informant bringing her small son with her. Neither her husband nor her son knew about her visit.

Settled women also have disagreements amongst themselves, independent of their husband's affairs, and these are reflected in the visiting patterns. For example, two women were close neighbors in the village. Their husbands were cousins and visited each other frequently in the evenings. One of the women accused the other of appearing unveiled in front of her husband. The two women did not visit each other or speak to each other for some months. When one of them gave a circumcision party the other did not attend it, although her husband did.

Settled women tend to visit their mothers more frequently than semi-nomadic women, particularly if they married amongst their father's sub-tribe for they then probably live quite near their mothers. They visit not only on the religious holidays but also whenever there is a family crisis of some sort. One of the effects of residential density is that more events are public and that gossip travels faster. For example, one mother of four married daughters had visits from three of them within two days of each other when the fourth one came home after a marital crisis. On another occasion a mother was insulted by her daughter-in-law. Two of her married daughters heard about the incident and came to visit her the next day. They wanted to hit the daughter-in-law in retaliation. Whereas all settled women visit the wives of their husbands' agnates frequently, women who marry their cousins and live nearby are able to visit their mothers and sisters often. They are able to express their solidarity with them at moments of crisis and help each other when necessary. Thus, women use their visiting patterns to develop their own relationships and build up their own reputations amongst other women. Their visits not only foster patrilineal solidarity and uterine solidarity, but they also consolidate friendships and build up reputations of piety, generosity and honor.

Settled women who marry their relatives have different patterns of social interaction with their husbands' agnates than women who marry unrelated men. A woman who marries a relative is surrounded by her husband's agnates who are also her kin. A woman who marries a stranger is surrounded by her husband's agnates who are only her affines. This difference is less significant for semi-nomadic women who are isolated in camping units regardless of whom they marry. A settled woman who marries a relative has plenty of opportunity for interaction with her male relatives. When they visit her husband, she can remain present and participate in the interaction. They may visit her when her husband is not home, on their way to or from work. They may simply chat about each other's family or the man may do errands for his female relative. One informant mentioned to her brother that she would like an oven and he found her a secondhand one. Another informant wanted to visit a woman who had given birth but who lived four kilometers away. Her first cousin visited her and gave her a lift there in his car. Similar patterns of casual visiting develop between stranger wives and their husbands' agnates over the years. By the time the stranger wife is middle-aged and a mother of grown children, her husband's agnates and their sons visit her freely. During the early years of her married life she is much more isolated from them. The only man she interacts with freely is her husband.

Each woman can decide whom to visit and when. A settled woman can create her own reputation and popularity through her own social activities. Although her reputation and status are affected by her husband and her sons, it is also affected by her activities, personality, age and kinship position. A new stranger wife may be more punctilious about visiting other women after a childbirth than a widow with married children. The stranger wife wants to create social debts and wants to be accepted by her peers amongst the women married to her husband's agnates. Thus, settled women have more contact with other women and related men than their semi-nomadic counterparts. Through visiting each other they develop their own networks of social obligations, debts and credits. Their visits to each other may emphasize the links between them as wives of men of one agnate group or as neighbors, or they may express uterine solidarity, their husbands' political and kinship links, their own personal likes and dislikes, and their concern for other women at crucial periods in their lives or their children's lives.

There has been some discussion on Arab village women's visiting patterns and social networks (Dobkin 1967; Rosenfeld 1974; Sweet 1974). Rosenfeld maintains that women's visiting patterns are reciprocal and non-hierarchical: "Although not entirely unambiguous, the way in which women understand the give and take of reciprocity emphasizes the basic equality that exists among them. That is, there is no status hierarchy between peasant women in the village other than that which may exist within an extended family." Dobkin writes about social rank amongst women in a Muslim Turkish village. She maintains that age and relative standing within a lineage are relevant to a woman's social ranking. This view in no way conflicts with Rosenfeld's argument, for age and lineage position are the two factors which are relevant within an extended family.

Settled Bedouin women's visiting patterns are reciprocal, but there are social differences. These are based not only on age and relative standing within their husband's lineage and their own, but also on behavior, personality and the political interests of both her husband and herself. These visiting patterns have three main implications for the scope of women's power and influence in Bedouin society. They increase her social independence from her husband. She is able to visit other women without her husband, not necessarily with his knowledge or permission. Her access to other women also enables her to venture into town without a male chaperon. Other women also help her to extend her economic resources.

These visits provide women with access to considerable information about other families' economic and social activities. Their possession of this information does not, however, enable them to extend their power and influence over their men. If a semi-nomadic women had this amount and type of information at her disposal, it would extend her power and influence. Her husband would find it extremely useful for he depends heavily on his agnates and affines for access to water and land, and for social support. Settled Bedouin have less need for this type of information since they are more economically independent from and less socially involved with their relatives. Settled Bedouin men spend less time within the domestic and tribal context and more time in their work environment and the town. Both of these activities are foreign to the women and beyond their control. The tribe is becoming less important to the settled men whose lives revolve around their work and their families in the context of their sub-tribes. They sometimes fail to honor the obligations of "balanced reciprocity" by not giving circumcision parties or by failing to attend the parties of those who were present at theirs, or they come to them reluctantly. Their women folk, on the other hand, are meticulous about honoring their social obligations. Thus, the increased residential density accompanied by an increased segregation of sex roles has resulted in more intensive and extensive visiting patterns between women which enables them to extend their power and influence amongst themselves, but does not affect their influence amongst their men.

ECONOMIC RESOURCES AND STRATEGIES

Negev Bedouin women all have similar economic resources. Their utilization, however, differs according to whether they are semi-nomadic, living from a mixed-economy, or settled. All Bedouin women are given jewelry by their fathers, mothers and husbands. As women grow older they begin to wear less adornments. They give their daughters their discarded jewelry, such as coins from their head-dress. Fathers often buy their teenage daughters pieces of jewelry, such as a bracelet or a nose ring. Jewelry for the bride is part of the bride-wealth. The groom's family buys it and gives it to the bride's mother before the marriage. One informant felt that the gold necklace and bracelets purchased by the groom for her daughter were of inferior quality. She exchanged them for gold she considered to be good enough. Husbands also buy jewelry for their wives. One informant received a pair of bracelets from her husband when she was pregnant with their first child. Another received a pair of bracelets from her husband when he took a second wife. Another informant received six gold hairpins (*āibkūl*) when her husband sold their flock.

This jewelry is theirs for life and it provides them with status and security. They wear the necklaces on festive occasions, while their bracelets, nose rings and hairpins are worn daily. In later years they either give it to their daughters or sell it when they have no money. Two widows in the Tel Sheva area sold their jewelry bit by bit over the years to enable them to support themselves and their children. One widow decided to buy a house. She planned to pay the mortgage from her pension and she raised the cash deposit for the house by selling her ten sheep, winter tent, carpets, silver bracelets and gold coins.

All Negev Bedouin women own a few livestock. Semi-nomadic and mixed-economy women own a few goats or sheep which their husbands or fathers have given them. These are slaughtered or sold whenever the women wish them to be. The animals are given to them by men, and slaughtered or sold by men according to the women's wishes. Settled women also own livestock. They may own a few goats or sheep but usually they own a collection of poultry — chickens, turkeys, geese. Unlike semi-nomadic women they do not receive them from their husbands. They buy them themselves or receive them as gifts from other women. One informant gave her sister two geese. Another informant bought a gander from another woman in the area when she saw that her goose was broody. The poultry provide fresh eggs and meat for the family and their guests.

All Negev Bedouin women also have money of their own which comes from various sources. One source is the fines that their husbands pay them after a domestic dispute, another source is the gifts other women give them at their marriage, after childbirth and on their sons' circumcision. Settled women receive more gifts than semi-nomadic women since they have more visitors on these occasions. In the Tel Sheva area, in 1974, one informant received IL 800 from other women on the birth of her daughter, and IL 1,075 on her sons's circumcision. Each woman gave about IL 15-20. This indicates that between forty to fifty women visited her after she gave birth, and about fifty to seventy women visited her when her sons were circumcised. Another source of money is state benefits. An increasing number of Bedouin women claim their children's allowances and their pensions. Settled women are more likely to claim these, since their menfolk work and have more knowledge of their social rights.

Settled women not only have more money of their own than semi-nomadic women but they also have a greater variety of ways of spending it. Semi-nomadic women may ask their husbands to bring them a dress from the market or they may purchase jewelry for themselves on the occasions that they go to the market with their husbands. Settled women are able to go to the market themselves more frequently by going in groups. If they cannot go themselves, they may ask an older woman to buy things for them. They may request a kid, some chicks, or some sewing silks and material. They are also able to purchase goods without leaving their homes. There are a number of itinerant female traders who come daily from Gaza to pass from door to door at regular intervals. They sell perfume, nightgowns and dresses, and are willing to take orders from women for specific articles. For example, one informant requested a red chiffon nightgown. By being able to spend their money themselves, the women can acquire garments they would never have asked their husbands for and livestock which perhaps he may not have agreed to. They thus exercise more control over what they wear and how their money is spent by spending it themselves or giving it to other women to spend for them.

All Negev Bedouin women have some control over the preparation of food. Settled women not only prepare the food but also purchase it themselves. The grocery shopping patterns of settled Bedouin differ from those of semi-nomadic and mixed-economy Bedouin. Semi-nomadic and mixed-economy men shop in the market once or twice a month. They purchase household necessities and food in bulk (e.g., fifty kilo sacks of flour and sugar, tins of tomato puree, several kilos of lentils and macaroni). Settled men shop more often and in smaller quantities since they are in town more often, going to and from their place of work. They purchase more perishable goods like fruit, vegetables and fish. There are also small grocery stores near most groups of settled Bedouin. Women have begun to shop by proxy from these local stores. In Tel Sheva there are two stores and the women both in the village and around the village send their children there to buy groceries. The children also buy the goods on their way home from school. They may buy packets of tea, a kilo or two of sugar, detergent, or perishable goods such as yoghurt, milk and bread. Most of the families buy on credit and the husband foots the bill. The settled women are thus using the new options available to them in their changed environment. They exercise more control over their family's diet, but they do so in a socially acceptable way. They never come to the local store in person. The shop is spatially and socially outside the women's sphere.

All semi-nomadic and nomadic and mixed-economy Bedouin women process the products from the flock. They make yoghurt, cheese and butter from the milk, and weave tent strips and carpets from the flock's wool. Settled families have no flocks. Their women no longer process the milk products but they do continue to weave. Since they no longer have a flock the fleeces are bought in the market. If the settled family lives in a goat's hair tent, the husband will buy fleeces in the market which his wife will then wash, spin and weave into tent strips. Occasionally settled men will buy tent strips but these are extremely expensive. Whereas relatively few settled women live in tents and weave tent strips, they all weave carpets whether they live in tents, huts or houses. The husbands generally buy the fleeces for the carpets for the home and the women often purchase additional fleeces with their own money. They may do so themselves in the market or ask an older woman who regularly goes to the market to buy fleeces for them, or they may buy them from a neighboring family who have a flock.

Settled women sell their carpets secretly. They may sell them to women traders who come from Gaza, and pass from dwelling to dwelling selling and buying during daylight hours when husbands are out at work. The carpets are also sold through other women who have contact with people who are probably willing to purchase them. For example, an older woman lives near an archaeological site which is visited by many tourists who frequently drink tea in her tent. She is given many carpets by women in the area and she sells them to the tourists. When her sons ask her who made the carpets, she refuses to divulge the names. She then gives the money to the women concerned. I was frequently asked to buy fleeces or to sell carpets, and each time I was pledged to secrecy not to tell their husbands or neighbors. One woman wanted to sell two carpets because she was ill and needed money for frequent trips to the doctor. Another was planning to buy a cow with the proceeds from the sale of a rug and two goats. Another rug seller was a teenage girl whose parents had died and she lived with her brother. Whilst he was away at work, she wove a carpet which she sold through an elderly woman. She planned to buy herself a pair of silver bracelets.

The pattern of rug selling has a number of significant aspects. The settled women are continuing a traditional domestic activity but utilizing it in a radically new way. In a semi-nomadic or mixed-economy household, rugs are woven from the flock's wool and are used only by the family. It is one of the women's activities which fit into the total system of production. In a settled household the women use this skill not only for their own households but for their own advantage. The fleeces may be bought with their own money. The rugs are sold and the women use the money received for their own ends. This pattern of rug making for sale has "low visibility." Jopling (1974) has described how Mexican peasant women embroider shirts at home for sale and how their sewing has "low visibility" not as an activity but as an industry. Sewing is an activity that women are expected to perform. Similarly, Bedouin women spin and weave in their leisure time. They may set up a loom and weave a long rug in five days. They they may cut it in half and keep one for the home and offer one for sale.

The fact that women sell their rugs secretly indicates that they are aware that although the activity is traditional and acceptable, their sale of them is not. Similarly, settled women embroider dresses for relatives and neighbors. They may do this with their sewing machines or by hand; the money they receive is their own and talked about amongst women but not men. Thus, settled women are beginning to utilize their domestic activites and skills to earn money. They do this, however, privately, within the home and amongst other women. Only six informants work "publicly" outside the home. One was educated in Gaza and taught embroidery for a few months to other girls. The other five are young girls who finished high school in the last few years. Two work as nurses, one is a teacher and two are secretaries at tribal elementary schools.

Settled women are more active in the purchase of food, clothing and household goods than semi-nomadic or mixed economy women. They spend their own money when they go to the market in groups, or when they buy from door-to-door merchants, and they spend their husband's money when they buy at the local store. Settled women have more cash income of their own and, therefore, more spending power through their state benefits, their gifts from other women and their covert sale of carpets. They spend their money on themselves for clothes, domestic livestock, material for sewing and weaving, and jewelry. Thus Bedouin women derive their economic resources from the domestic sphere, other women and the state. They use them solely within the domestic sphere and amongst other women. Settlement has resulted in their being less dependent socially and economically on their menfolk.

CONCLUSIONS

This analysis has focused on the roles, resources and strategies contributing to Bedouin women's power in two different dimensions of their lives. The first section dealt with their access to power through the roles they occupy during their life cycle in the domestic sphere; the second section focused on their use of their social and economic resources. Their access to power and the extent of it varies according to their stage in their life cycles, and also by settlement and wage labor.

Several conclusions can be drawn concerning the basis and exercise of Bedouin women's power. Bedouin women's power is based in and exercised from the domestic sphere. They utilize their roles and their social and economic resources to influence their husbands, children, kin and affines. Their resources increase as they get older and become both mothers-in-law and widows. Their power and influence is not, however, simply restricted to the domestic sphere. They often influence their husbands' and children's decisions and actions outside the home.

Settlement and wage labor clearly affect Bedouin women's power. The increased segregation of the sexes which accompanies wage labor has two contradictory effects on women's power. On the one hand, women have increased social and economic independence which they use to increase their power in the domestic sphere and amongst other women in their visiting circle. On the other hand, their increased economic and social independence does not give them increased power over men related to them. Women's power and influence over men would seem to be thus partially derived from their shared activities and interests. These decrease with settlement and wage labor. In settled families, the women's labor is no longer required in the care of the flock or land. The men become the sole wage earners and the women are solely responsible for the care of the home and the children.

Thus, segregation increases women's power over other women and gives them more exclusive control in the home, but does not give them more power over related men. Negev Bedouin women's power is based in and exercised from the domestic sphere but extends beyond the confines of her home. Those persons over whom she has influence and power, live and act in other homes.

NOTES

1. No official statistics exist concerning the number of semi-nomadic Bedouin in the Negev. The author estimates that 10 percent are semi-nomadic, 30 percent are mixed-economy and 60 percent are settled.

2. C beat D because A had beaten B (his sister), and one of the principles of a sister exchange manage is equal treatment. D felt that C was justified in beating her. Since this case is used to illustrate the way women protest the infringement of norms and not the properties of sister exchange marriage, there will be no discussion of the second beating.

3. A household is defined as a group of persons who have common purse management and eat together, even though they may live in separate dwellings.

Changes in Employment and Social Accommodations of Bedouin Settling in an Israeli Town

Gideon M. Kressel

This article discusses Bedouin who have settled in the towns of Lod (Lydda) and Ramla. It examines their migrations northwards since the establishment of the State of Israel in 1948, and some of the changes that have occurred over the years. The research first centered on the housing development project in Kiryat Jawarish in the suburbs of Ramla, Shikun Jarushi and Shikun haBedouim. Since late 1974 research has been undertaken in the Bedouin neighborhoods of the Lod Railway Station, at Gan Hakal bordering Lod and Ramla, and the dwellings scattered throughout the fields and plantations close to the towns.[1]

In 1952 the Israeli authorities started the construction of Shikun Jarushi which spread over four main development stages. Initially, 52 houses were built and occupied by Bedouin of Lybian origin who had settled in Palestine two generations ago, as well as several peasant families from the Southern coastal plain. In 1957 the construction of an additional 18 units was completed and were assigned to Bedouin families from the Negev. In 1965 the Minorities Department of the Ministry of Housing built a further 25 houses and by 1967 they had added another 27 units, all of which were designed to accommodate Bedouin families from the Negev. The housing complex built during the 1960s is referred to as "Shikun haBedouim" in order to distinguish it from Shikun Jarushi; the "Kiryat Jawarish" includes both of the neighborhoods. The Ministry of Housing also set up a Mother and Child clinic, kindergarten, primary school, youth club and shopping center which serves both sectors of the quarter.

By 1968 some additional residential units had been built in Shikun Jarushi and were renovated privately. The community then numbered 160 families and included some 850 individuals. By late 1976 there were

200 families and the population was estimated at 1,350 people. The increase was the outcome of a large number of marriages (several of which were polygynous), high birthrates and the arrival of new families from the South. Bedouin dwellings in other parts of the towns were unplanned. At first people rigged up tents or squatted in abandoned houses and then patched them up using pieces of wood and corrugated iron. Later huts and concrete partitioning found in the surrounding villages were used and eventually they built houses of reinforced concrete and building blocks. Neither public buildings nor municipal services were provided.

By the early 1950s many Bedouin could be found living in abandoned packing houses in the plantations in the central part of the country, and they made their living by working in the nearby orchards. Many had worked and lived there before 1948, prior to their enforced removal to the Bedouin Reserve which was carried out by the Military Government. They now returned in order to renew old contacts with plantation holders in an attempt to establish new sources of income. The former employers were mainly private orchard-owners who did not restrict employment in accordance with the prevailing socialist ethics of that time and therefore, in comparison with collective and cooperative cultivators, were less susceptible to supervision and public control.

In the early 1960s the Military Government lifted several restrictions on movement and consequently Bedouin migration from the Negev northwards increased considerably. Those who took advantage of this new situation came with their herds during a dry summer, and frequently stayed on since the men could find employment in citrus-fruit packing and construction jobs. Other members of the family and the herds would return to the south. In 1966 all restrictions on the Bedouin's movements were lifted. Former personal relations between the Bedouin and the farmers living in Central Israel played an important part in promoting the first land-tenure transactions concerning irrigated areas, the leasing of fields for farming or crop-harvesting or, on a partial basis, pasture land. Abandoned buildings were made available for the Bedouin in return for their guarding of the crops.

Young Bedouin males were the first to remain in the Ramla district but after they obtained regular work, others followed in their footsteps. Men called on their brothers and other relatives to participate in the more demanding tasks such as cultivating the plantations, and women worked in the vegetable gardens. When permanent grazing land was acquired in the north, the old folk, women, children and herds settled there. Inevitably the center of gravity of family life shifted from the Negev northwards.

Much of the leased arable land was irrigated and usually belonged to cooperative villages (moshavim and kibbutzim). During the early 1960s many similar leasing transactions were effected even though these organizations were forbidden to do so on account of their agreements with the "Nir" Worker's Settlement Cooperative and their political institutions. The handing over of land was fundamental to the principle of self-labor or the prohibition of hired labor. Similarly, leasing of land for cultivation by a third party was forbidden, especially in the case of an Arab lessee. Nonetheless, extensive areas of unirrigated crops were cultivated even though a complex network of pipes had been installed. In other areas cultivation had been neglected owing to the increasing scarcity and rise in costs of Jewish labor. The Military Government's restrictions on the movement of Arabs prevented them from competing with Jewish immigrants in the labor market and from taking over stateland (Ben-Porat 1966). However, the movement restrictions were lifted at the beginning of the 1960s, and as a result Arab labor became available and formerly neglected fields underwent intensive cultivation.

Daman (guarantee) arrangements or the leasing of land to a sub-contractor for cultivation purposes, was widely practised and undertaken on various terms. Sometimes contractors would purchase crops prior to their harvesting and market them themselves, and in other cases crops were purchased in the early stages of their growth — during ripening — and then prepared for harvest. Occasionally the early stages of cultivation were carried out by one contractor and sold to another who would continue and prepare the crops for harvest. For example, a contractor who bought a tomato crop at trellising time would, after completing this stage, sell it to a second contractor who would pick and market the crop. An arrangement that differed slightly from the *daman* enabled arable lands to be leased for contractual work on the basis of a previously agreed overall price. Cultivating or gathering vegetables; pruning and harvesting orchards; trimming and harvesting vines and so forth, were the responsibilities of a contractor or "foreman" who would carry them out with the help of his laborers. The term "foreman" (in Arabic, *rais*, meaning "leader") became popular in Israel during the 1960s and was widely used.

Within a short period of time most of the agricultural work in the region shifted from Jewish to Arab hands. The proportion of Bedouin among the latter was very high since they usually experienced great difficulties in obtaining employment, and took advantage of every suitable opportunity. Those who worked long distances from home usually had to sleep near their places of employment, and the Bedouin were more suited to the rigors of temporary lodging than were the local peasants. This arrangement allowed their employers to save on travelling expenses.

The contractor's willingness to assume responsibility for agricultural jobs was agreeable to both parties, far more than the complete leasing of land or cultivation with the help of hired labor. Several factors help to explain this trend. As regards the Jewish farmer, land that he was unable to work himself was put to use and he was spared the trouble of finding and supervising laborers. Many members of cooperative villages were, at that time, already engaged in profitable outside work in addition to their agricultural enterprises. This arrangement allowed the farmer to forgo the necessity of paying National Insurance on behalf of his workers. Furthermore, he evaded the supervision of the authorities since the laborers left the area after each stage of cultivation had been completed. As far as the Bedouin (most of whom were Bedouin peasants) were concerned, they had exchanged extensive dry-farming areas in the Negev for irrigated lands producing high yields (cf. Marx 1967). In addition, they substituted tenancy conditions in which they were ruthlessly exploited by the sheikhs, for more favorable business partnerships with the Jewish villages.

The organized employers were subject to legislation, which for the first time in the history of the country introduced a wage scale equal for all laborers. Moreover, after a certain trial period, the Bedouin were able to choose among various agreements and avoid less profitable deals. The extensive and large labor market in the coastal plain provided a number of opportunities for business enterprises, and laborers became more aware of the implications of individual freedom.

The Bedouin were able to increase the proceeds from their work over several years due to a number of factors: they constituted a relative advantage as regards the number of available agricultural laborers and they were impartial as to their form of employment. Moreover, their women and children were able to help them and their living expenses were minimal. However, the relative advantage of Bedouin work in the Ramla region declined during the 1960s. Firstly, the demands for labor in the primary and secondary sectors was satiated owing to the economic recession of 1966-67 and partial employment was widespread. Members of agricultural settlements who could no longer support themselves by means of outside work returned to their farms. In addition, the Labor Exchange directed many workers to the infrastructure industries.

Secondly, the Bedouin who had moved north gradually improved their standard of living. The economic success they enjoyed in the 1960s brought about changes in their consuming behavior. This change was noticeable even when they first settled on the outskirts of permanent settlements, and lived in tents and tin-huts. However, their transfer to the actual settlements caused them to discard many traditional customs. Living in buildings, whether temporary or permanent, involved the consumption of electricity and running water which necessitated the purchase of appropriate household appliances. Gradually, with the increase in the scope of work, second-hand (though later new) vehicles were acquired for the transport of laborers. The purchase of tractors and mechanical equipment for agricultural work, chiefly for earth-moving, crop-spraying, the transport of fruit containers in the orchards and so forth, quickly became a worthwhile investment.

Nowadays owners of orange groves and orchards prefer to rent machinery by the hour than personally acquire it. Many young Bedouin have gained experience in using agricultural machinery, have acquired their own, and now offer their services to farmers. The purchase of expensive agricultural equipment first involves a downpayment followed by monthly installments. These payments, in common with housing mortgages, property insurance and similar expenses, brings about an increase in financial demands.

The changes in Bedouin consumption patterns and the higher prices for their labor are accredited to social contacts with people who maintain higher standards of living. Daily encounters with Jews and Arabs from the permanent settlements have brought about improvements in dietary and clothing habits and have promoted new health standards, pedagogic concerns and related issues which were previously non-existent.

The third factor was of an administrative nature. Increased prices for Bedouin labor in Ramla resulted from large-scale supervision on the part of the regional labor exchanges. Coercive legislation to restrict unorganized labor expanded during the economic slumps of the mid 1960s. This limited the Bedouin's freedom of seeking employment, but at the same time resulted in increased wages and improved their social conditions.

The aftermath of the Six Day War witnessed a situation of full employment in an over-heated economy. Once again the demand for labor rose. Jewish workers were requested in the security services and industry, and the Arabs in the infrastructure industries. All the Bedouin who had migrated north were absorbed in the rapidly expanding work force. Irrigated fields which had been abandoned at the turn of the 1960s underwent massive cultivation during 1965-67, but after autumn 1967 were once again neglected.

Furthermore, construction projects did not attain their planned momentum owing to labor shortage, and as a result building activity declined. Bedouin migration from the Negev came to a stop. Development enterprises in the south were in full swing and employment could be found in the labor markets of the Beersheva region. Special work permits were no longer required in many parts of the Negev.

However, the vast demand for labor in the central region was short-lived. Within six months of the 1967 war, large numbers of workers arrived from the occupied territories. The advantages of this situation were realized with great alacrity (Lifshitz 1970). For example, in April 1968, at the height of the Valencia orange harvest, the new labor force enabled work to be completed on time. The massive labor potential that had been bound to the West Bank and especially the Gaza Strip, crossed the pre-1967 border and moved towards the centers of econmic activity, thus relieving the labor shortage and lowering wages. Owners of industrial plants, building contractors, agriculturalists and other employers benefited from this situation. However, there were severe repercussions in those sectors of the economy which were open to unorganized labor, namely construction and agriculture. The majority of the Bedouin migrants were employed in these sectors.

Tenured workers, especially those employed in work places registered with the labor exchanges, were scarcely affected. However, the number of tenured workers living in Kiryat Jawarish was very small. The transfer from agriculture to protected work places or obtaining tenure in the primary sector was a slow, protracted process. This was due to the fact that labor organizations, in conjunction with employers, labor exchange officials and security authorities, were interested in forestalling this development. Measures taken to prevent cheap labor from flooding the market and to maintain proper standards of remuneration and social benefits for workers, came to little avail in the infrastructure sectors of the economy.

The effectiveness of a trade union is partially determined by the extent of the damage caused by strikes. Service workers hold an advantage over production workers in as much as they are exclusive and cannot be replaced easily. Strikes and sanctions serve as an efficient means of improving work conditions and have increased since 1968. On the other hand, strikes in the manufacturing industries are far less frequent even though working conditions have taken a turn for the worse. During 1960-69, fewer work days were lost in strikes in agriculture and construction than in industry and public services (Michael and Bar-El 1977, pp. 328-29).

The professional struggle designed to protect and maintain production levels is of little avail in the primary sector owing to the growing proportion of Arab employees. Furthermore, the trade unions dealing with agricultural workers and the General Labor Federation dealing with construction workers, are not particularly influential. The professional protection granted by the Federation to large numbers of Jewish immigrants who were employed in infrastructure projects also took care of Israel's Arabs (until 1968) so long as their number remained relatively small. When the supply of unskilled labor increased, Jewish hired laborers were the first to leave the infrastructure industries. The Israeli economy's demand for labor from the occupied territories was regulated by certain objectives. For example, measures were taken to alleviate the plight of the Arabs in the occupied territories without harming Jewish labor and immigration. Consequently, sectors based on manual labor could be developed and skilled Jewish workers could be transferred to relevant professional occupations where their marginal utility would be higher (Bregman 1974, chap. 1).

As regards the issue of unskilled labor, the trade unions proved unsuccessful in their attempts to maintain basic work conditions. This is because, firstly, the supervision of unorganized labor is beyond the scope of the union, particularly when work places are abundant and dispersed throughout the country. Another problem is that the number of laborers is extremely large, that they have a low standard of living, and are not concerned with protecting their social rights at work. Agreements between employers and work contractors weakened the potential of supervisory authorities. Since supervision is interpreted as "estrangement from unemployed brothers" — all the more so under increasing political pressure for inter-Arab cohesion — union strength is sapped.

Secondly, the operation of the organizational apparatus is largely in Jewish hands. If independent union steps taken on behalf of work conditions are interpreted as nationalistic acts, they are not likely to succeed.

Thirdly, the relevant perception of socialism must be taken into consideration. Traditional socialist idioms such as "the worker's ownership of his labor," "the right to strike" and so forth are infrequent in Arab society. The leftist sympathies common in various countries in the Middle East are inseparable from nationalism (see *The New East* 1965, vol. 15, pp. 341-72). Professional and social conflicts such as attempts to limit religious influence, the fight for women's liberation, measures taken concerning environmental control and so forth, are at the best subordinate to nationalistic issues. The spearhead of the Arab leftist movement's struggle is lately directed against the State of Israel. More often than not sanctions and strikes are measurements of nationalistic demonstrations.

Last but not least is the devaluation of manual labor over the years. Technological sophistication is designed to replace unskilled labor, and science's prestige increases with its growing contribution to the welfare of society. Professional skill is considered more important than muscular strength. The discovery of oilfields served to strengthen this conception and has left its imprint on the Middle Eastern way of life. In simplistic terms: the added value of the work necessary to refine crude oil is incomparably smaller than the value of the work saved by using refined oil (*The New East*, vol. 15, pp. 341,72).

The efforts of the Ministries of Defense and Labor to adjust the excess supply of labor in the new economy were only recognized by the government in August 1960, some eighteen months after their initiation. The Ministerial Committee for the Occupied Territories then proceeded to normalize the working conditions of 20,000 laborers from the occupied territories employed in Israel.[2] The security forces provided the supervisory personnel to regulate the influx of the workers from the West Bank and the Gaza Strip, and regulated the influx of workers according to demand. Daily or weekly permits for residents of the restricted zones located east of the "Green Line" were issued by the security forces in coordination with various work contractors. At a later stage monthly and 3-month permits were issued.

The economic realities of 1968 proved harmful to the Bedouin and the threat of an economic recession pushed them to seek other possibilities, the chief one being to leave agriculture. Work that was relatively protected from the workers of the occupied territories and available to Israeli Arabs included the construction industry and service industries such as driving, guard duties, policing, service at petrol stations and maintaining buses. Light industries such as the food industries, cardboard products, citrus packing centers and the prefabricated housing industry took on Arab workers in considerable numbers. The construction industry is open to cheap labor but less so than agriculture.

The second possibility was to obtain security of tenure at work which prevents sudden dismissal, while allowing an inclusive monthly wage and other social benefits. In several cases workers with tenure or "seasonal tenure" were placed in charge of the plantation and were authorized by the owners to engage other laborers. A number of benefits can be derived from this although security of tenure is not granted in compliance with the workers' desire since only few of them achieve it: many orchard owners dismiss their workers for a few weeks each summer and vinegrowers release their permanent workers each winter. This tends to prevent the accumulation of seniority. The men are then re-hired, but only for the forthcoming season. This illustrates the fundamental significance of the concept of "seasonal tenure."

A third realistic possibility is to buy (or rent) a vehicle or tractor and to be an independent employer. People connected with agricultural work purchase a small wheeled tractor with all its mechanical equipment for cultivating orchards and plantations. A fourth path to economic independence is to lease lands for growing vegetables, though this requires a certain amount of capital. Those with means prefer this way since it offers success based on the employment of cheap labor. A fifth possibility of avoiding competition with the workers from the occupied territories is to remain in the field of temporary agricultural enterprises in the role of a middleman who supplies labor but is not physically involved in manual tasks. This proved to be an attractive solution to the more energetic Bedouin. Workmen and women, mainly from the Gaza Strip, who arrived looking for work and somewhere to stay over night, became sub-tenants in the Jawarish housing developments. By 1969 their number had already exceeded 100. Empty rooms in houses and huts were let to Gaza people (*Ghazazwah*) in return for small sums of money, or various household services or produce from fields and plantations. On arrival they would usually make contact with the local foreman who provided them with work. If they did not find any work locally they would gather near the grocery store the following morning and offer their services to prospective hirers. Local contractors gradually went straight to the laborers at Kiryat Jawarish and neglected the regional offices of the Ministry of Labor.

The *rais* or foreman had to maintain contacts with employers and security organizations in order to give work to the laborers from the occupied territories. Furthermore, he needed to be equipped with a vehicle to transport the men. Israeli Arabs had an advantage over those from the occupied territories as suppliers of work in that they knew the Hebrew language and were familiar with the local work conditions. Their knowlege of Arabic and familiarity with their fellows from the occupied territories also helped. The historic advantage of the Arab foreman over Arabic-speaking Jews (mainly those who had immigrated from the Arab world) lay in the fact that the latter had recently neglected these professions. Finally, the Arab foremen were suitable for their role because of a shared Palestinian identity. They are capable of supplying workers who would not otherwise have found their way to farms. Former acquaintances and family contacts with the inhabitants of the refugee camps facilitated the task of mobilizing labor, particularly as regards women. Girls who work outside the home are only entrusted to a very reliable person.

During 1968-69 the commission of the sub-contractors originally amounted to the greater portion of the wage differential between Israel and the occupied territories. The wage of an agricultural worker in the Gaza Strip, for example, was IL 2-3 per day at the beginning of 1968 and reached IL 4 at the beginning of 1969. The differential between this wage and that common for an agricultural worker in Israel (IL 14.75–15.85 gross) was about IL 11–13. The worker from Gaza would be offered IL 5–6 per day, and thus earn two pounds more than previously. As regards unorganized laborers, the employer paid the foreman between IL 11–13 and so saved between IL 3–5 by comparison with his costs for an organized laborer. The foreman earned between IL 6–8 per day for every laborer he engaged. Even though travelling expenses of IL 1–2 per day per worker were deduced, his relative share of the wage differential remained large.

The form of economic success described above did not, however, last for long. First, changing agricultural seasons bring about the movement of workers to other industries. Also, fluctuations in the security situation affected the availability of workers from the occupied territories and failure to maintain the terms of the work contract involved compensation payments to the employer. Secondly, economic success immediately attracts hangers-on who wish to benefit from its fruits; officials from the national companies for orchard cultivation, the Jewish Agency, "Hadrey Tidhar," "Pardes Co.," "Syndicate," "Mehadrin" and others appointed as senior contractors to supervise the work of the Arab contractors. For transferring workers' wages from the company to the sub-contractor the senior contractor would deduct a commission, consequently the sub-contractor would only receive IL 5.50 or IL 6 for a container of Jaffa oranges. Some agents of the Police or Security Service who tacitly allowed the foreman to operate, also received their cut of the fruits of the success. For example, an indirect yet perfectly visible payment was the costs of entertaining and providing for the big Muslim festivals and family occasions that served to promote work transactions. This was a conspicuous outlay often costing thousands of Israeli lirot (Marx 1973, pp. 411-27). New foremen who appeared on the scene from time to time increased the competition and also cut into the profit margins. The number of commercial vehicles (vans and trucks) in the Bedouin community grew from 3 to 15 in two years. A few men who were not contractors earned money by transporting laborers.

The biggest competitors who incessantly pressurized the foremen were the labor exchanges. With the rise in the demand for laborers from 1970 onwards the labor exchange did not pretend to satisfy it, but did what they could to solve technical, administrative and security problems to enable large labor operations. They provided transport, concerned themselves with the safety of the passengers when terrorists threw handgrenades at them,[3] arranged an office-bank routine, wage payments and dealt with other similar concerns. These public services were available to employers and laborers who were unable to make contact with each other by their own efforts or through the foremen. The middlemen and potential competitors, and the authorities and the private labor contractors complemented each other's shortcomings.

The state services were relatively more clumsy and their costs were higher than those of private services. The employers transferred the full wage of their workers according to the regulations of the Employment Service (equivalent to the wage of Israeli workers) to the appropriate authorities who paid the workers in their home towns after deducting a commission. An unmarried agricultural laborer received between IL 6–8 for a day's work in the years 1968-69, and IL 10–11 at the beginning of 1972. The official justification (1969) for the deductions and their high rate (up to 50 percent) was explained as expenses incurred in the organization of the laborers' arrangements, travel and so forth. Another portion of the deductions was explained as being kept for the workers in a "blocked fund" until it was clarified how it could be passed on to them (cf., *Davar* newspaper, 1 November 1969). A third qualitative explanation was bound up with the need to maintain the wage system in the occupied territories themselves. Inevitably a scale of preferences quickly emerged: workers and employers who made contact with each other via the employment services earned less than those who made contact through private middlemen. Laborers (especially the young and more ambitious) who wished to increase, even double, their income by working according to production norms, would find their way to a *rais*. Those who preferred to work under less strenuous conditions applied to the Employment Service. Laborers and employers who made contact with each other without any middlemen clearly earned the largest incomes.

Relatively small landholders who were capable of putting up the workers in their farms did not pay the obligatory deductions of social security nor the agency fees of the Employment Service and the foremen. Laborers from the occupied territories risked punishment by working without a permit but they received very high wages.[4] They lost the social benefits but avoided the obligatory deductions. Events took their natural course and the independent contacts between laborers and employers continually increased. The laborers were quick to adapt, to grasp work conditions, pick up Hebrew and, in particular, to take risks.

Eventually the middlemen profit from labor ceased. The authorities and the foremen were affected, although the opportunity for profit taking had ostensibly increased with the growth in the number of laborers from the occupied territories in Israel. The foremen responded by reducing their profit margin and paid a worker (winter 1971) IL 4.50-5 for a container of Jaffa oranges, or IL 1 for pruning a mature citrus tree (summer 1971). At the same time they tried to get the employers to make up the difference and pressed, in the first instance, for a wage increment for agricultural work. A moderate increase of labor costs was noted already at the end of 1970. The small sub-contractors (engaging 5 or 6 laborers) became less conspicuous owing to economic reasons and tightening supervision.

At the turn of the 1970s, in order to increase clients' dependence on the state Employment Service, the authorities intensified their activities against their three partners in labor transactions and their potential competitors: the laborers, the employers and the foremen. Different administrative steps were taken against each and for different normative reasons. The authorities applied both deterrent and incentives in their dealings with the laborers from the occupied territories. Initially, using security as a pretext, supervvision was tightened up but without success. There were three reasons for this. First, it is difficult to verify the current validity of permits amongst tens of thousands of laborers, particularly when it was necessary to renew them after short time periods. Secondly, the security forces were unable to deal with the vast number of violators and, thirdly, the courts did not have means of punishment to dissuade them from doing it again. In one of the cases that I recorded, unlicensed laborers were given the option of an IL 80 fine or several days in prison. They chose to go to prison rather than pay. When the strong-arm treatment turned out to be insufficient, an incentive was used. The amount of enforced deductions was reduced and became effective post-factum from April 1971. The details are as follows: standard daily travelling costs — IL 3, i.e., 18.6 percent of the agricultural worker's salary; income tax, 10 percent of the salary; national insurance, 3.4 percent; agricultural workers' insurance fund, 4.5 percent; organization tax, 1 percent. The total deductions came to 37.5 percent of the salary. In addition to the basic salary of workers from the occupied territories, which so far had been paid as though they were all unmarried, a children's allowance (IL 17.50 per child) was now paid, as is customary in Israel. An annual two week vacation allowance was also granted.

Despite the fact that (1) retroactive repayments were not proposed for deductions during the period prior to April 1969, (2) the conditions for accounting with the Israeli tax authorities for retroactive reimbursements were unfair to laborers from the occupied territories, and (3) their chances of remaining at work through the Employment Service until pensionable age (in order to draw their moneys from the retirement funds) were minimal, improvements in their social conditions were remarkable. In November 1971 the deduction for travel expenses was discontinued and only 18.9 percent of the worker's salary was taken as tax. The obligation to pay for transporting the laborers was shifted from the laborer to the employer, as the latter were a safer address to refund the expenses of the Employment Service, or an easier target to hit when they circumvented its services. During the course of 1971 the Employment Service collected tens of thousands of Israeli lirot as fines from employers of unorganized laborers from the occupied territories. The ideological reason given for restricting the employers' activities at the same time as employing the law against them was social in kind. They were presented as people who avoided to pay for the social benefits of their employees. Kibbutzim caught violating the Employment Service Law were accused of being socialists who did not observe their own teachings. By way of apology, actions of the Jewish employers were described as erring or as taking the easy way out as suggested to them by the foremen. The Arab work contractor was presented as being antagonistic towards the Employment Service (*Davar* newspaper, 4 August 1974). He was described as a seducer who "buys" daughters from their fathers and wives from their husbands, while the foreman was described as "lining his own pocket" with half of his laborers' wage. During 1971 imprisonment and fines were the means used to restrict their activities.

Only the biggest and strongest of the contractors, who had extensive connections with laborers, employers and representatives of the ruling power, were able to continue against such tactics. In order to do so they made various semi-legitimate arrangements. Of the 18 contractors and sub-contractors for agricultural work in Kiryat Jawarish at the end of the 1960, only 7 remained by spring 1971, most of them members of the most influential families. A *rais* who mobilizes his laborers himself, transports them in his own vehicle, and collects their wages from the employer, facilitates the burden of the labor exchanges, so long as the demand for cheap labor is on the rise.

Four years after the Six Day War the labor organizations appeared to have stabilized. There was a steady increase in the demand for laborers, but the supply too seemed to be unlimited. Work conditions were fixed in unwritten agreements among employer authorities and foremen. Only the fourth element, the manual workers themselves, were not yet able to influence conditions and were in a relatively weak position. Considering the rise of the cost of living, it appears that many of those in the Bedouin neighborhoods found it difficult to maintain their former standards in comparison to the few who grew rich. The aspiration to improve the situation is expressed in the movement of the Jawarish workers during April 1968 to April 1971 (see table 1). The variety of jobs grew, but nevertheless, the workers tended to concentrate in a limited number of occupations.

General conclusions that can be made from table 1 and the other data presented in this paper are as follows:

(a) A shift from agriculture (63.6 percent of the workers in 1968 as against 36.9 percent in 1971). There is a conspicuous reduction in jobs not requiring skilled labor.

(b) On the other hand, there is a shift to industry, crafts and

Table 1

Distribution of breadwinners in Kiryat Jawarish as of April 1968, April 1971 and April 1976

	1968		1971		1976	
	N	%	N	%	N	%
Men, hired in agriculture						
Temporary unskilled	87	43.0	40	17.0	23	7.4
Temporary skilled (operators of agromechanical equipment)	21	10.3	20	8.5	11	3.5
Tenured	14	6.9	15	6.3	23	7.4
Women, hired in agriculture[a]	7	3.4	12	5.1	15	4.8
Men, hired in industry and crafts (including apprentice youth)						
Metal branches	15	7.9	22	9.3	17	5.5
Wood branches	—	—	—	—	4	1.3
Mechanics	—	—	—	—	21	6.8
Food production and packing of agricultural products	—	—	—	—	6	2.0
Women, hired in industry (seamstresses)[b]	—	—	—	—	10	3.2
Men, hired in constructions						
Unskilled	4	2.0	23	9.8	16	5.2
Skilled	—	—	—	—	24	7.7
Men, hired in services						
Drivers	4	2.0	8	3.4	10	3.2
Policemen and guards	12	5.9	9	4.2	25	8.0
Vehicle maintenance	1	0.4	9	4.2	16	5.2
Teaching and clerical	—	—	—	—	3	1.0
Salesmanship, gardening	—	—	—	—	3	1.0
Women, hired in services	2	1.0	7	3.0	7	2.2

Table 1 (continued)

Self-employed						
Commercial enterprise	2	1.0	5	2.1	4	1.3
Lorry owners	—	—	—	—	9[c]	3.0
Owners of tractors and agromechanical equipment	4	2.0	16	6.8	8[d]	2.6
Owners of a sheep herd	7	3.4	5	2.1	1	0.3
Cattle owners	4	3.0	3	1.2	3	1.0
Owners of arable land	6	2.9	4	1.7	3	1.0
Leasing field for vegetable growing	1	0.4	4	.7	5	1.6
Construction work	—	—	3	1.2	6	2.0
Agricultural work	3	1.4	7	3.0	4	1.3
Service work (lubrication, washing buses, guarding, etc.)	1	0.4	4	1.6	5	1.6
Agency and mediation	—	—	—	—	5	1.6
Beneficiaries; insurance and welfare	7	3.4	19	8.0	23	7.4
Total	202	100	235	100	310[e]	100

[a] The women included here were single, mostly unmarried girls (banāt).

[b] Few married women were engaged in textile industry when supplied with the machinery to work at home.

[c] Three lorry-owners owned more than one vehicle.

[d] Three tractor-owners owned more than one tractor.

[e] The number of those who earned their own living was in fact only 304. Six persons were counted twice, as they were both employed and self-employed at the same time, e.g. a lorry-owner who also leases fields for cultivation; herd-owner and policeman, etc.

21 of the workers counted in April 1971 have not been counted in April 1976; 4 workers died and 17 workers now live and work elsewhere.

construction (9.9 percent in 1968 as against 19.1 percent in 1971) and to the services (8.3 percent in 1968 as against 14.8 percent in 1971).

(c) The proportion of self-employed rose (from 13.1 percent in 1968 to 21.4 percent in 1971) relative to that of hired hands.

(d) The proportion of hired women (young girls, widows and divorcees) also rose (from 4.4 percent in 1968 to 8.1 percent in 1971).

(e) At the same time the number of applicants for welfare and national insurance benefits increased.

(f) The overall number of those who went out to work grew (from 202 to 235), a figure that includes youngsters who came of working age and particularly the mobilization of those who had not previously worked (including females).

New work opportunities that became available in the Negev halted the migration northwards prior to spring 1974. Seven families sold their homes. Three of them returned to their original tribe, al-Huzail, and four left the district changing their established houses for shabby dwellings. Regret over the deal to settle in Kiryat Jawarish underlies the following story. At the beginning of 1972 I was sitting together with Kiryat Jawarish resident Khalil, in the *shiq* (where the older members of the family sit), around the fire and coffee pot.[5] I asked how things were, and he replied:

> You want to hear? It is an old-folks' story, but some say it is also correct: in old days, before the cars and the telephone appeared, when we still had some peace of mind, there was a poor man who made a meager living by packing (*barda'ah*) grain and straw sacks on the backs of the animals returning from the fields. He was poor and complained to his Creator and said: "You who created us and then abused us, it is You who is bound to us and not we to you." Thus he would bargain with his Creator, until He appeared to him in a dream. He showed him the wall of a gorge (*wādi*) in which were springs of water ... but perhaps it wasn't a *wādi* wall, perhaps it was just a wall with taps ... in some of the springs there was a strong flow, in some a weak one, while others just dripped, and people were drinking. Some of the people near the large taps were drinking a lot without effort. Those by the small taps were making an effort and drinking a little. There was a large fellow standing guard over the taps in the wall and however much they spoke to him (to increase the flow), they never knew if he had heard, for nothing changed. So the man guarding the wall said to him: "This is your spring" and showed him a spring that dripped one-and-a-half drops a minute. When he saw it, he already knew that he would never receive more than the grush (a coin) and a half that he earned each day. However, he would have this pitiful amount of a grush and a half a day to the end of his days. The next day, he pushed the straw into the sacks, and sang: "I have seen everything with my own eyes and no man told me anything."
>
> Not far from there was a palace of a king (or maybe a sheikh or an officer) whose daughter used to steal out at night to

meet a man in the threshing yard. When she heard the poor man's song she immediately understood that "the singer" had seen them and knew everything. Towards noon she prepared a roast partridge (*shonārah*) stuffed with rice and sent it to him. She placed a golden dinar inside, in the hope that he would understand and keep quiet.

Then somebody passed by, either Khalil (the story-teller), or Ednan (one of the listeners) or Gideon (pointing at me), who was hungry and asked him to sell the roast. The poor man thought "I am used to my bread and onion, and can make do with a little this time as well." So he sold it to him for five grush. The following day he was in an even better mood and sang his song in a louder voice than previously. The girl heard and was even more afraid and this time sent him not a partridge but a roast chicken and inside it two dinars not just one. But the passer-by Khalil, Ednan or Gideon, had not continued on his journey. Having found the dinar the previous evening he returned to try his luck once more, but this time he sold it to him for ten grush not just five. Consequently, the next day he was in an even happier frame of mind working and singing in a loud voice. The girl, afraid for her head, sent him not a chicken, but a duck, and inside were five gold dinars not just two. And that passer-by meanwhile had considered settling in the place and came and bought it for twenty grush.

The girl, who was so frightened that she could not sleep at night, realized that there was no way of keeping him quiet other than getting him to move from there. So she ordered that he be brought to her parlour. He came, and fell on his knees for it seemed inevitable that he would be killed. He immediately started crying and praying for his life. Then she ordered him to get up and tell her what he had seen. He told her his life story about his family and his job and the vision that he had seen, of the spring that dripped, and the promise that it would never run dry. Her mind was now easier but she was not completely sure, so she asked: "Is that all you dreamt, nothing more?" He answered: "Nothing more." Then she said that she believed him but that, nevertheless, he would have to leave his work and his home. If he did not agree, he would die; but if he complied and left, she would give him silver. She had no sooner said it than she had filled up his sack, or maybe it was a suitcase and not a sack (this

> was told with demonstrated indifference), with more gold than he had ever seen in his life.
> And what should he do? Should he not take it? She would kill him. Should he take it? Allah might see, or might not. And if He should see, would he be forgiven and saved? At that point he became confused, grabbed the sack and ran outside.
> But Allah, of course, always sees and knows. As the man left the parlour the Angel of Death, U'zrael, who takes men's souls in his hands, met him. He was found by the servant-girl who told Her Highness, but she did not believe what her ears heard until she came and saw for herself. They had no choice but to call the Sheikh and the Dervish; they also phoned the police, the doctor, the officer, the mayor — all of whom came. They examined him and didn't undertand! His body was healthy and he wasn't that old, and they were astonished. Then Allah sent the Angel Gabriel to speak to them, and this is what he said: "We made him poor so that he would be happy, and you have enriched him so that he will lie — like you. We have killed him today and you, if you could, would bring him back to life."

Her Highness, the princess or Sheikh's daughter, the mayor and the officer, were presented to us listeners as the authorities, while the poor man reminded us of the Bedouin peasants who live in the north. The authorities, in common with the man in the gorge, want to determine man's destiny. Like him they are deaf to the claims and protests of people. They are like a girl (not even a male) who is disobedient. She does what she likes, is an accomplice with U'zrael and brings catastrophe on her fellow men. The similarity between the name of the Angel of Death (U'zrael) and the Arabic pronounciation of Israel (Israil) emphasizes the meaning of the story and its moral.

I asked the storyteller whether the princess had in fact killed the poor man. Pensively he replied:

> She did what she did (prostituted herself), and she was afraid of what she was doing (of being caught and put to death), but she did not murder the poor man. In the last resort, when he grabbed what was forbidden to him it was as if he had committed suicide. If he had not taken it, would it have been possible for the girl to have killed him? Could she have killed him while he was a guest in her house? I think that she

> definitely would not have carried out the threat. He should have thought a little more. Satan speaks about the glistening object as though life were impossible without it. But look, whether the man really thought and only erred in the accounts, or really committed suicide, we do not know. Anyway, this is only a story of old men.

The conciliatory note at the end did not ease the harsh impression left by the story. The ancient folk story in its modern form points an accusing finger.[6] Because of my presence the storyteller did not identify the murderers nor the argument that must have broken out. Alternatively he suggested a shadow of doubt regarding the address of the charge. But even so the tendencies for compromise in 1972 declined after the Yom Kippur War, as shall be explained later on.

Between the 1973 War and the summer of 1975 considerable improvements took place in the Bedouin's economic situation throughout the central region. At the same time, and apparently paradoxically, their negative attitude to their surroundings became more extreme. During the short emergency, the men did not leave their houses. The temporary population of the Negev and the occupied territories were evacuated and did not return to the central area for many days after the end of the fighting. During this time, stringent supervision on the roads, particularly those leading from the occupied territories, served to restrict population movements. Many of the Bedouin's former occupations became unavailable and as the months of full mobilization stretchedd out, seasonal agricultural work fell behind, and work in construction and services was disrupted. The great demand for vehicles that were not requisitioned by the army opened up new work markets, resulting in unprecedented profits. At the same time second hand vehicles were offered for sale at bargain prices. Thus, a profitable new economic activity came into being. At the beginning of 1975, the community of Kiryat Jawarish and its surroundings owned 14 lorries, 30 commercial vehicles used for transporting passengers and goods, and nine tractors.[7] This investment possibility released large sums of blocked savings. The directions and scope of the consumer investment at that time also testify to the withdrawal of savings, as shall be shown at a later stage. But economic success came only to a few people and did not last long.

The speedy rise in the cost of living and vehicle maintenance costs since the summer of 1974 and the gradual return of the workers of the occupied territories began to harm the small entrepeneurs, subcontractors for agricultural and construction work. Since the laborers from the Gaza Strip[8] were the first to return to the farms of the south (particularly the Western Negev), it was the Bedouin of the Negev who were hurt first. Entrepeneurs from the Negev again made their way northwards. The contractors' difficulties were due to the fall of wage rates for unorganized labor in 1976 in the fields of the south: IL 25 for a man and IL 15-20 for a woman in the south, compared to IL 45 for a man and IL 25 for a woman in the central region. The very dry years of 1974-76 added to the damage and speeded up migration northwards. Bedouin encampments are dispersed throughout central region. The herds are kept in the hilly regions stretching from Kfar Daniel and Gezer, and southwards, parallel to the railroad.[9] The work-seekers camp on the outskirts of villages and towns in the large rectangle between Ashdod and Holon to the west, and Gedera, Ramla and Lod to the east. Competition is difficult for the veteran Bedouin settlers of the area as is reflected in the work situation in April 1976 (see table 1).

The general picture presented by table 1 throws light on the following issues:

(a) Although the employment fell within restricted boundaries, a variety of professions is to be discerned; but agriculture is no longer the dominant occupation as it was in the past.

(b) Most types of agricultural work are now available. The proportion of agricultural laborers (hired hands — 23 percent; self-employed — 6.2 percent) reaches 29.3 percent and there is a large number of tenured hired workers. There are fewer skilled and unskilled hired laborers, contractors, lessees and herd-owners.

(c) In contrast to the above, growth is noticeable in the proportion of employees in service jobs. The proportion of hired laborers is 20.6 percent.

(d) The proportion of construction laborers grew. The total of hired workers (12.9 percent) and self-employed (2 percent) comes to 14.9 percent.

(e) The proportion of laborers in industry and crafts grew to 18.8 percent.

(f) The proportion of the various self-employed workers showed an overall drop (from 20.8 percent in April 1971 to 17.7 percent in April 1976) in relation to the hired labor, a fact that is to be explained on one hand by a reduction in the number of small contractors, and on the other hand by an increase in the number of hired workers.

(g) The overall labor force grew from 235 in April 1971 to 310 in April 1976. This reflects the addition of young men (mainly) and young girls to the labor force.

(h) The number of female workers grew slightly, a phenomenon explained by the development of the sewing industry. Three of them go out to work in nearby plants while the others work at home for a clothing manufacturer. Another explanation can be found in the laxity of implementation of the compulsory education law. Nowadays many families are terminating the education of girls earlier than before and sending them to work. Despite the great demand for the work of women, the only ones sent to work are the young girls and a few widows. They are placed under the supervision of local contractors.

(i) Within industry and crafts there is much interest in engineering and carpentry. The salary of class A mechanics, for example, was nearly IL 4,500 at the end of 1975, and indirect increments increase the amount considerably. However, at that time there were only three top-rate mechanics, the remainder being apprentices with a lower professional grading.

(j) The salary of skilled workers in the building trade approached as much as IL 5,000-6,000 per month (August 1975) but work could not be found regularly, and the slow-down in the trade was expressed in a drop in working days during 1976. The situation was relatively better in specialized construction jobs (plasterers, floor-layers, and so on), but there were only a few who do this work.

(k) Many moved into vehicle services, but the number of those who turned to guard duties is most impressive and parallel to the development of the "thieving industry" in the district.[10]

(l) Independent operators of a new type were recognized for the first time, namely agents and middle-men involved in drugs and prostitution. A particularly important new branch is transport. Several lorries were purchased but, at the end of 1976, as licensing conditions and vehicle insurance became problematic and petrol more expensive, this activity declined. The small operators, owners of a single lorry, were the first to be hurt. The larger ones overcame the difficulties and branched out into new activities. The large scale enterprises were in the hands of an owner of three lorries and a transport office that specialized in supplying straw from Israel to the farmers in occupied territories.[11] Another entrepreneur specialized in spraying plantations and at the same time leased irrigated lands from moshavim in the area for growing hay which was sold in the occupied territories.

Agro-mechanical work in leased lands and direct trading in agricultural produce brought forth high profits. Contacts were made with Jewish settlers in the central region who leased their lands (usually the fee was obtained from cultivation of their plantations) and with the wholesalers in the occupied territories who dealt with agricultural produce. Since October 1973, however, this situation has witnessed several changes. Since this time representatives of settlements lease out extensive tracts of land, whereas before individual Jewish farmers used to hire out small plots. The Israeli Arab *rais* has now become the mechanized tenant-farmer, a laborer from the occupied territories is nowadays a sharp-witted merchant. The three parties have circumvented the limitations of their traditional fourth partner, the slow authorities, and now tend to leave them out of the picture. Large transactions take place without government supervision or taxation. A comparison of the income of the aforementioned group with that of the agricultural wage earner and the worker in vehicle services (i.e., minimum wages) reveals a growing social gap. The maximum incomes are earned by individuals but are shared by extended families. The young sons of such families work as hired hands in the various branches and benefit indirectly from the profits of the business, but the gap between the families is now more perceptible than ever before and is a cause for agitation. Antagonistic behavior is not directed towards more affluent people but towards the Israeli authorities and institutions. It is not surprising that extreme hostility is shown by the small sub-contractors, the entrepreneurs and independent employers who are sliding back into manual work themselves, and have become hired laborers.

The accusatory charge against the state is somewhat surprising considering its welfare policy (i.e., provision of the basic essentials to all). The benefits are not large (elderly couples received nearly IL 1,200 per month in the summer of 1976) but the income coming from their working children and the fact that this generation is used to making do with a little, render this amount reasonable. The children's allowance is not large, yet quite significant since little is invested in each individual child. Its importance is shown by the fact that the average number of children per woman over the age of 40 was 7.7 in 1971 (Kressel 1975, pp. 131-32) and rose to 9.2 in 1976. The payment designed to improve child care thus encourages the traditional trend for larger families (Schmelz 1981). The National Insurance pays IL 1,800 a month (summer 1976) for 10 children. Increasingly crowded living quarters, accompanied by lower standards of living, arouse the Bedouin's indignation especially since conditions are far better in neighboring Jewish residential areas. Expectations for increased support on part of the settlement authorities have as yet not been fulfilled.

Hostility toward the authorities also increases as a result of friction between the Bedouin residents and the continuing waves of immigrants from the Negev.[12] For example, the new school in Kiryat Jawarish, opened in the summer of 1969, was unable to accommodate its pupils by autumn 1974. The number of children from encampments in the vicinity exceeded expectations and proved harmful to school life. Prefabricated classrooms were erected in the yard desgined for games. Parents and teachers expected the Ministry of Education to require that "new pupils" were to enroll in their registration area (i.e., the Negev). This procedure had been enforced when new Bedouin had set up unplanned concrete houses and had not acquired permits. However, the planning departments of the Ramla and Lod municipalities turned a blind eye and gradually abandoned the Bedouin in their districts. The Ministry of Housing which had supported Bedouin housing development in Ramla and the "Neve Yereq" development in Lod, virtually put an end to any activities in the Bedouin sector although housing projects for Jewish citizens were continued. The Israel Lands Administration, which had obstinately prevented the issuing of further building permits in the veteran Bedouin housing develooments, and even more so in the agricultural regions bordering the towns, were taken by surprise and did not react to the new situation. Neither was any move taken by the district officer. Violations of sanitation standards and construction irregularities were rife and the municipal health departments paid little attention to them. In several cases frictions between the veterans and the newcomers developed into open disputes and police were requested to evacuate the ("new") Bedouin encampments from the doors of the ("veteran") Bedouin housing development.

Illegal building spreads with alacrity; scores of structures are erected regardless plan or order. The blocked savings find a new constructive channel. Those with means put up multi-level villas sometimes covering over 300 square meters. The know-how acquired in the building industry serves well as the workmen and contractors build their own homes. Theft of building materials harms construction sites throughout the region and surpluses are traded off in the occupied territories, so that the demand for Bedouin watchmen grows. People fence their houses with concrete walls that usually encroach upon public land, and it is becoming increasingly difficult to recognize the original architectural plan. It can be argued that this development encourages the growth of slums. Bedouin residential districts in Gan Hakal near the railroad joining Ramla and Lod, and Pardes Nir,[13] which were never planned as concrete-covered housing developments, became urban suburbs accommodating hundreds of families. Gan Hakal developed due to permission given to Bedouin workers to live in the corners of abandoned plantations, where they worked under the patronage of the Custodian of Absentee's Property and were considered as residents of Ramla in order to receive urban services.

Pardes Nir's development was mainly due to Bedouin who were alloted irrigated plots and orchards there and were eventually allowed to take up residence in the vicinity. Later they were officially recognized as residents of Lod. Subsequently, cultivation of the plantations was neglected since the settlers (most of whom were descendants of tribes from Sinai and the Negev)[14] preferred cattle-raising and wage-earning jobs rather than utilizing the land and water that were made available to them. Also, the cultivable plots were sold illegally to Bedouin newcomers for construction purposes. The population of Pardes Nir grew from about a dozen families in the mid 1950s, to 80 families by the end of 1976. The availability of the very best irrigated soil for building did not provoke reaction from the Committee for Preservation of Agricultural Land of the Israel Lands Administration and this was regarded as tacit agreement. Jewish financiers quickly arrived from far and near in order to invest, and land transactions prospered with the increase in construction activities. Considerable pressure has been involved in making the scheme recognized as a legal settlement. The Lod municipality was concerned about extending its services, but helped the children of Pardes Nir to find their way to educational institutions, and was finally forced to pave various connecting roads. At the beginning of 1976 the electricity corporation connected several unlicensed houses to the national grid. A grocery store was opened in the autumn. Construction projects ruin any chance of an effective operation designed to restore the plots for cultivation. In a similar fashion, active and influential Bedouin prevent the rehabilitation of the slum areas in Lod (rehabilitation activities have not yet been started in the old Arab quarter in Ramla) by squatting in buildings designated for destruction. The force called in to evacuate them was particularly incompetent. Destruction orders were not carried out, thus enabling those who moved to new housing developments to indulge in the improper sale of old houses.

In the aforementioned cases, hostility to authority can be regarded as defensive in nature as well as the direct outcome of violating the law (e.g., illegal building and provocative evasion of mortgage and tax payments). The collection rate which was lowest in Kiryat Jawarish of all Ramla suburbs, has lately dropped to 6 percent of the municipal rates and 1.5 percent of the water rate (Kressel 1975, pp. 58-59, 68-69).[15] Those who paid in the past are dilatory with their payments; others did not pay and are not paying now. The evasion of tax payments including income tax and employers' tax started with most of the local job contractors. Job transactions and commercial deals involved breaking other laws such as the employment of minors, thus violating the compulsory education law. Removing girls from school (not necessarily for work purposes) is now more common than ever. Another offense which has been spreading since 1968 is polygyny: 12 cases were reported amongst the elder generation up to the mid 1950s (a short time after the 1951 law was introduced) as against 15 cases in the period 1968-71 (ibid, pp. 133-39), and a further 14 cases were brought to light by the summer of 1976. Most of the polygynous are young foremen (35-40 years old) who have ready cash available and status aspirations. Semi-legitimate transgressions or a selective application of laws, which in effect means the existence of two civilian legal systems, can be discerned. Selective application of military service law[16] throws light on this matter since army service can be reviewed either as an imposition or as a privilege. Convenience and the ability to work and earn as an alternataive to military service are acquired at the price of foregoing the rights of army veterans. The ambivalence of the law also finds expression in the criminal code to the extent that the offenses are internal when both the injurer and injured belong to the Bedouin community.

Police involvement and judicial decisions concerning damage to property, physical violence and murder attempts are only called on when the parties are unable to come to terms within the traditional mediation forums (Kressel 1975, pp. 85-86). Cases of murder or suicide due to circumstances of "preserving the family honor" for example, entail a police investigation and a court case. But with due consideration given to principles of Eastern culture, murderers do not generally receive severe sentences. Complaints lodged by Jewish settlers concerning damage done by the Bedouin are dealt with in a similar fashion. The grazing of herds on cultivated areas does not always call for police interference, imprisonment or fines. Incidents of theft are dealt with loosely and the thieves' daring is on the increase. The victims are trying to organize increased vigilance.[17] A survey showed that the veteran Bedouin tend to prefer unplanned settlements. In Pardes Snir, several Bedouin argued that just as Jewish immigrants are absorbed, they too "absorb immigration." Apparently, letting herds graze on fields and plantations was in some cases an intentional act of provocation. In several instances the herdsmen violently refused to remove their herds claiming that the field had belonged to their forefathers. Cases of intentional arson have also been reported.

Radicalization of the relationships among the Bedouin, the authorities and the Jewish settlement since the October 1973 War, bears considerable importance as regards the Israel-Arab dispute. So far the material relations and their bilateral dimensions have been discussed as though the only relationships were those of a Jewish majority and an Arab-Bedouin minority.[18] However, the fact that Israel is part of a wider region, mainly Arab, leaves its imprint on the relationships among

Israel's population. The ever stronger ties with the veteran Arab population in the towns has increased the Bedouin's susceptibility to nationalism. Certain indications of this tendency were cleary expressed in the parliamentary elections held in December 1973.[19] In the Bedouin residential districts the number of those voting for the Israel Communist Party rose slightly. Latent support for the "left" increases as a result of the general development in the Arab sector but does not obscure the traditional community structure. The Greek Orthodox community is the nucleus in Ramla for Communist support. The effects of "Land Day" (Spring 1976) are less amongst the Bedouin, since their sympathies are purely nationalistic and not with strictly "leftist issues." This paradox is expressed in the following example: one of the active party sympathizers is 36-years-old, a *rais* for vegetable cultivation, employs women from the "territories" (in the main), is married to two wives and is a father of nine children. This way of life is not compatible with the ideologies of the "New Left" in the West, but is acceptable to the "Arab Left", its organs and its officials.[20] In places where the impact of "leftism" is restricted, radio and television broadcasts serve important functions.[21] Their frequent discussion of Israel and imperialism as the source of social deficiency in the country encourages social reformers to act. Making Israel the Left's main target, with the worldwide encouragement of the Kremlin, has brought about support from a variety of sources and appeals to urban Bedouin.

Unlike the authorities who try to formulate a policy for dealing with the Bedouin, the man in the street develops his relationship with them post factum, and this is conditioned by the changing reality of day to day life. The complex of changes described above is expressed by a sharp transition from amazement, indifference and pity, to suspicion. The press writes about "the wild attempts at settlement" and since winter 1976, attention is alternatively focused on land arrangements in the Negev and the faits accomplis in the central region. In the middle of the election campaign, suspicion suddenly concentrated on foreign Arab elements, who are extending their sphere of influence by supporting this illogical process, as a part of the general combat over the land. Consequently, the relationship between excessive rights and excessive obligations in the state has become more obvious; the lesson being that "What is forbidden in North Tel Aviv, is permitted in the South; what is forbidden in South Tel Aviv, is permitted in the Arab Sector, and what is forbidden in the Arab Sector is permitted in the Bedouin Sector."[22] Attention is being paid to the effect of the laborers from the occupied territories on Israel's social structure.

The disregard for the law was condoned in light of the important function that the Bedouin fulfill in the regional employment system. The matter of breaking arrangements was determined essentially by the great dependence on cheap Arab labor, the lesson being that this was the additional price that had to be paid. This gave rise to various charges and counter charges among factions because the price (of cheap Arab labor) had to be paid for by public assets.

SUMMARY

The great number of manual laborers imported produced immediate profits, but gradually harmed industrialization trends which characterized the Israeli economy throughout the 1960s. The citrus industry, for example, witnessed a constant increase in work norms and a drop in the number of workers as a result of the use of containers for crops and hydraulic loading. Other changes having drastic results included working equipment for boulevard pruning in veteran orchards, mechanization of spraying (including spraying from planes), transfer to irrigation by fixed semi-automatic plastic pipes, and so forth. The creative capacity of agricultural research institutes did not cease in the 1970s. They continued to develop new strains, fertilizers, means of pest-control etc.; only the cultivation methods became outdated. Consequently, the demand for innovations dropped. Despite the fact that contractual workers damage the orchards since they break so many branches, dependence on them is growing.

The fabric of labor relations in the economy was damaged due to the increasing gap among the specialist, administrative and working grades. A relative worsening in the conditions of manual labor and its status caused Jewish laborers to seek alternative employment. The socio-cultural exclusiveness of the Bedouin and laborers from the occupied territories caused negative labeling of places of work and of the Jew who remained to work in them ("just like Arabs"). Furthermore, labor relations were disrupted. One of the first claims to be raised in factories was to separate the conveniences for the Jewish workers and for the Arab workers. Only too quickly, functions and personal status in the factories were determined by nationality. The Jews who had not left concentrated in administrative and supervisory roles. For example, the 600 workers of "Kargel," one of the largest places of work which are open for Arab labor, were classified (summer 1976) as follows: 380 tenured workers in responsible positions, 335 of whom were Jews, 28 Israeli Arabs, and 240 temporary workers employed in unskilled jobs, all of them from the occupied territories. In the local moshavim, ever since the Arabs started driving tractors, the settlers rarely use them as means of transportation as they did in the past.[23] Apparently the source of pressure is the children who are ashamed of their fathers when they "drive around on tractors like the Arabs."

Initial developments in agriculture occured also in the construction and industrial sections. Most of the veteran (tenured) Jewish workers stayed on, but the temporary staff turned to the services or to work with a security classification.[24] With the increasing threat of unemployment from spring 1975 onwards, socio-ethnic tension grew worse. The choice of regressing to those branches that absorb cheap Arab labor was initially offered to the unskilled laborers, most of whom are immigrants from the Islamic countries. For the first time the biting accusation "First you ("first Israel") took us (the Oriental communities); then you put Arabs in our place" was voiced. Employers settled their laborers' complaints by referring to "work ethics." How could a Bedouin contractor and a disciplined laborer from the occupied territories be replaced now by these privileged folk. The Government responded by emphasizing its overall responsibility to its citizens in the occupied territories. Increased attention was directed to the autonomous economic growth in the Israeli Arab sector and in the occupied territories. Proposals were presented concerning the construction of intensive farming units for Bedouin as well as industrialization of villages etc. This time the development of the Arab sector was viewed from aspects which could be potentially beneficial to Jewish settlements.

The pitiful appearance of the Bedouin and their temporary dwellings on the outskirts of the agricultural settlements gave rise to guilt feelings among the Jewish settlers. In the early days they extended most of the settlement's services to the Bedouin; use of the local road, water supplies, electricity, postal services, the settlement's name for the purposes of population registration, the local store, clinic and auditorium. However, feelings of discomfort gradually came to the surface and the social contact was avoided. One of the pressure sources was the parents who were forced to indulge in apologetics when their children asked them about their good clothes and homes. On the other side of the coin they found it difficult to teach their children independent work habits. The sensitivity to international coverage of the destruction of an Arab house tends to encourage a policy of lighthandedness. The Bedouin take advantage of these limitations imposed on representatives of the law. For example, polygynous men now facing trial are tried with compassion if they state that the second wife is a relative who was betrothed to them at birth, but they had not been able to marry because of the circumstances of the war and its aftermath. This proves to be an effective line of defense, but in most cases lacks any factual base.[25] Similarly, property offenses that are exposed are explained as unavoidable because of privation and hunger, and again these usually result in a lenient sentence. The Bedouin way of dressing and their homes are often viewed as though they are indicative of deprivation rather than a culture per se.

The Bedouin settlements on the periphery of the urban district exerts a considerable impact on the entire system of social relationships. The three-class web of Ramla and Lod as "mixed population" cities — Jewish immigrants from the West and from the East, and a veteran Moslem and Christian Arab population — absorbs an additioonal component as the Bedouin settlement becomes denser. Eventually it becomes a five-class web owing to the influx of laborers from the occupied territories. The numerical increase of the infrastructure layers quickly becomes conspicuous in the streets and plays an important part in widening the cultural rift between east and west. Those with professional skills look for jobs in the Tel Aviv metropolitan area. In the first stage commuterism increases, and in the second stage those who are successful go to live in the Dan Region and other nearby urban centers which are not "mixed." In fact, the process is one of "negative migration". The population groups coming to the city are of a lower socio-economic status and have relatively inferior means than those who leave. The first to leave are people of western origin and young intellectuals. The city becomes "easternized," in the sense that a commercial life, society and culture develop where men and women perform very different roles. The open markets (in contrast to the supermarket),[26] urban politics, restaurants and cafes, entertainment centers and the repertoire of performances are indicative of "a men's world".[27] The dance clubs in Ramla are closed to Arab males who come without a partner. The next stage witnesses feelings of mutual discomfort and concludes with the regression of the "modern" minority. The phenomenon of permissiveness, reserved for men only, togehter with the influx of strange men — who work and sleepover in the city and who have ready money — gives rise to whoredom which functions on the basis of national division. The main clientele are Arab laborers, the girls are Jewesses from the Oriental communities (mainly second generation Moroccan immigrants), and the pimps are local veteran Arabs. Prostitution in the streets is highly offensive for parents of teenagers, and prompts them to go and live elsewhere.

Negative migration harms the quality of life. Public areas are neglected, housing deteriorates, the tax collection system collapses and the municipal services slacken. Limitations of supervisory authorities tend to increase crime rates. Insecurity in the streets also pushes those with the means into leaving, thus creating a self-perpetuating cycle.

NOTES

1. The initial field work was carried out during December 1967 and July 1970. It then continued intermittently until 1972, and was renewed on a more intensive basis in 1975. The support of the Truman Institute of the Hebrew University, the Desert Research Institute of Ben Gurion University of the Negev and the Israel Commission for Basic Research, is gratefully acknowledged.

2. The number of laborers from the occupied territories working in Israel grew to 30,000 by Autumn 1970 and reched 44,000 by the end of 1971. By the close of 1972 there were 52,400 workers and this grew to 61,300 by the end of 1973. At the close of 1974 a total of 68,700 workers had been registered and by 1975 this had jumped to 70,300. For further details see: *Administrated Territories Statistics Quarterly*, Vol. VI 2, p. 32 (1976).

3. The official policy of the Arab underground organizations in the occupied territories was to prevent their brethren from working in Israel, claiming that their work released Jewish labor for fighting. In various cases that I noted they offered the laborers the equivalent payment for cooperation with them.

4. The offices of the Military Governors in the territorries were overcrowded and selective methods were applied, which disappointed many. To ensure a permit and save time it was necessary to bribe the local organizers who went in and out of the licensing officer's room. Sometimes the cost of a work permit or renewal could run to IL 20-25.

5. The story teller was about 50-years-old, married with 11 children, and had lived in the Bedouin housing development since 1965, leasing land from settlers in the vicinity. He grew vegetables with workers from the occupied territories.

6. The lesson of the story is to recommend frugality, and submission to one's fate, as attempts to change the future may have frightening results.

7. I also counted vehicles owned by former residents of the neighborhood who were still living in the area.

8. The origin of most of the laborers from the occupied territories working in the central region, is the Gaza Strip. The proportion of workers from the West Bank increases from the Southern Sharon and northwards.

9. Forest areas in the Modi'in region and north (as far as Rosh ha-A'yin) are prohibited for grazing purposes, but nevertheless herds can be seen there and near Petach Tikva. From Rosh ha-A'yin northwards, the old border between pasture land and the cultivated plain, has been portioned off. Preferences in the labor market are given to foremen from the "Triangle" and their workers from the West Bank.

10. See *Ma'ariv* (Israeli daily newspaper) of 2 September 1978.

11. The large transactions reached IL 2 million per annum.

12. A large and violent dispute that took place in November 1976 was reported in the press: "The insurgence of Bedouin into Shkhunat Jawarish in Ramle was referred to the attention of the police." See *Ma'ariv* newspaper of 22 December 1976.

13. Pardes Nir is named after the nearby settlement of Nir Zvi. In Bedouin documentation, it is sometimes referred to as "Pardes Snir" and "Pardes Shnir".

14. Several residents are of peasant origin and make their living by cultivating the land.

15. The collection rate in Ramla reached only 30 percent of the highest rate in autumn 1976, and 45 percent of the water rate. The water bills were highest in those Bedouin areas where plots of land adjacent to the houses are utilized for vegetable growing. The bills do not reflect actual consumption since many consumers are connected directly to the water mains.

16. Recruitment to the I.D.F. (Israeli Defense Forces) is compulsory for Jewish youth (men and unmarried women), Druze and Circassian men. Christians and Muslims can volunteer for the army.

17. An investigation of the murder of an owner of an avocado plantation, on the border of the Bedouin development, in October 1976, lead to the discovery of a large quantity of insecticides was found in an abandoned wharehouse in Gaza. They had been stolen from settlers in the south over many years and the thieves had planned to sell them.

18. The tendency to analyze Arab-Jewish relationships in Israel on a minority-majority basis, is common in the social sciences in Israel. Usually, minimum attention is paid to the influences of surrounding Arab circles and cultural differences. This is discussed by Jacob M. Landau in *The Arabs in Israel: A Political Study*, Oxford University Press, London, 1969. See also Sammy Smooha (1976).

19. An indication (of sorts) can be found in comparing the election results to the general Labor Federation (September, 1973) with those to the Knesset in December, 1973. In Ramla, 120 voted for the communists in September and 283 in December, although the opposite outcome might have been expected.

20. The Al-Itihad newspaper of the Communist Party minimizes requests for correcting the arrangements made in Muslim society, even in its internal pages.

21. Arab broadcasting stations are more popular than Israeli stations. Programmes from Cairo are the most popular and are seconded by broadcasts from Amman.

22. The version of an official of the Israel Lands Authority.

23. My notes regard particularly Yashresh and Nir Zvi.

24. The Israel Aircraft Industry, the largest employer in the region, employs very few Arabs.

25. In six out of seven cases that I recorded dealing with this claim, the wife was not a kin and had been unknown to the husband previously.

26. A supermarket has been opened in the new residential quarter of Lod. Ramla has, at present, one store which was opened in the autumn of 1978 for its 38,000 inhabitants. By way of comparison, Nes Tzionah, with half the number of inhabitants, has three general stores.

27. Theatre performances are occasionally held in the new "Orli" cinema in Lod, but not in Ramla. Concerts are not held in either town. Cinemas screen mainly sex and action films.

‘Arab al-Ḥjerāt: Adaptation of Bedouin to a Changing Environment

Rohn Eloul

This paper[1] analyzes the adaptation of a Galilean Bedouin tribe, the ‘Arab al-Ḥjerāt,[2] to its socio-political environment over the past 70 years with a special emphasis on the period since the establishment of the State of Israel in 1948. Although during this period the material culture and daily life of the Ḥjerāt have undergone considerable modifications, these changes have not necessitated a collapse of their tribal organization and kin ideology (Awad 1959, p. 26). On the contrary, this paper will show that changes in the economic and political spheres enabled the tribe to adapt to its new environment. I do not, of course, rule out the possibility that rapid and major changes in a cultural complex may cause it to collapse and organize along different principles in the future. The ill-effects of such changes, however, are not to be taken for granted since contradictions between state organization and kinship-oriented society may promote tribal solidarity. In fact, this seems to be more often the case. The group's leadership realizes the bargaining power of a united vote in a parliamentary state, and recognizes that it can use its tribal power-base to act as a mediator between the state administration and the local population.

In the following paragraphs I will describe some of the more salient changes which have occurred as the Arab al-Ḥjerāt have adapted to their changing environment. I will first introduce the tribe and briefly discuss its history, in order to present a diachronic perspective. I will then discuss the changes which have occurred in the tribe's economic and political organization since 1949 and show how these changes, together with the rise of Ḥjeri leadership from tribal to regional political supremacy, were adaptive responses.

THE ḤJERĀT

By the end of 1976 the Ḥjerāt numbered about 3,500 people. The majority of this population currently resides in three permanent villages in the lower Galilee: Bir al-Maksūr, al-Mikmān and al-Dhmydeh (see map 1). Of the three, only Bir al-Maksūr was planned by Israeli state agencies and lacks the characteristic appearance of a Bedouin settlement (Amiran 1953, p. 255; Amiran and Ben Arieh 1963, pp. 177-79). Other than these settlements, segments of the tribe also reside in the east part of the town of Shfar'am, on the outskirts of some villages, notably 'Ozer and 'Iblīn, and in their old camping grounds in the Yotvat Mountains (al-Ẓahara).

All these locations are close to the industrial centers of Haifa and Nazareth, a fact which bears considerable impact on their current economic activities. They also maintain two permanent herding camps: one in Wadi Mzagga (north of Tiberias), and one in Umm al-Zeynat, southeast of Haifa. Single families can be found in the districts extending from Kiryat Shmona in the north to Ḥadera in the south and from the sea of Galilee in the east to 'Akko (Acre) in the west. In this respect the Ḥjerāt is the most widely distributed tribe in the northern half of Israel. This has resulted from the general state of personal and material safety and the tribe's good relations with its Jewish neighbors, particularly with the state authorities.

The judicio-political boundaries of the tribe (i.e., the territory to which the tribe can forbid entry to one of its members as punishment and within which it is held responsible for the safety of its guests) is much smaller and follows the Yagur–Aḥihud Road to the junction with the Sakhnin Road in the west; then stretches along the Sakhnin Road in the north. Its eastern boundary runs along the Mghar–'Ilabun Road to the Golani Junction where it turns southwest toward Nazareth and continues on the Migdal Ha'Emek–Yagur Road in the south (see map 1).

The Ḥjerāt are divided into three *ḥama'il* (lineages): the Ghadāyreh whose center was in the Ẓahara and is now in Bir el-Maksūr; the Ṣawalḥeh whose center is in al-Mikmān; and the Dhyabāt, which is closely associated with the former. All three are subdivided into smaller named units which may be further subdivided into sub-units some of which have names. Thus:

GHADĀREH	Ghadāyreh (Ghadāyreh/Ramalāt + two unnamed ones) Samrāt (+ two unnamed ones)
DHYABĀT	D'ayfeh Ta'aweneh

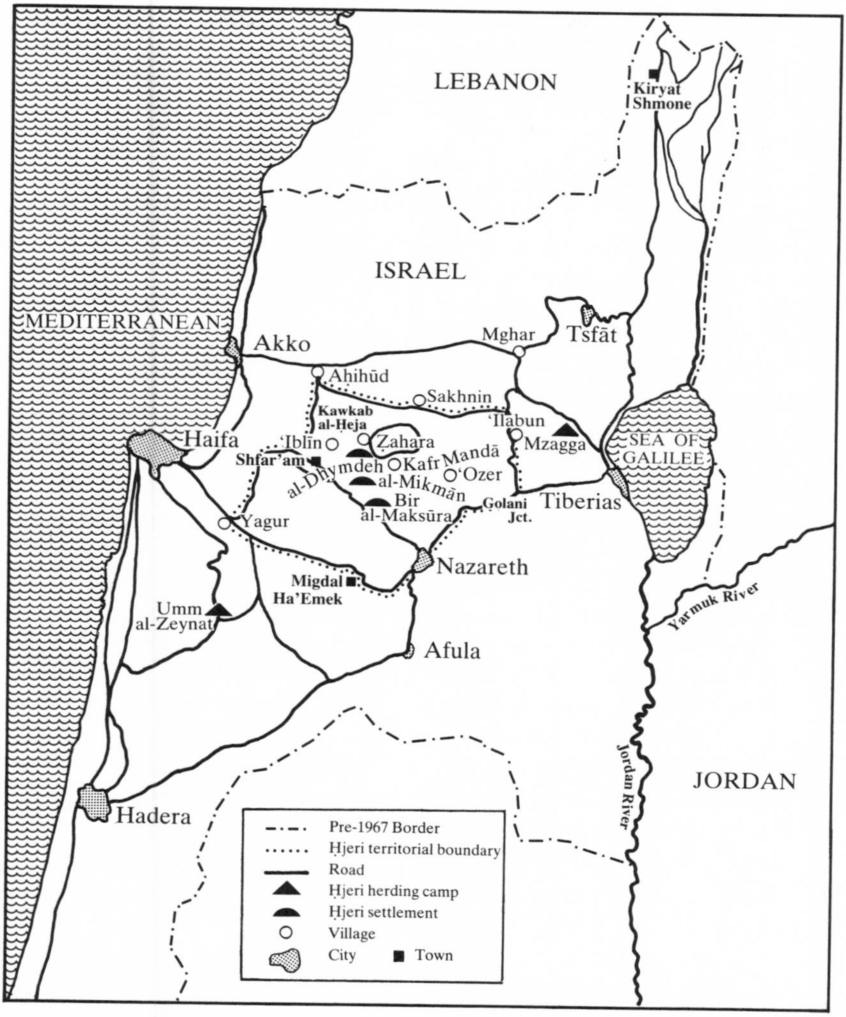

Map 1: Northern Israel showing the tribal territory of the 'Arab al-Ḥjerāt with towns and settlements relevant to the Ḥjeris

ṢAWALḤEH	Ulad Ḥasan al-Sāleḥ
	Maḥamīd
	Jawāsreh
	Sama'neh
	Masa'id
	'Awābdeh

Although familiar with the term *khams* (Marx 1967, p. 64), the Ḥjerāt in common with other tribes in the Galilee do not recognize them as a valid socio-political unit. Instead, the Ḥjerāt have absorbed new members and have used an alliance with two other small tribes to amass enough men for protection. All three members of the alliance form a "co-liable group" (ibid.). The alliance which the Ḥjerāt heads includes the members of the 'Arab al-Ka'abiyeh and the 'Arab al-Ḥelf. This alliance is attested by a putative common ancestry between the Ḥjerāt and the Ka'abiyeh, cemented by the exchange of women between the two groups and the Ḥelf.

Ḥjeri leadership is composed of two closely cooperating institutions. The first is the traditional leadership, the informal Council of the Elders (the Khatyariyyeh) led by the sheikh (or First Elder), which deals primarily with the resolution of internal conflicts and the formal representation of the tribe vis-à-vis other Arab social groups. The second is the state inspired mukhtarship (local headmanship). The Ḥjerāt has two mukhtars: one for Bir al-Maksūr and the Ẓahara, and one for al-Mikmān. Of these only the first, who is the senior of the two by force of his personality and by virtue of his position as head of the largest ḥamula, is oriented toward the state and its agencies and serves as the link between these and the tribesmen.

DEVELOPMENT PRIOR TO 1949

Like most Galilean tribes (Sharon 1964, p. 10) the Ḥjerāt claim origin from a father and his two sons who were banished from the Ḥajara tribe of the Leja in Syria some nine generations ago, or about 175 years ago. Like other such mobile Bedouin (Golani 1966, p. 2), they established themselves first near Tel Shummam in the valley of Yizrael and then in an uninhabited area bordered by Sakhnin (north), Kafr Mandā (east), Kawkab al-Heja and 'Iblīn (west), and Shfar'am (southwest). The main center was the Ẓahara area where the tribe started clearing away some of the forests for tent and pen sites, and later for growing barley and wheat as supplements to the diet derived from their herds of goats and cattle. They became involved in this kind of mixed economy because there were too few of them to raid the villages for these products (as in the case of the stronger tribes), and too poor to barter for them on a regular basis. Legally, the Ẓahara lands belonged to the fellahin (peasants) of Sakhnin. However, they rarely bothered to voice complaint about the take over by the Ḥjerāt, since a peasant during that period usually cultivated about 10 dunams, and never more than 30. Sakhnin also had more than enough lowlands in the valleys of Sakhnin and Beit Netofa. With no shortage of land the peasants were reluctant to start a conflict with the Ḥjerāt who, although small in number, were aggressive and "bandits" as one of them recounted.

By the end of the nineteenth century the D'ayfa established themselves in al-Dhmydeh where they bought land from 'Iblīn. Later, about 1930, the Ṣawalḥeh likewise established itself in al-Mikmān by buying some land from Kafr Mandā. By the time World War I broke out, the Ḥjerāt as a whole were conscious of the value of land as an insurance against herding hazards and of the ability of a landowner to reach independence in a subsistence farming economy. Furthermore, since many already cultivated the land, they overcame the Bedouin ideological barrier which depicts agriculture as a despised occupation. Nonetheless, the richer Ḥjeris hired the poorer members of the tribe to cultivate their land as sharecroppers. During World War I the Ottoman Army frequently took the villagers' supplies and animals. This enforced "war taxation" left the peasants with no animals to plough their land. Some Ḥjeris exploited the situation and exchanged an ox or a cow for 8-10 dunams in the Valley of Beit Netofa thereby acquiring good lowlands. In 1942 they bought the lands of Bir al-Maksūr cheaply and on good terms. In between these major acquisitions, and since 1942, more land was bought by different individuals. Consequently, this tribe nowadays has the largest land-holding among the Bedouin tribes of the Galilee, approximately 7,500 registered dunams. They also maintain squatters' rights to some 25,000 dunams of state lands (Dīb 1971, p. 1).

Until 1949, the Ḥjerāt subsisted primarily on a mixed economy of cultivation and herding. They also bartered in the villages, and provided transportation services with their camels. Some Ḥjeris became freelance trackers who were hired to find stolen goods and animals. Many Bedouin are skilled trackers. The Ḥjerāt, however, are reputed to be the best trackers in the north of Israel and claim that they needed to perfect this skill to compensate for their small size vis-à-vis other tribes. The ability to locate any property which was stolen from them and reacting immediately and aggressively, enabled them to maintain their independence before and during the British Mandate Period (1922-1948) when most other local tribes paid *khawa* (protection fees) to the larger and stronger tribes, notably the 'Arab al-Ṣbeyḥ. Tracking also served as their first entry into the wage labor market and their good relations with both the Mandatory and Israeli Police forces. In 1923, the first two Ḥjeri trackers joined the British Police Force in the north. Later these two introduced seven others, so that by 1948 nine Ḥjeris had served in the force. One of them (today's Sheikh) promoted cordial relationships with the Jewish policemen of the Nahalal Station where he was posted. This friendship proved useful towards the end of Israel's War of Independence when, in July of 1948, the Ḥjerāt were planning to escape to Syria. At that time the Sheikh went to Nahalal, which served as the regional headquarters of the Israeli Intelligence Services and received assurances that no harm would come to the tribe. Furthermore, he was asked to persuade the Ḥjerāt to remain in the newly formed state.

With the end of the British Mandatory Rule in 1948, several changes in the economic sphere of Ḥjeri culture were beginning to emerge. They had acquired land which they cultivated, had settled in houses, and were engaged in wage labor. At that time the socio-political sphere witnesssed only insignificant changes which involved the office of the Mukhtar. Originally it was the Ottomans who instituted this office in the villages, and its general purpose was to mediate between the villagers and the authorities. More specifically, a Mukhtar served in a capacity similar to that of a Notary Public, Public Registrar, and helped the authorities in taxation and police work in return for a part of the taxes levied from his village (Ashkenazi 1957, p. 59). In accordance with their policy of "indirect rule" (Watson 1973, p. 2) the British instituted this office among the Bedouin tribes as well, because it permitted them to deal with a single person instead of a whole tribe. The British authorities requested the Ḥjeri elders to recommend a rich and important man for the office, and they nominated the most influential one from among themselves who, incidentally, was illiterate. (So much for the clerical duties of the Mukhtarship.) Similarly, another Mukhtar was instituted in al-Mikmā after the Ṣawalḥeh moved there in 1930.

These Mukhtars, however, did not change the funtioning of the socio-political organization of the tribe which continued to be led by the Elders who represented the different units of the tribe. An Elder did not inherit his position in the Council but achieved it through his personal qualities. Nor was the Khatyariyya, for that matter, a formal council. It convened ad hoc, with whoever was involved in the case at hand and any others who happened to be present. In fact, any male member who was present in such a meeting could express his opinion. During the Mandate period the Mukhtar was simply the leading member of the Council of Elders.

DEVELOPMENT SINCE 1949

In order to understand the changes which have occurred since 1949 attention must be paid to the state authorities. If the British favored "indirect rule," the Israelis favored a "direct" one, because they intended to build a Jewish state and not a colony or a Mandate. Yet, when dealing with the Arab sector, the authorities encountered the same problem which the British had generally succeeded in avoiding: the problem of the basic differences in the organizing principles of a state society on the one hand and those of a kinship-oriented community on the other hand. If in the westernized Jewish sector most people were able to function in the anonymous and time conscious milieu which characterizes modern state organization, the rural Arab population could not easily contend with realities which were alien to its cultural heritage. Interpersonal interactions in traditional society place much emphasis on courtesy in order to prevent infringing on a peer's personal freedom which can be equated with his honor. Furthermore, since the making of a request places the one who makes it in debt relations to the one who grants it, one will make a request at the very end of a long and often insignificant conversation in order to belittle its importance. He will also explain the reasons for his request in great detail and in such a manner as to present it as a necessity caused by others which is not in his power to avoid.

Procedures such as described above, which for an Arab are the dictates of proper conduct, were considered time consuming and wasteful by the western minded Israeli officials. Because of the personalized character of most interactions in traditional society it was very hard for an Arab to function in the anonymous milieu of the administration. He attempted therefore to establish a personal relationship with the officials he was dealing with, and this was in discord with the norms of behavior of the western officials. Needless to say, as much as the Israeli westernized concepts were alien to the traditional Arab so were those of the Arab alien to the Israeli official. The disparity between the accepted behavior patterns of the two cultures led the Israeli administration to deal with the Arab population by means of local people. Two types of persons functioned as mediators: those who saw and understood these contradictions and could function in both milieus, providing indispensable services for both sides, and those who collaborated in order to provide for themselves rather than for the population they represented.

Two institutions played a major role in the life of the Arab Sector. The most important was the ruling Labor Party (formerly Mapai), until it moved to the parliamentary opposition in 1977, and secondly the Military Government until its abolition in 1966. The Military Government was set up in order to solve the problem of having a population whose cultural and religious brethren were in a state of war with Israel. At its inception the Military Government was very strict and practically every transaction economic or otherwise, needed the local governor's stamp of approval. The country was divided into regions and permits to move from one region to another were needed. During the first years of the military government permits were effective for 24 hours (i.e., the carrier had to be back in his settlement by nightfall). The permits were used not only for state security reasons, but also to prevent competition between Jewish labor and the cheaper Arab labor when the country was in an economic slump and short of jobs. As the economy stabilized and the Arab population was not very politically active, this stringent rule was relaxed. Concurrently, the Arab labor force grew owing to natural increases. It thus became necessary to enable these excess workers to look for jobs in the Jewish sector. Movement permits were therefore extended, first for a week's duration and then for a month, until they were abolished altogether in 1963.

The Labor party was less obtrusive than the Military Government in everyday life, yet the Arabs were aware that it influenced the latter's activities. This realization was not hard to come by as once every four years, during the elections, party activists would canvass influential Arab personages and grant their requests so as to gain their allegiance. Many of the requests made in those days were for permits and jobs which the Military Government were often reluctant to grant.

These conditions provide the background for the rising importance of the Ḥjerāt among the Galilean tribes, and bear upon the changes which have occurred in their way of life.

During the first years of Israeli rule the daily life of the Ḥjerāt remained almost unchanged. They tended their herds and cultivated their land, and a few of the more daring among them made their livelihood by exploiting their tracking talents and becoming successful smugglers. In 1949, after the War of Independence, the Israeli authorities required the inhabitants of the Ẓahara to surrender their weapons and reinstituted the office of the Mukhtar. The job was offered to the Sheikh who refused it and suggested his 17-year-old firstborn son in his stead (he also handed over the old muzzle-loading Turkish rifles the Ḥjerāt possessed, while clandestinely keeping the more modern, bolt action, British types.) One of the men on this mission was the Sheikh's old Nahalal policeman friend who had become an officer and was trying to recruit the former Ḥjeri members of the police. He asked the Sheikh to join the force and the latter consented for several reasons: (1) being with the police during Military Government was very advantageous when a tribesman got into trouble and needed help; (2) for the same reason, coupled with the customary reciprocity for help, he increased his family's influence within the tribe and especially so with his son as Mukhtar; (3) it was also advantageous vis-à-vis other Arab communities: the fellahin with whom long-standing disputes were an ancient tradition, and the Druze with whom the Ḥjerat had tense relations and, as the result of a recent feud, the status quo was still unclear; (4) even though he was well-off the extra money could be put to use in the post-war depression. Later, other Ḥjeris joined the police which, thereby, became the stronghold of the Ḥjerāt in their competition for political supremacy in the Arab sector with the 'Arab al-Hēb and their traditional rivals, the Druze, who established themselves in the Israeli Army.

Most of the Ḥjerāt, however, kept to their small herds and land plots and turned to wage labor to complement subsistence production. Their first access to salaried jobs was through the Jewish National Fund Forestation Department for which they planted trees (if they were poor) or became forest guards (if they came from influential families). These jobs were created primarily to absorb the unemployed Jewish unskilled labor during the economically lean years of the early 1950s. It was the Mukhtar who first convinced the Ḥjeris to take such work and then convinced the Military Government and the Jewish National Fund to let the tribesmen have these jobs in order to supplement their incomes. Presumably one of his reasons in having the Ḥjerat take these jobs was the creation of another link with the authorities, as the Jewish National Fund was administering some state lands at the time.

In the mid 1950s, when their Mukhtar had established influential relations with the Military Government, the Ḥjeris were able to obtain seasonal work in agriculture. The introduction to the market took place in a somewhat roundabout manner. The Mukhtar would obtain movement permits for his tribesmen which allowed them to stay in other regions for prolonged periods in order to use pasture. As a result they were usually closer than other Arabs to Jewish agricultural settlements which, even during the off season, frequently needed extra working hands or plantation guards. Their proximity and the long slack periods in herding schedules made it possible for them to take on these jobs while their Mukhtar's good standing with the Military Government, Police and the Jewish National Fund enabled him to get them the necessary recommendations and permits.

Working as watchmen held benefits, other than being employed, consistent with Bedouin ideology of proper male occupations. They were also able to gain access to stubble pastures. By the end of the 1950s weekly movement permits were issued and more Ḥjeris entered this labor market. Many tribesmen who looked for an independent and steady income turned to the construction industry. Over the years many of these acquired experience in that industry and by the mid 1970s some had become small-scale independent contractors.

These processes only became apparent during the late 1960s owing to limitations on movement imposed by the Military Government and the slow development of the economy. In 1966 the Military Government was abolished and all its restrictions were lifted. However, the economy was experiencing the severe effects of the slump of the mid 1960s. The year 1967, however, marks the beginning of acceleration in the changing Ḥjeri economy. The extended borders and the activities of the Palestinian guerrillas after the Six Day War created an increasing demand for trackers to serve in the army. Consequently, increasing numbers of young Ḥjeris volunteered for the army. By 1977 some 200 men or about 30 percent of the tribe's males had been or was serving in the forces. Several reasons account for their recruitment: (1) this type of work becomes the traditional image of the Bedouin as a fighter; (2) the salaries were quite good, especially in comparison with the industrial sector; (3) the life in an army camp, away from the village, allowed youths to enjoy considerable freedom which they could not enjoy otherwise; (4) the young men felt that they achieved something on behalf of the whole tribe in its rivalry with the 'Arab al-Heb by moving into the latter's traditional stronghold.

Another outcome of the 1967 war was the economic boom that followed and which increased the demand for labor in industry. This enabled many Ḥjeris, and especially the younger men, to be employed in occupations other than construction. By 1977 Ḥjeris were employed in the textile and food industries, and several worked as operators of heavy highway construction equipment. Others were employed as car mechanics, metal workers and one even became a professional hotel waiter. In 1974 some young unmarried females started working and were later joined by several married women.[3] The women do however go to work under the watchful eye of a labor contractor who is, invariably, a trusted and respected tribesman so that no damage is caused to the female's family honor. Nonetheless, the more relaxed inter-sexual behavior in the factory milieu tends to relax these young females' traditional concept of shame and family honor.

While participation in the wage labor market has increased and diversified, herding has declined steadily for several reasons the most important of which is the shortage of pastures. This situation has been caused by an expansion of cultivation on the one hand and increased competition for the diminishing pastures on the other. The first is the outcome of the establishment of new Jewish agricultural settlements which cultivate large areas formerly left fallow. The second was caused by the entry of Jewish corporate groups such as kibbutzim and private companies into the beef-raising trade. Being economically corporate they can establish large herds which utilize the pasture more economically than the much smaller Bedouin herds;[4] and being Jewish they exert greater influence on the authorities who allocate state land for pasture. An additional factor in the decline of herding is the shortage of labor, that is shepherds. Prior to 1967 all the small herds were herded by the herd-owners' sons. The increase in job opportunities, the Bedouin cultural ideal of achieving economic independence even from one's own father, and increasing embarrasment at being called "shepherd," have caused many of the youth to leave herding for wage jobs. The shortage of shepherds has partly been alleviated by personnel from the West Bank, but due to the increase in wages this labor pool is open only to the well-to-do herd-owners. These factors have prompted increasing numbers of small herd-owners to sell their herds, settle, and join the wage labor market. Thus, the large Ḥjeri herd-owners who are able to compete with their Jewish counterparts for the available pasture and are able to hire shepherds, become large livestock traders, whereas the smaller Ḥjeri herd-owners sell out and leave the trade altogether.

Although herding is slackening off, the other traditional occupation, agriculture, has been developing and increasingly orienting itself toward the commercial market. The Ḥjeris not only cultivate their own land (and most families have some), but they rent more available arable land, be it private or state-owned. They have mechanized cash cropping, although they consciously avoid mono-cropping. Their choice of crop combination is conditioned by market profitability, household needs, and the risk involved. One of the external reasons causing this market orientation has been the assistance received from the Ministry of Agriculture.

Regardless of the great increase in the Ḥjeri population from 1,220 individuals in December 1955 (Ashkenazi 1957, p. 215-16) to about 3,500 persons by the end of 1976, an increase of close to 370 percent, no severe pressures were imposed on the tribe's economic resources. Two factors seem to account for this phenomenon. First, most of the 1976 population is still juvenile and, hence, is not currently competing for the available resources. Second, and most important, since the tribe is enmeshed in the regional economy and is deeply involved in industrial wage labor, the tribal resources do not have to absorb all of the Ḥjeri active labor force. In fact, this latter factor suggests that it may be futile to follow the traditional analysis of population size versus a society's resources when that society forms part of a large economic system and is highly involved in an industrial wage labor market which has the potential of absorbing its excess labor.

Several processes in the Ḥjeri economy can be distinguished: (1) a shift from independent herding and farming to wage labor, so that by 1977 some 70 percent of the tribe were employed in wage labor and only about 30 percent were still working in the more traditional occupations; (2) a process of occupational diversification in both the production and service sectors of industry; (3) a rise in the upper age limit of the active labor force as former herdsmen, who traditionally would have held managerial positions while their sons would have been the workers, now enter the labor market and work until they reach the age of 65, when they receive their retirement benefits; (4) an increase in individualized participation in the economic sphere. Previously, most of the salaried jobs came through the Mukhtar due to his connections with the Military Government, whereas nowadays all the jobs in the industrial sector are found on an individual basis although they often make use of the tribe's informal information network. Jobs in the security organizations, however, are still arranged through the Mukhtar whose recommendations are highly respected and demanded by the officials in that field.

The processes outlined above emerged gradually, gaining momentum as time passed. The Ḥjeri way of life gradually adjusted and the tribesman took the cars, houses, new types of jobs, education, electrical appliances and family planning in their stride. The ability of the Ḥjerāt to absorb these changes with no apparent difficulties, appear to be rooted in their ability to maintain tribal unity and cohesion despite personal rivalries and interests. I contend that this is due to their leadership and the way it has adapted to the new environment.

It was mentioned before that the Ḥjeri leadership is composed of two closely interrelated institutions: the Council of the Elders and the Mukhtarship. Of these, the latter is the major force, as each tribe in the Galilee has its elders but only a few of them have Mukhtars who have been successful in maintaining their tribe's unity when no external threat to their existence has been apparent.[5] Despite his youthfulness and lack of experience, the Mukhtar of the Ḥjerāt perceived the gap that lay between the traditional Arab society and the westernized state administration. Moreover, he was able to function in both milieus. Hence, he stepped into the role of mediator between the two traditions, thus expanding both his political and economic power.

During the early 1950s the Mukhtar established his leadership of the Ḥjerāt in face of some internal opposition by causing some of his opponents to move to Bir al-Maksūr (which at that time was just a hamlet) and having others leave the tribal territories. He was able to bring the rest of the tribe into line by concerning himself with their welfare, solving their problems and finding them jobs and pastures. He did it with the assistance of the Military Government which he helped by curtailing the activities of the Ḥjeri smugglers (some of whom were among his opponents) and keeping the tribe quiet and cooperative. His main asset to the Military Government, however, was the efficiency with which he conducted relations between the Ḥjerāt and the authorities.

The Mukhtar acted as a go-between on behalf of his tribesmen and external organizations, thus monopolizing the access to the authorities. The Military Government had tried to promote this form of control among other Mukhtars, but had met with little success. Secondly, having realized the authorities' limitations, he previewed the tribesmen's requests and only passed on those which could be handled by the Military Government. Lastly he aligned himself with the Labor Party in particular, and the state in general.[6] Both the Labor Party and the Military Government often granted his requests and participated in their implementation. Most of the requests in those days were concerned with movement and pasture permits, and jobs which his tribesmen were the first to enjoy. This middle-man activity permitted the Mukhtar to accumulate a fortune so as to comply with the requirements of hospitality and generosity which are expected of Mukhtars and which contribute to their political power. Needless to say these services obligated the tribe to him so that he was able to mobilize them as a small private army.

Such an army is essential if a successful *ṣulḥa* (reconciliation) is to be concluded since both quarrelling parties must realize that if a peace agreement is violated, they would be punished by the one who mediated and vouched for the contract. The Mukhtar not only had ready access to such force but also had shown himself to be a talented *ṣulḥa* mediator, a quality which was highly appreciated by the authorities, particularly the police. The latter were aware that violent conflicts between Arab *ḥama'il* were not infrequent and that arresting the culprits did not end the affair. Sooner or later the fight would inevitably flare up again. They had two alternatives, either to station some 20-30 policemen for an indefinite period to maintain the truce, or to resort to the traditional and more effective *ṣulḥa*. In fact, the latter was the only solution available to the police due to its chronic shortage in personnel. While tightening his reciprocal relations with the police in this way, the Mukhtar also gained prominence in the regional politics of the Arab sector as each *ṣulḥa* places at least one side (the weaker one) in debt with the mediator who ensures the duration of the peace. Often, however, both parties to *ṣulḥa* made by the Mukhtar were indebted to him because in order to assist in a successful conclusion the police, at his request, would drop charges on minor crimes connected with the case.

The Mukhtar's close relations with the authorities did not escape the attention of the Arab sector as a whole, and soon many non-Ḥjeris came to ask for help in their dealings with the authorities. Once helped, they remained in a moral debt to him, to his sub-lineage (which could also provide help either through their own connections or by approaching him on behalf of the applicant), and by extension to the whole tribe. Thus, a self-reinforcing cycle was formed: due to the unity of his tribe, its allegiance to the authorities, and his own services to them, the Mukhtar could provide it with more and better services which were distributed beyond the tribal framework. Consequently the Mukhtar, and by extension the tribe as a whole, expanded his sphere of influence in the Galilee. The more influence the tribe acquired, the more they could help the authorities in managing the region, and the more assistance they received from the authorities.

Being conscious of the importance of the power-base the tribe provides him with, the Mukhtar helps the tribe acquire modern services, while at the same time maintaining and perpetuating the traditional socio-political unity of the Ḥjerāt.[7] In this task he is supported by the Council of the Elders which adjudicates internal conflicts thus allowing him to deal with extra-tribal affairs and to avoid taking sides in internal conflicts which may increase the dissent against him if one of the parties to such a conflict happens to be his own sub-lineage. The Council also helps him in conducting *ṣulḥa* ceremonies as well as advising him in traditional legal matters should he need such advice. It may also mediate small *ṣulḥa*s on its own, thereby enabling him to participate in more important activities such as partisan politics. Thus, the Mukhtar does not operate in contradiction to the old leadership structure but having risen above it, maintains close cooperation with it in this way being less restricted to act on a national level. The Elders, for their part, support the Mukhtar as they still hold most of their former positions, enjoy increased regional influence and honor, and, due to the increase in population, are fully occupied with conflict resolution. Moreover, the Mukhtar's attempts to perpetuate the tribe's unity not only corresponds to the Elders' traditional role as conflict mediators thus making them allies, but also enhances their status vis-à-vis the younger members, many of whom need the help of the Mukhtar.

In brief, although the Mukhtar was originally appointed by the state, he has adjusted his office to the traditional tribal socio-political structure and established his power-base in the tribe rather than relying on the state. By so doing and with his loose patron-client style of operation, he has elevated his office, thereby increasing the complexity of Ḥjeri political organization. Prior to this there was one body, the Council of the Elders, which handled all the political functions. Now there are two bodies: one which primarily manages internal affairs, and the Mukhtar's own office which loosely oversees the Council of Elders and manages the extra-tribal relations.

NOTES

1. This paper, written in 1977, is based on 22 months (Sept. 1975-July 1977) field work among the 'Arab al-Ḥjerāt. The project was not supported by any institution and would not have been possible but for the hospitality and generosity of the Ḥjerāt and their Mukhtar. I would also like to thank Dr. Avshalom Shmueli for helping me find a part-time teaching appointment, and Dr. Yehoshua Yitshaki who entrusted me with it. Were it not for this appointment, which kept me from the tribe for two days a week during three semesters, I would not have been able to defray the costs of the project. I would also like to thank Professor William Schorger, Robert Whallon, and Henry Wright and Mr. Jon Hofmeister who read the manuscript and made many helpful remarks.

2. In transliteration I have used the spoken dialect of the Ḥjeri. Although the correct written form is Ḥujayrāt, the pronounciations are Ḥjerāt and Ḥjeri.

3. The Ḥjeri women, as well as those of other Galilean tribes, have not been as secluded as the more tradtional Negev Bedouin women. A Ḥjeri woman, for example, can receive guests even if her husband is not at home although she will immediately be joined by at least one other women.

4. According to the Mukhtar, Bedouin have difficulties in forming partnerships. When asked why the Ḥjerāt do not form partnerships which will enable them to compete with the Jews for pasture lands, he replied "*lawā sharāki mliḥah lakān kul thnen shāraku bḥormah*" ("if partnerships were good, every two men would be partners to a wife").

5. The Bedouin need for unity is expressed in a saying which I heard several times from different Ḥjeris: "*al-Ḥaqq mā lo sayf yibri mā hu ḥagg*" ("Justice without a sharpened sword is no justice") meaning that if one cannot back up his demand for justice by force he will be robbed of it. It can also mean that if the authorities are not strong their law is valueless.

6. At the time both were conceived as being identical.

7. For example, in 1975 one tribesman killed another in an act of self-defense. First, the confrontation was limited to the sub-units of the killer and the deceased, and other sibling sub-units were consciously barred from joining in, thus preventing the escalation of the conflict to include the whole tribe. Second, although the killer was aquitted by the Criminal Court, his family was made to pay twice the accepted amount of blood money and he was banished for seven years from the tribal territories. When I questioned members from both *ḥama'il* about the severity of the punishment, I was repeatedly told that the Elders and the Mukhtar wanted to make it so severe that if another tribesman found himself in the same or similar predicament "he will think five times before he picks up a stick" because such occurrences "split the tribe."

Changing Employment Patterns of Bedouin in South Sinai

Emanuel Marx

In the wake of political upheavals the employment situation of Bedouin in South Sinai during recent years has undergone several dramatic changes. When Sinai was occupied by Israel in 1967, all the Bedouin lost their work. Gradually employment became available and opportunities multiplied, and by 1973 work was again available to all. After the 1973 war between Egypt and Israel all these Bedouin again found themselves out of work and by the middle of 1974 only half the former number of workers had been reemployed. The Bedouin appeared to take all these abrupt changes in their stride. During the periods of unemployment there were no food scares, no social unrest, and even no clamor for work. An analysis of the various employment situations in their social context, provided an explanation to the Bedouin's behavior on one hand, and made me reflect on some of the economic concepts of employment on the other.[1]

I shall first explain why, in my opinion, a straightforward economic approach can give some, but not all, of the answers to these questions. I shall also argue that while a precisely defined concept of "employment" is essential for our investigation, that of "disguised unemployment" is not very helpful. I shall then proceed to analyze the impact of the varying employment situations on Bedouin of South .Sinai. It will be seen that while the Bedouin subsisted mainly on their income from wage labor, they could not afford to neglect other sources of income, even when they were relatively "unproductive." In the face of political and economic uncertainty they had to keep these economic alternatives open and to foster the social relationships that made them possible. Such matters as unrewarding subsistence farming and herding may be uneconomical in a sense, but the anthropologist can view them as sound long-term economic considerations.

The employment situation provides one of the basic indicators as to the state of a society. Although there are many ways to study employment problems, I wish in this essay to examine contrasting approaches found among economists. Most economists are interested in the conditions of production, and for them labor is only one among several factors affecting it. However, a welfare economist usually regards labor as the most important factor (whether scarce or not), because he is first and foremost concerned with what happens to people and their livelihood. This seems to be a reasonable standpoint in the highly industrialized societies normally studied by economists where one or more members of practically every household is engaged in a very specialized productive activity outside of the home, and obtains money in return for his services.

When a person is unemployed for more than a few weeks, he is not only unproductive but may also suffer real deprivation. For a while he may rely on the help of friends and relatives, and eat up his savings, but before long he becomes a "burden on the taxpayer," that is he has no other way to make a living but to reenter the productive process. Now it is interesting to note that some welfare economists adopt the opposite approach when dealing with non-industrial nations. Here they become "ordinary" economists concerned with production and economic growth, and consider men merely as one of the factors of production. Thus, when referring to "disguised unemployment" they often mean that given the existing state of factors of production, the labor potential has not been maximized. When this attitude is taken, sound reasons for limiting economic growth, for eliminating costly production processes, or for giving precedence to human needs may be disregarded, and the social context of production may be studied partly in order to be manipulated for the sake of increased production. The underlying rationale seems to be that economic growth is that society's main problem and as it remains unsolved it causes all-round suffering, and that such a society can take care of most personal problems of a non-economic nature because people live in close-knit communities. However, economic growth is often connected to greater movement of people, and as a result social networks become looser. It would therefore make sense for welfare economists to adopt the same approach for both industrial and non-industrial societies, and to put the interests of their individual members first.

Economists who employ the concept "disguised unemployment" not only proceed from the assumption that able-bodied adults, and particularly men, should spend much of their time in the production of goods and services; they also seem to know how much work is good for a man, what kind of work is productive and what a man's minimum wage should be. They will not commit themselves lightly to a definition of optimal employment, but they appear to know when over and under-employment exist, and also when there is "disguised unemployment" in any of its constituent parts. In this sense "disguised unemployment" exists on the micro level either when individuals or groups do not achieve an ideal Western standard of efficiency in the use of material resources or time, or receive insufficient remuneration for their work, and on the macro level when the economy does not provide the resources that would allow workers to reach these standards. In both cases the economist decides what that standard is, taking an industrial society as his model.

On the macro level Western industrial nations should, however, not be viewed as nearly autarchical systems, but rather as parts of a world-wide economy in which resources are distributed unequally. Industrialized nations are those which have been able to harness a large share of these resources and to convert them into products, services, skills and mechanisms designed to obtain even more resources. The undeveloped countries, or the stagnant sections of industrialized countries, must be viewed as those parts of the world-wide economy which get less than an equal share, either because they obtain smaller return on their resources, or because they cannot even enter into economic exchange with the more industrialized nations or companies. These matters are often determined by differentials in political power. One example is the employment of foreign labor in the major industrial countries of America and Europe; only citizens of some countries are permitted to sell their labor and the employers set the rate of exchange for this commodity. Therefore it is unreasonable to compare the two types of economies, and even less so to set the standards of a developed country as those to which the poorer one must aspire. An integrated treatment of both types is needed — one which would attempt to explain the unequal distribution of resources and its consequent effects.

As an anthropologist I feel on safer ground in micro-sociology. On this level too, though for other reasons, I feel one should not set standards for employment. To make this point clearer let me first try to show what employment is about. Definitions of "employment" often vacillate uncertainly between two approaches: should only the gainfully employed be dealt with (i.e., those whose contribution to the economy is easily measured and can be translated into dollars and cents), or should every kind of economically significant activity be dealt with, even when it is not directly productive. In recent years there has been a growing recognition that housewives do an important job. This has been the result of increasing participation of women in the labor market with a resulting scarcity of women willing to remain unpaid housewives or to become low-income and insecure domestic staff. We still have to learn that many other unpaid activities which one tends to dismiss as non-economic, may facilitate the so-called economic activities and may indeed be indispensable for their proper execution. If we were to pursue this approach to its logical conclusion, every activity contributing to the production of approved goods and services, and serving the welfare of society, would eventually be included. This would not only make the field virtually coextensive with the whole universe of social interaction, but would also constitute a return to the functionalist view of society where every social act has the end of maintaining the body social. Besides, it would introduce somewhat prematurely the anthropologists' views about what is good or bad (functional or dysfunctional) for society. Therefore I tend to prefer the first approach and to use the concept only for gainfully employed persons. In this usage a peasant's wife, for instance, is "employed" only while she works on the farm or sells farm-produce. Her labors in the household go unrequited, and therefore do not count as employment. Needless to say this includes every activity, whether full-time or part-time, in which goods, services or money change hands. Under this heading come such items as crime, prostitution and gifts.

This approach has obvious shortcomings, which can be compensated for in two ways. First, henceforth each employment situation must be fully described, so that the reader understands its social context. Second, even a full description is not enough, for a full understanding necessitates a precise definition of all factors affecting employment. While the attention is focused on the employment situation, it is essential to take the natural and social environment into consideration and the way it shapes and conditions employment. When this approach is taken such matters as seasonal variations in employment, shifts from one type of work to another, "unwillingness" to work or, indeed, full employment can often be explained. Thus a person may prefer during politically unsettled times to cultivate relationships with his close associates rather than enter the labor market, he may willingly forego opportunities to earn good wages and revert to a subsistence economy. On the other hand, climatic conditions play a large part in determining whether seasonal unemployment may alternate with periods of strenuous work. Alternatively the state may coerce men and women to work, even when the type of employment is unsuited to their capabilities and training, and is only available in distant regions — thus full employment of a kind may well be achieved. The Bedouin of South Sinai have in recent years experienced several abrupt changes in the labor market and their situation can, therefore, illustrate the argument.

The southern half of the Sinai Peninsula extends over an area of 17,000 square kilometers. Most of the country is made up of bare rugged mountains reaching a height of 2,600 meters. The main roads (asphalt) run along the seashore and sturdy motorcars reach the interior via several mud tracks running generally from east to west. Public transportation is provided by a fleet of over a hundred American jeeps, Russian military vehicles and assorted pickups, mostly in rundown condition and owned by individual Bedouin. Many areas are inaccessible by car and can only be reached by camel or by foot.

Rain falls in very small amounts; the annual average in the low-lying areas is around 10 millimeters and in the high mountains about 60 millimeters. In addition, rainfall is very irregular so that the low-lying areas may frequently remain dry during two to three consecutive years. Sometimes most of the annual rainfall comes in a single downpour which may cause much havoc. One torrential rain in May 1968 destroyed thousands of palm trees, houses and gardens, and ruined a number of major motor tracks. Rainfall is restricted to the cooler winter months, between November and March. Temperatures in the mountains occasionally fall to minus 10°C (12°F). In the summer temperatures are uniformly high — in the low-lying areas often going up to 40°C. (105°F) and in the mountains to around 30°C. A rare freak rainstorm may occur in early summer.

This arid climate produces little natural vegetation, and few plants are able to survive in the dry, hot summer. Horticulture is confined to the main valleys which retain ground water. This water is tapped by wells dug by individual Bedouin and used to irrigate small gardens. A few deep wells have been sunk by the government and all Bedouin have equal access to these wells.

South Sinai is inhabited by about 7,000 Bedouin, giving an average population density of one person to two square kilometers. Permanent settlements were few until the 1950s. Up to this time the little port of al-Tur on the Red Sea, where most of the residents were sailors and fishermen, was the main settlement. It had a quarantine station for Moslems returning from the annual pilgrimate to Mecca. The other settlement is the monastery of Mount Sinai, a venerable institution founded in the sixth century, usually maintained by up to a dozen Greek monks. In the 1950s the Egyptians established army camps and an airfield, built roads along the west coast of the peninsula, and exploited the oilfields on the Red Sea coast, and gypsum and manganese deposits on a commercial scale.[2] These enterprises employed relatively few Bedouin. Egypt has an almost infinite reservoir of men who had first claim on available work. Bedouin claim that about 4,000 Egyptian workers were employed in Sinai, excluding military personnel, as against some 300 Bedouin. Thus the biggest industrial plant in Sinai, the gypsum factory at Ras Mal'ab was reported to have employed nearly 2,000 workers of whom only 65 were local Bedouin. The Abu Rudes oil installations and the Umm Bogmah manganese mine together employed roughly 150 Bedouin, and a few men were employed in government offices and in the Mount Sinai monastery. A handful of well-diggers and builders were also employed by other Bedouin. During the pilgrim season the quarantine station in al-Tur supplied work to as many as 500 to 600 men, but only for four to eight weeks.

The Bedouin could not rely on wage labor in Sinai. Many of them exploited the meager natural resources, raised goats and camels, and engaged in some gardening. Some complemented these activities by smuggling hashish and opium. Many of the younger men sought employment as unskilled laborers and menials in Egyptian cities. These men used to stay away from home for months on end, and sometimes for several years. Some tribesmen settled permanently with their families in Egypt, while others returned home when their children were old enough to replace them as laborers.

The Jebaliya can further illustrate this argument. They are the second largest tribe in South Sinai, with around 1,200 members. Traditionally they are the weakest and most unwarlike of the tribes, and inhabit a small area in the high mountains near the ancient Saint Catherine monastery. The monastery claims ownership of the land and until 1967 the monks collected an annual tithe from Jebaliya orchards and gardens located close by. The tribesmen claim a longstanding special connection with the monastery. When the Byzantine emperor Justinian built the monastery in the 6th century, they say, he sent their Wallachian ancestors to serve the monks. This ancient tradition is confirmed by the monks. To this day there are complex relations between the Jebaliya and the monastery: in a world that is all too insecure the monastery stands as a rock, and tribesmen rely on it in time of need. The monastery employs between 20 to 30 tribesmen (customarily only few members of other tribes are employed) and while it pays low wages — less than half those currently obtainable in wage labor — its employees often remain in their jobs throughout their working life. The monastery lays claim to the tribe's land, and thus helps to prevent encroachment by the more powerful tribes.

Gardens can provide the Jebaliya's basic requirements. In the not too distant past they had to be satisfied with their garden produce, part of which they consumed and the rest was transported by camels to al-Tur. With the proceeds of the sale of fruit and nuts they were able to buy enough grain to last them through the year. In addition they earned cash from working in the quarantine station for pilgrims returning from Mecca. The pilgrim season lasted several weeks, and with the money earned they could buy some basic necessities such as tea, sugar and clothing. The prevailing attitude of Bedouin was then expressed by the saying that "The Bedouin loves freedom and hunger," for toward the end of summer they often ran short of basic commodities such as grain.

During periods of abundant wage labor the Jebaliya view the gardens as summer retreats. Each family owns at least one garden (some men own several gardens in different locations) and spends part of the hot summer months in the shade of the trees. The gardens are watered fairly regularly and many men grow some vegetables in plots between the fruit trees. But they consider neither the fruit nor the vegetables as valuable economic resources. They are viewed as delicious additions to the diet, but not considered as staple food. Wage labor has brought them higher incomes and created new needs. Nowadays they buy more food, a wide range of canned food stuffs, more and better clothing and household goods, as well as transistor radios and watches. A comparison between the expenditure on food alone in the days of the gardening economy and the present shows that standards have risen about three times, from an average of about $10 a month per household to $30.

In the early 1950s the smuggling of hashish and opium which had for generations contributed to the economy of the Bedouin became even more important. It brought more money into the locality and created the incentive to raise standards of consumption. As a result ever more Bedouin sought employment, mostly as menial laborers in Egyptian cities. The tendency to seek employment has increased under Israeli rule, for three reasons: smuggling declined because too many risks were involved; industrial work in Sinai which had previously been reserved for Egyptian laborers now became available to Bedouin and Israeli economic activities provided new jobs in Sinai; the market for their garden produce had vanished and it thus became almost imperative for Bedouin to seek wage labor. Although work is now found nearer to home, it is still at some distance from the tribal areas. A pattern of commuting has developed in which men remain at work for six to ten weeks and then spend two to four weeks at home. When at home they may easily decide to stay on for a longer period, often for as long as cash and provisions last.

Jobs are not secure and a Bedouin may be dismissed without notice. The unpredictable political situation adds another element of insecurity. As a result Bedouin consider their work to be temporary, and although they do not usually accumulate cash reserves (and certainly not in Israeli currency) they do keep stocks of food to last them through several months. For the same reason men do not move their families to the area of employment, but are content to go on their own, while their women take care of the household and the small flock of goats that serves largely as an emergency supply of cash and food. Even though the wage laborers do not try to improve their gardens, they at least maintain them in good shape and are thus prepared for the possibility of "unemployment" in the wage labor market.

From 1971 to 1974 I was able to observe the situation in the labor market, both from the Bedouin viewpoint and that of the employers and the authorities. During this period the employment situation experienced several extreme changes. Until October 1973 the number of employed Bedouin grew from month to month, until it comprised most of the able-bodied adult males. In parallel with this increase the demand for work by the unemployed increased as well as the demand for better wages. The authorities tended to consider the Bedouin to be a self-sufficient population of pastoralists and horticulturalists, and tried to reduce their flow to places of employment by fixing the maximum wage employers were allowed to pay. They also attempted to improve livestock and introduced better farming procedures, as well as digging new wells to increase the water supply and opening up new grazing areas.

In the wake of the 1973 war between Egypt and Israel, most Israeli economic activities in south Sinai were interrupted for about five months. Even after this time nearly 500 Bedouin, a third of the labor force, who had been employed in the Abu Rudes oil installations were not reinstated. Bedouin used the money and food they had accumulated during the previous work period. Since everybody was at home social relationships were intensified and people who had large stocks of provisions shared with others. Credit at the local shops stopped but food prices remained stable because the authorities rushed in a large supply of grain even during the fighting. This factor facilitated the sharing of food among kinsmen. The level of consumption remained almost unchanged and yet no demands for employment were reported. Universal unemployment was understood as an inevitable result of the war, and Bedouin were pleased to have escaped unharmed although fighting had come pretty close to their area. Later, after the first shock had passed, they felt that the political future of Sinai was in the balance. They felt it was wise to stay close to their families so as to forestall any enforced separation. Since this was not the time to work in the gardens, I could not observe whether Bedouin were now paying more attention to horticulture.

After the war the attitude of the Israeli authorities toward the

Bedouin changed. They had been convinced by the volume of Bedouin labor on the eve of the war that the Bedouin were not herders and gardeners, and that they needed work. They also attributed the Bedouin's passivity during the war to their correct administrative treatment, and were eager to retain their friendship. Following the assumption that Bedouin were in need of work, the Public Works Department recruited 900 men to repair roads, until such time as economic activity returned to normal. Almost overnight the expectation of work was raised and Bedouin returned to the places of employment. A month later the number of Bedouin employed in public works was drastically reduced to 300 and tribal chiefs made dramatic appeals to the authorities to alleviate the situation. At the same time Bedouin flocked to the towns, and while many of them obtained work some of them were disappointed. The overall employment picture is summarized in table 1.

Table 1

Bedouin employed in South Sinai 1972-74, by major regions of employment*

Region	*Aug. 72*	*Sept. 73*	*Nov. 73*	*Apr. 74*
Sharm al-Sheikh	222	250	66	555
Abu Rudes	400	482	—	42
Saint Catherine	79	101	43	52
Eilat	—	480	20	105
Government employees	35	45	45	48
	736	1,358	174	802

* The figures were compiled from the monthly returns of the employment office of the South Sinai civilian administration.

Both the fluctuations in total employment and the effects of administrative steps are evident. When the South Sinai civilian administration permitted Sinai Bedouin to enter Israeli territory without special permits in 1973, Eilat quickly became a favored center of employment and nearly 500 Bedouin joined the work force. By 1974 the new town of Sharm al-Sheikh (Ofira) had grown to such an extent that it had become the largest employment center in Sinai, and adequately compensated for the loss of work opportunities in the Abu Rudes oil installations. A by-product of both these developments was that the economic center of gravity shifted from the west coast to the east coast of Sinai, and while the eastern tribes benefited from the advantages, the western ones became dissatisfied. Another point worth noting is that during all the upheavals, government employment was stable and increased slowly and steadily. We shall see that this apparent job security is not enough for government employees; they still faced the risk that a change in the political regime would cost them their jobs.

The changes in the wage labor market affected a majority of households. There were, however, some people who never sought work including many of the former organizers of smuggling activities. In the pre-1967 period these men had often handled large amounts of goods and money, and had employed many people. Some of them had amassed fortunes which, of course, they could neither deposit in banks nor use for the acquisition of property. Some of the money they hid in caches, and some of it they used to establish villages in inaccessible mountain areas not far from smuggling routes. They hired Jebaliya masons to build small stone houses for use in winter, and dug wells which they equipped with modern gasoline and diesel pumps. They also planted orchards with a considerable variety of fruit trees. At first sight this appears to be a striking example of "conspicuous consumption." In reality these villages served a purpose: they were hideouts for the smugglers, and allowed them to stay together and prepare for the next haul. The various fruit trees supplemented the food supply throughout most of the year. Soon after the Israeli occupation, smuggling declined since it had become too risky. The rank and file smugglers easily adapted to the new situation and sought employment. The smuggling organizers were faced with a harder decision: whether to go out to work or to maintain their organization on the alert so as to resume operations. Most of them chose the second option, because the Egyptian authorities knew of the smuggling activity before the Israeli occupation and they would have to go into hiding if the political situation changed. In the meantime their reserves were dwindling. One smuggling organizer put it concisely: "Today there is no smuggling or commerce. Now you can only work as a laborer."

The prevailing political and economic conditions are reflected in the behavior of individual Jebaliya tribesmen. The households discussed in the following examples largely depend on income from wage labor, and yet their members do not devote all their efforts to earning money. They are also concerned with activities designed to protect themselves against the dangers of political and economic instability. The first case, that of Salama Muss, throws some light on the insecurity of work.

Salama Musa is a 35-year-old widower. His son is being raised by his sisters and brothers living in the Saint Catherine area. His statement that he has been "working in Zalman Moshe's hotel in Sharm al-Sheikh for the last four years" omits the fact that in 1973-74 Salama was out of work for five months. He also can be dismissed from work without notice. Salama is assistant cook, works a 16-hour day, and earns IL20 (about U.S.$5) daily. His wages are paid on a monthly basis, and are usually at least one month in arrears. Salama eats and sleeps in the hotel, and has no interests or friends in Sharm al-Sheikh. In his words, "In the intervals between work shifts I only sleep." He works continuously, without days of rest, for two to four weeks, and then takes up to four weeks leave. Salama always spends his vacation at home in the Saint Catherine area, and often times it so as to coincide with seasonal events: once he returned home for Id al-Adha, the major Moslem holiday, another time, in mid-summer, because he wanted to stay with kinsmen in the gardens in the high mountains. When at home he stays with his siblings whose houses are all located in a tight cluster, and helps them with their daily chores. While in Sharm al-Sheikh Salama wears a shirt and trousers, at home he dons the flowing dress (*galabiya*). When at home he is even reluctant to talk about his work. He has never considered taking his young son to Sharm al-Sheikh, a place for men, where no Bedouin woman or child lives. Salama maintains strong ties with his kinsmen: much of his earnings are passed on to them in the form of gifts of staple food such as coffee, biscuits and canned vegetables; he coordinates his visits home with kinsmen working in other places; and he retains a share in the family garden in the mountains. Home for Salama is the place to return to in any contingency, if for instance he should lose his job about which there is no doubt in his mind that sooner or later he will. This has now become clearer than ever: the October 1973 war left him stranded in Sharm al-Sheikh. The hotel and all other civilian installations closed down, and the Bedouin workers made their way home by foot, walking up to three days in the mountains. The hotel was reopened five months later and Salama went back to work. During those months he stayed with his brothers who maintained him and even helped him arrange a new marriage.

A Bedouin construction worker in Sharm al-Sheikh spoke quite explicitly about the two kinds of insecurity to which every Bedouin was exposed, and which made him leave his family and household in the mountains: "Any Jewish workman can throw you out of work, even if we have been three years on the job and he arrived just recently. We are not safe here; what happens if there should be another war? When the October (1973) war broke out we were left stranded here and walked three days in the mountains without food or water before reaching home. In the mountains we are safe, so we prefer our families to remain there."

Many Bedouin realize that wells, gardens and even flocks may bring them little gain, and may even cause them losses. Auda Saleh, one of the chiefs of the Muzeneh tribe, expressed the following view concerning Bedouin horticulture: "People lose when they invest in wells and plant gardens; they only live on wage labor. Whoever cultivates a garden and digs a well is mistaken (*bitih*, literally 'errs in the desert'); he can only obtain food (or water) from them, but cannot make a profit." Yet all Bedouin wish to own gardens and animals. A Jebaliya man like Mahmud Faraj who has steady and well paid employment near his home still takes a keen interest in his gardens and intends to acquire more. Mahmud is about 30-years-old, married, and has five children, the eldest of whom is a 12-year-old girl. He works for the civilian administration as a driver-mechanic. As a young man he spent nine years in the service of the monks at Saint Catherine's and then operated a small store for three years. Mahmud is energetic and versatile, and works long hours on his job. Even so he always finds time to irrigate his garden, one of the few left in the vicinity of the monastery and proudly points out the contrast between the vivid green of his fruit trees and the relatively neglected trees nearby. Mahmud owns two female camels which for most of the year range freely over the countryside. Unlike most of his relatives he owns no goats, though his eldest daughter often herds the kids belonging to his kin. One day while driving along the trail leading from Saint Catherine to the Firan oasis, Mahmud pointed out a small orchard in a gully high up the mountains. There were three or four large almond trees in it. Mahmud explained that the orchard had been planted by a monk many years ago. When the monk died the orchard fell into neglect. Water drips from a small crevice in the rocks (*nagat*), though it is not enough to water the trees. He was going to take over the garden, to which no one was laying claim, build a small water storage tank in it and generally attend to it so he could come and relax there whenever he wished. This may have been a daydream, but it shows that Mahmud attaches much importance to orchards. Whilst regarding them as a pleasure retreat, Mahmud also views them as a possible stand-by food supply that would be useful if he ever lost his job. Consequently he is willing to invest cash in improvements. As his income is relatively high, his standards have risen and he now considers it necessary to own a larger garden area.

The mutual help given among kinsmen is practically unlimited. It may be given grudgingly but it is not usually withheld, as is demonstrated in the case of Salem Atesh. Salem is about 25-years-old, recently married and has no children. In 1973 he worked as a subcontractor for a small firm in Sharm al-Sheikh producing cement building blocks. He claims that he made up to IL60 (U.S.$15) daily, about three times the wages usually earned in this type of work. He returned home in August 1973, ostensibly for a week's vacation. But he did not return to Sharm; instead he stayed on to help his elder brother Suliman who maintains an extensive garden by Bedouin standards, in the outlying Wadi Baghaber. Salem remained in the mountains for the next eight months, much against his will, because of the war. Most of the time he stayed in the vicinity of Saint Catherine's and twice a month he hauled supplies to his brother's camp. Salem did not help his brother in the garden, but after entreaties he sent his wife to Wadi Baghaber to help herd the family's flock of fifty goats. During that entire period Salem was supported by his brother. In March 1971 he went to work in Eilat. When I saw him at that time, he complained about the demands his brother made of him, and expressed a distaste for living in Wadi Baghaber "which is far from people, where there is no one to talk with and it is difficult to get supplies." Now that Salem is back at work, he fells free to complain about the dependence on his elder brother, but he would not think of severing their ties. While the relationship makes heavy demands on the brothers, both of them consider it to be beneficial. The conditions of South Sinai require that family relationships must remain intact.

Several conclusions can be drawn as regards the employment situation of the Bedouin of South Sinai.

A useful concept of "employment" should refer to any kind of work that is performed for subsistence, or activities carried out in exchange for money, goods and services. These activities should be studied in their social context. A study of this nature should consider the fluctuating conditions of work and the constantly changing physical and social environment in a single framework. Work behavior can only be understood if all the activities designed to make a living are considered in an interrelated manner. Thus among the Bedouin of South Sinai, pastoralism can only be understood in connection with wage labor and smuggling.

Whilst being employed a person must also prepare for various contingencies that may befall him. There is, of course, a problem of limited information — not all contingencies are foreseeable, but people often do have a very good idea of what is likely to happen. The Bedouin are well aware of two basic dangers, political upheavals and insecure employment, and try to forestall them by fostering their kinship ties and gardens. Examples of similar contingencies are recurrent in professional literature. The Red Xhosa in East London, South Africa (see Mayer 1961), immediately come to mind. Those men who cannot obtain secure jobs in the city cultivate relationships with their fellow-villagers and maintain their usually unprofitable farms; their families too remain in the countryside. The other East Londoners of London, England (see Young and Willmott 1962) also maintain intimate relationships with their kinsmen neighbors as insurance in case they should lose their jobs, and are willing to forgo mobility and higher incomes.

Even while basic structural traits of a society may appear to be unchanged, constant changes bearing considerable impact occur within it as well as in its physical and social environment. Thus while the two "basic dangers" were ever-present to the Bedouin, they are also affected by overall fluctuations in the demand for labor. When the danger of war receded and more jobs became available, Bedouin paid somewhat less attention to their kinship ties and their gardens. They did not neglect them, but they voiced complaints about the demands made upon them by kinsmen, and maintained their gardens without improving them.

In general if income and consumption vary from one person to the next and change rapidly within short periods, it becomes very difficult to determine standards however minimal. And if it is so hard to set standards for a particular society, meaningful comparison is almost out of the question. It makes little sense for different nations to use a gross measure of employment suited to one specific environment.

NOTES

1. Field work in South Sinai was carried out between 1971 and 1974. I spent six months in the field and during 1973-74, Miss Shuli Hartman participated in field work. The Ford Foundation, through the Israel Foundation Trustees, supported the project, and this help is gratefully acknowledged. I gained much from the help and advice of Moshe Sela. I would like to thank Yoav Gai, Dani Zadik and Mahmud Faraj Abu Msa'ad for their help.

2. Manganese mining began in 1918. In 1956 the operation was nationalized. See U. Wurzburger, "Minerals in Sinai — a general survey". In *South Sinai*, Tel Aviv: Nature Preserves Authority, 1973 (Hebrew).

Bibliography

Abou-Zeid, Ahmed M. "Migrant Labour and Social Structure in Kharga Oasis." In *Mediterranean Countrymen*, edited by J. Pitt-Rivers, pp. 41-53. Paris: Mouton, 1963.

Abu Lughod, L. Janet. "Migrant Adjustment to City Life: The Egyptian Case." *American Journal of Sociology* 67 (1961): 22-32.

Abū Zahra, Muḥammad. *Al-Aḥwāl al-shakhṣiyya*, Dār al-Fikr al-'Arabī, Cairo, n.d.

Aharoni, Yochanan. *A Historical Geography of the Holy Land During Biblical Times*. Jerusalem: Bialik Institute, 1962 (Hebrew).

Amiran, D.H.K. "Dura — The Nature of Settlement in the Bedouin Frontier." *Bulletin of the Israel Exploration Society* (1948): 30-48 (Hebrew).

——— "The Pattern of Settlement in Palestine." *Israel Exploration Journal* 3 (1953): 65-78, 192-209, 250-60.

Amiran, D.H.K., and Ben Arieh, Y. "Sedentarization of Bedouin in Israel." *Israel Exploration Journal* 13 (1963): 161-81.

Anderson, J.N.D. "Recent developments in *sharī'a* law: V, the dissolution of marriage." *The Muslim World* 41 (1951): 271-88.

——— "Recent development in *sharī'a* law: VIII, The Jordanian Law of Family Rights." *The Muslim World* 42 (1952): 190-206.

'Ārif,'Ārif al-. *Al-qaḍā' bayn al badu* (Bedouin Justice), Jerusalem, 1933.

Asad, T. *The Kababish Arabs: Power, Authority and Consent in a Nomadic Tribe*. London: C. Hurst, 1970.

Ashkenazi, T. *The Bedouin*. Jerusalem: Rubin Mass, 1957 (Hebrew).

Aswad, B.C. "Key and Peripheral Roles of Noble Women in a Middle-Eastern Plains Village." *Anthropological Quarterly* 40 (1967): 139-52.

Avi-Yona, Michael. *The Roman and Byzantine Eras*. Jerusalem: Bialik Institute, 1952 (Hebrew).

Awad, M. "Settlement of Nomadic and Semi-nomadic Tribal Groups in the Middle East." *International Labour Review* 79 (1959): 25-56.

Baer, Gabriel. *Population and Society in the Arab East*. London: Routledge and Kegan Paul, 1964.

——— *Studies in the History of Modern Egypt*. Chicago: University of Chicago Press, 1969.

Bailey, F.G. *Stratagems and Spoils: A Social Anthropology of Politics*. Oxford: Blackwell, 1969.

Barth, F. "Principles of Social Organization in Southern Kurdistan." *Universitets Etnografiks Museum*, Bulletin No. 7, Oslo: Brodrene Jorgensen AOS, Boktrykkeri, 1953.

——— *Nomads of South Persia: The Basseri Tribe of the Khamseh Confederacy*. Boston: Little Brown, 1961.

——— "A General Perspective on Nomad-Sedentary Relations in the Middle East." In *The Desert and the Sown*, edited by C. Nelson, pp. 11-21. Berkeley: University of California, Institute of International Studies, 1973.

Baxter, Paul T.W. "Some Consequences of Sedentarization for Social Relationships." In *Pastoralism in Tropical Africa*, edited by T. Monod, pp. 206-28. London: International African Institute, 1975.

Ben-Porath, Yoram. *The Arab Labor Force in Israel*. Jerusalem: Falk Institute, 1966.

Ben Zvi, Izhak, *Eretz-Israel Under Ottoman Rule*. Jerusalem: Yad Ben-Zvi, 1967 (Hebrew).

Berque, J. "'Amal" (3). In *Encyclopaedia of Islam*(EI^2), pp. 427-29. New edition, Leiden and London, 1960.

Black-Michaud, J. *Cohesive Force: Feud in the Mediterranean and the Middle East*, Oxford: Blackwell, 1975.

Bousquet, G.-H. "*'Āda*" (I-II). In *Encyclopaedia of Islam* (EI^2), pp. 170-71. New edition, Leiden and London, 1960.

Bregman, Arie. *The Economy of the Administrated Areas 1968-1973*. Jerusalem: Bank of Israel, Research Department, 1975.

Bresslavsky, Moshe. *Do you know the Country. B: The Negev*. Tel Aviv: Hakibbutz Hameuchad, 1946 (Hebrew).

Bujra, Abdalla S. "The Social Implications of Developmental Policies: A Case Study from Egypt." In *The Desert and the Sown*, edited by C. Nelson, pp. 143-57. Berkeley: University of California, Institute of International Studies, 1973.

Chelhod, Joseph. *Le droit dans la société Bédouine; Recherches ethnologiques sur le 'orf ou droit coutumier des Bédouins*. Paris: Rivière, 1971.

Cole, Donald P. *Nomads of the Nomads: The Al Murrah Bedouin of the Empty Quarter*. Chicago: Aldine, 1975.

Conder, C.R. *Tent Work in Palestine*. 2 vols. London: Bentley, 1879.

Conroyer, B. "Histoire d'une tribu semi-nomade de la Palestine." *Revue Biblique* 58 (1951): 75-91.

Colson, E. *The Plateau Tonga of Northern Rhodesia: Social and Religious Studies*. Manchester: Manchester University Press, 1962.

——— "Social Control and Vengeance in Plateau Tonga Society." *Africa* 23 (1953).

Coser, L.A. *The Functions of Social Conflict*. London: Routledge and Kegan Paul, 1956.

Coulson, N.J. "Muslim Custom and Case-law." *The World of Islam* 6 (1959): 13-24.

——— *A History of Islamic Law*. Edinburgh: Edinburgh University Press, 1964.

——— *Succession in the Muslim Family*. Cambridge: Cambridge University Press, 1971.

Cunnison, I. *The Baggara Arabs: Power and Lineage in a Sudanese Nomad Tribe*. Oxford: Oxford University Press, 1966.

Dalman, G. *Arbeit und Sitte in Palästina*, Vol. 6, *Zeltleben*. Gütersloh: Bertelsmann, 1939.

Dan, Joel, and Raz, Zvi. *Israel: Map of Soil-Groups*. Tel Aviv: Ministry of Agriculture, 1970 (Hebrew).

Deng, F.M. *The Dinka of the Sudan*. New York: Holt, Rinehart, and Winston, 1972.

Dīb, K. "A Survey of the Ḥjerat." Unpublished report to the Israel Lands Administration, 1971 (Hebrew).

Diqs, Isaak. *A Bedouin Boyhood*. London: Allen and Unwin, 1967.

Dobkin, M. "Social Ranking in the Woman's World of Purdah: A Turkish Example." *Anthropological Quarterly* 40 (1967): 65-72.

Durkheim, Émile. *The Division of Labor in Societey*. Glencoe: Free Press, 1933.

Evans-Pritchard, E.E. *The Nuer: a Description of the Modes of Livelihood and Political Institutions of a Nilotic People*. Oxford: Oxford University Press, 1940.

Feldman, Yossi. "Ancient Agricultural Oases in the Dead Sea and Jordan Valley Areas." In *Judea and Samaria — Studies in Settlement Geography*, edited by A. Shmueli, D. Grossman and R. Ze'evi. Jerusalem: Canaan, 1977 (Hebrew).

Fishburne Collier, J. "Women in Politics". In *Women, Culture and Society*, edited by M. Rosaldo and L. Lamphere, pp. 89-96. Stanford University Press, 1974.

Frank, F. "Ramla, the Backyard of Tel Aviv." *Lihyot Ba'ir* 4 (1976): 30-35 (Hebrew).

Friedl, E. "The Position of Women: Appearance and Reality." *Anthropological Quarterly* 40 (1967): 97-108.

Gichon, Mordechai. "Sites of the Limes Palaestinae in the Negev." *Bulletin of the Israel Exploration Society* 12 (1975): 149-66 (Hebrew).

Ginat, J. "The Bedouin of the Negev in Agan Ayalon." In *The Western Ayalon Basis*, edited by S. Martin. Tel Aviv: Hakibbutz Hameuhad, 1970 (Hebrew).

——— *Women in Muslim Rural Society*. New Brunswick: Transaction Books, 1982.

——— "Meshamas — The Outcast in Bedouin Society." *Nomadic Peoples*, 1983.

——— "The Role of the Mediator — With Special Reference to Blood Revenge." To be published in a forthcoming issue of *Asian and African Studies*.

Golani, G. *Bedouin Settlement in the Alonim-Shfar'am Hills*. Jerusalem: Ministry of the Interior, Dept. of Minorities and Hebrew University, Dept. of Geography 1966 (Hebrew).

Glickman, M. "Kinship and Credit among the Nuer." *Africa* 3 (1971): 306-19.

Gulick, John. *Tripoli, A Modern Arab City*. Cambridge: Harvard University Press, 1967.

Hacker, M. Jane. *Modern Amman. A Social Study*. Durham: University of Durham, 1960.

Hardy, M.J.L. *Blood Feuds and the Payment of Blood Money in the Middle East*. Leiden: Brill, 1963.

Harel, Menashe. *Surveys in the Judean Desert and the Dead Sea Region*. Tel Aviv: Am Oved, 1971 (Hebrew).

Ibn Khaldun, 'Abd al-Rahman. *An Introduction to Historical Sciences (Muqaddima)*. Jerusalem: Bialik Institute, 1966 (Hebrew).

Jaussen, A. *Coutumes des Arabes au Pays de Moab*. Paris: Adrien-Maisonneuve, 1908.

Jopling, C.F. "Women's Work: A Mexican Case Study of Low Status as a Tactical Advantage." *Ethnology* 13 (1974): 187-95.

Karmon, Yehuda, and Shmueli, Avshalom. *Hebron: The Nature of a Mountainous Town*. Tel Aviv: Gomeh, 1970 (Hebrew).

Kennett, A. *Bedouin Justice: Laws and Customs among the Egyptian Bedouin*. Cambridge: Cambridge University Press, 1925.

Khuri, Fuad I. *From Village to Suburb: Order and Change in Greater Beirut*. Chicago: University of Chicago Press, 1975.

Klein, Shmuel. *The Land of Judea*. Tel Aviv: Dvir, 1939 (Hebrew).

Kochavi, Moshe. "Survey in the Land of Judea." In *Judea, Samaria and Golan — An Archeological Survey* (1968). Jerusalem: Ministry of Education and Culture, 1972.

Kressel, Gideon M. *Individuality versus Tribality: The Dynamics of an Israeli Bedouin Community in a Process of Urbanization*. Tel Aviv: Hakibbutz Hameuchad, 1975 (Hebrew).

Lamphere, L. "Strategies, Cooperation and Conflict Among Women in Domestic Groups." In *Women, Culture and Society*, edited by M. Rosaldo and L. Lamphere, pp. 97-112. Stanford University Press, 1974.

Lancaster, Fidelity. "Bedouin by Adoption." *New Society* 591 (1974): 245-46.

Lapidus, M. Ira. *Middle Eastern Cities: A Symposium on Ancient Islamic and Contemporary Middle Eastern Urbanism*. Berkeley: University of California Press, 1969.

Layish, A. "*Sharīʿa* and Custom in the Muslim Family in Israel." *Hamizrah Hehadash* 23 (1974): 377-409 (Hebrew).

——— *Women and Islamic Law in a Non-Muslim State: A Study based on Decisions of the sharīʿa Courts in Israel*. New York and Jerusalem: John Wiley and Sons, Israel Universities Press, 1975.

——— "Women and Succession in the Druze Family." *Asian and African Studies* 11 (1976): 101-19.

——— "The Contribution of the Modernists to the Secularization of Islamic Law." *Middle Eastern Studies* 14 (1978): 263-77.

——— *Marriage, Divorce and Succession in the Druze Family*. Leiden: Brill, 1982.

Layish A., and Shmueli A. "Custom and *sharīʿa* in the Bedouin Family According to Legal Documents from the Judaean Desert." *Bulletin of the School of Oriental and African Studies* 42 (1979): 29-45.

Lewando-Hundt, Gillian. *Women's Power and Settlement*. Ph.D. Thesis, University of Edinburgh, 1978.

Lewis, Norman. "The Frontier of Settlement in Syria 1800-1950." *International Affairs* 31 (Jan. 1955): 48-60.

Lichfield, et al. *Regional Development Plan for Ramla Subdistrict*. Jerusalem: Ministry of Interior, Central District, 1977-8 (Hebrew).

Lifshitz, Yaacov, *Economic Development in the Administrated Areas 1967-1969*. Tel Aviv: Ma'arachot, 1970 (Hebrew).

——— *Structural Changes and Economic Growth in the Occupied Territories 1922-1972*. Tel Aviv: Tel Aviv University, David Horovitz Institute, 1974 (Hebrew).

Linant de Bellefonds, Y. *Traité de droit musulman comparé*, Vol. 2. Paris: Mouton, 1965.

Marx, Emanuel. *Bedouin of the Negev*. Manchester: Manchester University Press, 1967.

——— "The Organization of Nomadic Groups in the Middle East." In *Society and Political Structure in the Arab World*, edited by M. Milson. New York: Humanities Press, 1973.

——— "Communal and Individual Pilgrimage: The Region of Saints' Tombs in South Sinai." In *Regional Cults*, edited by R.P. Werbner, pp. 29-51. London: Academic Press, 1977.

Mayer, P., and Mayer, I. *Townsmen or Tribesmen: Conservatism and the Process of Urbanization in a South African City*. Cape Town: Oxford University Press, 1961.

Meshel, Ze'ev. "South Hebron: The Influence of Natural Conditions on the Area's History." *Teva VeAretz* 3 (1969) (Hebrew).

Michael, A., and Bar-El, R. *Strikes in Israel 1960-1969; A Quantitative Approach*. Ramat Gan: Bar-Ilan University, 1977 (Hebrew).

Milliot, L. *Introduction à l'étude du droit musulman*. Paris: Editions Sirey, 1953.

Mohsen, S. "Aspects of the Legal Status of Women among Awlad Ali." *Anthropological Quarterly* 40 (1967): 153-66.

Musil, Alois. *The Manners and Customs of the Rwala Bedouins*. New York: American Geographical Society, 1928.

Nelson, C. "Women and Power in Nomadic Societies in the Middle East." In *The Desert and the Sown: Nomads in the Wider Society*, edited by C. Nelson. Berkeley, California: University of California, Institute of International Studies, 1973.

Nir, Dov. *On the Fringe of the Desert, Man in a Semi-Arid Environment*, Jerusalem: Bialik Institute, 1973 (Hebrew).

Patai, Raphael. *Golden River to Golden Road: Society, Culture and Change in the Middle East*, 3rd edition. Philadelphia: University of Pennsylvania Press, 1969.

Pehrson, R. *The Social Organization of the Marri Baluch*. Viking Fund Publications in *Anthropology* 43. New York: Wenner-Green Foundation, 1966.

Perevolotsky, A., and Perevolotsky, A. *Subsistence Patterns of the Jebeliya Bedouins in the High Mountain Region of Southern Sinai*. Tel Aviv: Society for the Protection of Nature, 1979 (Hebrew).

Peters, E.L. "Sex Differentiation in Two Arab Communities." In *Masculine and Feminine in Mediterranean Countries*, edited by J. Peristiany. Unpublished paper, 1966.

——— "Some Structural Aspects of the Feud Among the Camel-Herding Bedouin of Cyrenaica." *Africa* 37 (1967): 261-82.

——— "The Status of Women in Four Middle East Communities." In *Women in the Muslim World*, edited by L. Beck and N. Keddie. Cambridge, Mass., Harvard University Press, 1978.

Radcliffe-Brown, A.R. "A Further Note on Joking Relationships." In *Structure and Function in Primitive Society*. London: Cohen and West, 1952.

Reifenberg, A.A. *The Battle of the Desert and the Sown*. Jerusalem: Bialik Institute, 1960 (Hebrew).

Riegelhaupt, J. "Saloio Women: An Analysis of Informal and Formal Political and Economic Roles of Portugese Peasant Women." *Anthropological Quarterly* 40 (1967): 109-126.

Rosenfeld, H. "Determinants of the Status of Arab Village Women." *Man* 2 (1960): 66-70.
——— "Non Hierarchial, Hierarchial and Masked Reciprocity in an Arab Village." *Anthropological Quarterly* 47 (1974): 137-66.
Rustum, Asad. *The Royal Archives of Egypt and the Egyptian Expedition to Syria 1831-1841*, Beirut: American University, 1936.
Sahlins, Marshall D. *Stone Age Economics*. London: Tavistock, 1974.
Samooha, Sammy. "Arabs and Jews in Israel — Minority-Majority Relationship." *Megamot* 22 (1976): 397-433 (Hebrew).
Schacht, Joseph, *An Introduction to Islamic Law*. Oxford: Oxford University Press, 1964.
Schmelz, U.O. "Vital Statistics and Population Growth." In *The Arabs in Israel: Continuity and Change*, edited by A. Layish, pp. 11-45. Jerusalem: Magnes Press, 1981.
Scholz, Fred, *Belutchistan*. Göttingen: Goltze, 1974.
Segev, Yitzhak, "The Planned Sedentarization of the Rashaida Tribe." *Judea and Samaria: Studies in Settlement Geography*, edited by A. Shmueli, D. Grossmann and R. Ze'evi, pp. 567-71. Jerusalem: Canaan, 1977 (Hebrew).
Shalem, Natan. *The Judean Desert*. Jerusalem: Recanati Fund, 1968 (Hebrew).
——— *A Collection of Research Works on Israel*. Jerusalem: Kiryat Seffer, 1974 (Hebrew).
Shamgar, Irith. "Lod, Two Thousand Years of History, Twenty Years of Promises." *Lihyot Ba'ir* 2 (1975): 8-15 (Hebrew).
Sharon, Moshe, "The Bedouins of the Hebron Hills." In *Judea and Samaria: Studies in Settlement Geography*, edited by A. Shmueli, D. Grossmann and R. Ze'evi, pp. 548-57. Jerusalem: Canaan, 1977 (Hebrew).
Sharon, M. "The Bedouin in Israel during the 18th and 19th Centuries." M.A. Thesis. Hebrew University, Department of Islamic Studies: Jerusalem, 1964.
Shmueli, Avshalom, "Two Aspects of Sa'ir Village." In *Teva VeAretz* 3 (1969): 125-29 (Hebrew).
——— *Bedouin Sedentarization in the Judea Desert*. Tel Aviv: Gomeh, 1970 (Hebrew).
——— "The Background of Nomad-Sedentarization in the Jerusalem Vicinity." *Merhavim* 1 (1974): 70-79 (Hebrew).
Shwadran, Benjamin. *Middle East Oil and the Great Powers*. New York: Wiley, 1974.
Simmel, G. *On Individuality and Social Forms: Selected Writings*, edited and with an introduction by Donald N. Levine. Chicago: University of Chicago Press, 1971.
Smith, Adam. *The Wealth of Nations* (1776). Indianapolis: Bobbs-Merrill, 1961.
Smith, W.R. *Kinship and Marriage in Early Arabia*, 2nd edition,edited by S.A. Cook. London: Black, 1903.
Sweet, L.E. "Camel Raiding of North Arabian Bedouin: A Mechanism of Ecological Adaptation." *American Anthropologist* 67 (1965): 1132-50.
——— "The Women of 'Ain Ad-Dayr." *Anthropological Quarterly* 40 (1967): 167-83.
——— "Visiting Patterns and Social Dynamics in a Lebanese Druze Village." *Anthropological Quarterly* 47 (1974): 112-119.

Swidler, Warren W. "Adaptive Processes Regulating Nomad-Sedentary Relations in the Middle East." In *The Desert and the Sown*, edited by C. Nelson, pp. 23-41. Berkeley: University of California, Institute of International Studies, 1973.

Tyan, Emile. *Histoire de l'organisation judiciaire en pays d'Islam*, 2nd edition. Leiden: E.J. Brill, 1960a.

———— "*Ḥakam.*" In *The Encyclopaedia of Islam* (EI^2). Leiden and London, 1960b.

Vilnay, Ze'ev. *Ramla, Past and Present*. Ramla: Municipality of Ramla (Hebrew).

Watson, W. "British Colonial Policy and Tribal Political Organization." *IX International Congress of Anthropological and Ethnological Sciences*, Chicago, 1973.

Weber, M. *Economy and Society*. New York: Bedminster Press, 1968.

Weulersse, J. *Paysans de Syrie et du Proche-Orient*. Paris: Gallimard, 1946.

Zohari, A. *Geobotanics*. Merhavia: Sifriat Poalim, 1955 (Hebrew).

The Contributors

EMANUEL MARX is Professor of Social Anthropology and Head of the Social Studies Center at the Institute for Desert Research of Ben-Gurion University at Sede Boqer, and Professor of Social Anthropology at Tel Aviv University. He has worked among Bedouin in the Negev and in South Sinai. In recent years he has been concerned with urbanization among the Negev Bedouin.

Professor Marx's publications include: *Bedouin of the Negev* (Manchester 1967); "Circumcision Feasts among the Negev Bedouin," *International Journal of Middle East Studies*, 1973; *Bedouin Society in the Negev* (Tel Aviv 1974, in Hebrew); "The Organization of Nomadic Groups in the Middle East," in M. Milson, ed., *Society and Political Structure in the Arab World* (New York 1974); "The Tribe as a Unit of Subsistence," *American Anthropologist*, 1977; "Communal and Individual Pilgrimage: the Region of Saints' Tombs in South Sinai," in R.P. Werbner, ed., *Regional Cults* (London 1977); "Wage Labor and Tribal Economy of the Bedouin in South Sinai," in P.C. Salzman, ed., *When Nomads Settle* (New York 1980).

AVSHALOM SHMUELI (1925-1981) was Senior Lecturer in Geography at Tel Aviv University. He specialized in the human geography of Bedouin, and did extensive field-work in the Judean desert.

Dr. Shmueli's Hebrew writings include *The Settling of Bedouin in the Judean Desert* (Tel Aviv 1970); *Hebron*, with Y. Karmon (Tel Aviv 1970); *The End of Nomadism* (Tel Aviv 1981), as well as numerous articles and edited books.

ROHN ELOUL has recently completed his dissertation for the University of Michigan, specializing in culture change in tribal societies exposed to state administration. He has taught at the University of Michigan/ Dearborn; Wayne State University; and Eastern Michigan University in the U.S.A. and at "Beit Berl" College in Israel.

He studied anthropology (archaeology) at the University of Illinois/ Urbana-Champaign (B.A., 1970), and ethnology at the University of

Michigan/Ann Arbor (M.A., 1972). Professional interests include the dynamics of culture change, pastoral societies, sedentarization, ethnicity, and the application of a cybernetic approach to anthropology.

JOSEPH GINAT received his B.A. degree in Archaeology and Middle Eastern Studies from the Hebrew University of Jerusalem in 1964. From 1968 to 1970 he studied Sociology and Anthropology at Tel Aviv University and received his Ph.D. in Anthropology from the University of Utah in 1975. He was Deputy Adviser on Arab Affairs to the Prime Minister from 1968 to 1975, and Senior Researcher in the same department from 1976 to 1978. He is a research affiliate at the Shiloah Center for Middle Eastern and African Studies of Tel Aviv University and at the Institute of Middle Eastern Studies, Jewish Arab Center, University of Haifa, where he also lectures. In 1978 he was appointed by the Rocky Mountain Gerontology Center, University of Utah, as a Center Associate. He is the author of *Women in Muslim Rural Society* (New York 1982), and various articles.

During the academic year 1981/2 Dr. Ginat was a visiting professor at Concordia University, Montreal, Canada under the Canada–Israel Foundation.

GIDEON M. KRESSEL is a senior lecturer in the Institute for Desert Research, Ben-Gurion University, Sede Boqer, and teaches in the Faculty of Social Sciences of the Hebrew University, Jerusalem. Dr. Kressel was educated at the Hebrew University (B.A., 1962); the University of California at Los Angeles (M.A., 1965); and Tel Aviv University (Ph.D., 1973). He has done academic research for the Harry S. Truman Research Institute; for the Institute for Social and Labor Research at Tel Aviv University; for Ef'al, the Kibbutz Seminar for Higher Education; and has done applied research for Urban Planning. His interests are the impact of industrialization on egalitarianism in the kibbutz, the social adaptation and acculturation of Bedouin in the process of urbanization, and the micro-economy of Arab communities in Israel.

Dr. Kressel's publications include: *From Each According to his Ability...Stratification vs. Equality in a Kibbutz* (Tel Aviv 1974); *Individuality vs. Tribality: The Dynamics of an Israeli Bedouin Community in the Process of Urbanization* (Tel Aviv 1975); and *Blood Feuds among Urban Bedouin* (Jerusalem 1982).

AHARON LAYISH took his Ph.D. in Muslim History and Civilization at the Hebrew University of Jerusalem, and studied Islamic Law at the University of London. He was Deputy Adviser on Arab Affairs to the

Prime Minister from 1963 to 1966. From 1966 to 1968 he was Research Associate at the Shiloah Center for Middle Eastern and African Studies, Tel Aviv University. He is now a Senior Lecturer in the Departments of Islamic Civilization (its present chairman) and History of the Muslim Countries (its former chairman) of the Hebrew University of Jerusalem, and a Visiting Senior Lecturer in Islamic Law in the Faculty of Law of both the Hebrew University and Tel Aviv University. From 1976 to 1978 he was Co-ordinator of the Middle East Research Unit at the Harry S. Truman Research Institute of the Hebrew University. In 1979 he was elected a Visiting Fellow at Clare Hall, Cambridge (England) and was a visiting Professor in Department of Law, School of Oriental and African Studies, University of London (1979-80).

Dr. Layish is the author of *Women and Islamic Law in a Non-Muslim State* (Jerusalem and New York 1975); *Marriage, Divorce and Succession* (Holland 1981); and the editor of *The Arabs in Israel: Continuity and Change* (Jerusalem 1981). Since 1977 he has been editor of *Hamizrah Hehadash* (The New East), the quarterly of the Israel Oriental Society. In 1981 he was elected as Acting Chairman of the Executive Committee of that Society.

GILLIAN LEWANDO-HUNDT was born in London in 1949. She studied Sociology and Social Anthropology at Edinburgh University (M.A. Hons. 1972, M. Phil. 1978). She has been living in the Negev since 1972. She carried out field work among the Negev Bedouin during 1972-73, and since 1976 has been working in the Faculty of Health Sciences, Ben-Gurion University of the Negev. She is now concerned with the provision of mobile health services for Bedouin, and is doing research in applied medical anthropology.